Point of No Return

Point of No Return

AN AVIATOR'S STORY

Ralph E. Piper

IOWA STATE UNIVERSITY PRESS / AMES

To my parents for showing me how to choose a course
and to my immediate family whose inspiration helped me hold it.

RALPH E. PIPER is president of Ralph E. Piper &
Company Aviation Consultants. From 1946 to
1968 he was chief pilot and general manager of
the flight department for Monsanto Company.
He served in the Army Air Corps during World
War II and was awarded the Air Medal, the Distinguished Flying Cross, and the China War Me-
morial Medal.

Manufactured in the United States of America

♾ Printed on acid-free paper

First edition, 1990
Second printing, 1990

Library of Congress Cataloging-in-Publication Data

Piper, Ralph E.
    Point of no return : an aviator's story / Ralph E. Piper. — 1st ed.
    p. cm.
    ISBN 0–8138–0158–3 (alk. paper)
    1. Piper, Ralph E. 2. Air pilots—United States—Biography. I. Title.
TL540.P529A3 1990
629.13′092—dc20
[B]   89–27919

Contents

Foreword

Some sixty years ago, at the tender age of twenty-four, I teamed up with a fellow Aeronca C-3 pilot named A.T. Barrett to establish an aeronautical journal, largely because the big depression was on and we couldn't get decent jobs.

Ralph Piper's book begins with that same period of depression and postdepression aviation history. Piper grew up in Iowa and graduated from Iowa State Teachers College in 1934. After three years of teaching and coaching athletics he had the good fortune to meet up with the legendary Livingston brothers, Johnny and Bite, in Waterloo, Iowa. He learned to fly under their tutelage then went to work for them as an instructor in that first, historic national civilian pilot training (CPT) program that proved so vitally important to the World War II air power buildup.

Once America had entered the war, Piper joined the Army Air Force and wound up flying the Hump in the CBI (China-Burma-India) theater. He returned from the War highly decorated and went into civilian aviation, first with the famous St. Louis company Remmert-Werner and then as a corporate pilot and aviation department manager with Monsanto Chemical, taking up consulting work upon his corporate retirement.

Ralph Piper and I have had parallel interest in and involvement with what is known as, for lack of a better term, General Aviation, which has so often been either ignored or misunderstood by the general public. From the earliest days aviation documentation and coverage in the public media have been overwhelmingly devoted to the military and to scheduled air transport. Furthermore, general aviation has produced very few writers capable of documenting the history as well as the tremendous economic, social, and technological contributions general aviation has made — and continues to make — to our national fiber and industrial might. That's where *Point of No Return* comes in.

Knowledge of a speciality is one thing; knowing how to put that knowledge on paper is a completely different matter. Piper has both — the experience and the ability to write about it. He has used his rich aviation experiences to help launch and promote the application of airplanes to the realm of American business enterprise, especially when the airplane designers and builders finally engineered real utility into their products after the end of the big war.

When I checked out for antisubmarine service in 1942 I was lucky to find a highly competent editor to take over management of *Flight Magazine*. Tom Ashley was one of those rare journalists brought up under the hard-nosed, picturesque city editors of the prewar period. He had a passion for accuracy and could not tolerate mediocrity, sham, or propaganda. It was Ashley who discovered Ralph Piper as a writer after we had known him as a fifteen-plus-year volunteer veteran with the National Business Aircraft Association, one of the nation's top consumer trade organizations.

Ashley signed Piper up to write THE formula for pilots making the transition from props to jets. Published in 1965, Piper's words became the seminal directive on the subject. It was most timely because the year before many of the new corporate business jets were emerging from experimental stages toward FAA approval. Ralph had already picked North American's Sabreliner — a commercial version of a military design and certificated earlier — as the first jet for his Monsanto aviation department. He was breaking new ground as always, with the qualifications necessary to advance the cause of safety, promote specialized training, emphasize professionalism, and pave the way for progressive companies to establish flight departments in the rapidly expanding jet age that made obsolete the DC 3, the Lodestar, and the Convair 240, to name a few. Ralph had flown them all and was one of the first to transition to jets.

Not only is *Point of No Return* a major contribution to the documentation of general aviation in America, it also holds a preeminent position in aeronautical biography because it is easy to read, flowing with action and verisimilitude. Piper's life parallels the major developments of this century in the private, entrepreneurial, rugged-individualistic segment of the flying game. His is the world of learning to fly in hard times, living on good airport chili and hamburgers. With an obsession for professionalism, he attaches himself to the flying game using an adhesive composed of dedication, guts, faith, a generous amount of go-that-extra-mile attitude on every assignment, and of course, a bit of good luck along the way. All the young hopefuls for a life in aviation should be lucky enough to read this airman's odyssey. It's a cinch the old-timers will find it.

GEORGE HADDAWAY

Preface

The experiences recounted in this book are all true. Many readers may see themselves as part of the story. Any Midwest farm boy could feel some sort of kinship with the author. College athletes, coaches, and people who grew up in the depression years will see themselves. Those who were flight instructors during the early years of World War II will be back in the cockpit with students. The pilots who flew the Hump will certainly feel the cold, the dark, and the uncertainty of those long flights. And those who flew corporate aircraft before the days of push buttons and jets will know the growth pains and the problems facing the people in early corporate aviation.

My role is certainly not that of a hero, but rather that of the voice of many others, who will relate to the days and the experiences we all had as aviation came of age.

This is not meant to be a documentary, but merely an account of things the way they were while aviation grew. I hope you see some of the humor which appears through the veil of time, that otherwise may have remained just another experience. If this entertains you, then my story has been successfully told.

Acknowledgments

Without the help and inspiration of many people this book could never have been published. Typists, word process operators, proofreaders, editors, researchers, and people who just plain gave encouragement were all necessary. If any deserving person is omitted it is not intentional.

Some of the special people who must be recognized:

Ethel Rank Lynch, for giving me the basics of English in high school, and Ruth Zorn, junior college teacher, who taught me how to put it all together in a story.

Joe Garagiola, for his encouragement to write the book. When asked how he started his first book, *Baseball Is a Funny Game,* he replied, "You just sit down and start to write."

Linda Smith, who typed on the original manuscript for over six months, and my wife, Kay, for her meticulous proofreading.

Del Scharr, for valuable advice and for research regarding the days we spent together on the base at Romulus during World War II.

Editors and publishers such as George Haddaway, Leighton Collins, and Tom Ashley, for publishing some of my early writings.

Jack King and Torch Lewis, whose writings gave me encouragement to do something about my story.

My friend Paul Vance, for prodding me into doing many things I would not have done otherwise and for his many hours in the same cockpit with me on some of the most memorable flights.

Paul Murphy, for his expertise in handling the complicated art of word processing and the Meadows, for the use of equipment in times of stress.

Dwight Dinsmore, Bob Browne, and Dick Thurston, all Iowa pilots during the Cuero days, for their assistance in researching the Cuero data.

The personnel of the 94th Squadron in St. Louis, whose inspiration and memorabilia were great contributors to the atmosphere of this book.

My friend Dean Gaunt, for his early interest in aviation that drew me deeper into its mystique and for his picture of our hometown.

Ann Pellegreno, for her advice and guidance in getting the book published.

Jim Webb, who knew John Livingston and admired him as much as I, for his research and help in substantiating some of the data on John's early career.

Col. Harry Watt, retired, for camera work and advice.

The China-Burma-India Hump Pilots Association, for permission to reprint "China Flight" and "The Eager Beaver," from *China Airlift-The Hump* Volumes 1 and 2.

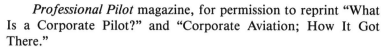

Professional Pilot magazine, for permission to reprint "What Is a Corporate Pilot?" and "Corporate Aviation; How It Got There."

Bill Kading of Boone, Iowa, for researching my Boone experiences.

Bob Artley, for providing custom artwork for the dust jacket.

Al Kiefer, for his research on Lambert Field history.

Introduction

The phrase "point of no return" has long been used by navigators. It is that hypothetical point beyond which you may not retrace your steps to the point of origin. Once the point is reached and passed, there is no turning back. The point of no return on a maximum endurance flight is a critical bit of information. On our trip from Natal, Brazil, to Ascension Island, it was at high noon when the navigator took the sun shot and stepped down from the celestial dome, made some calculations on the chart table, and announced we had passed the point of no return! That meant we were committed — we could not return to Natal; we had to go on and hoped to find that elusive little island way out in the middle of the South Atlantic.

"Point of no return" has many applications other than as a navigational term. People experience it at different times in their lives. For example, I have made several major moves, particularly during the war years. It was always somewhat traumatic to pull up roots and leave good friends and pleasant surroundings for something new and unknown at another location. Invariably I would find myself thinking how sorry I was to leave , but at the same time I would begin to look forward with anticipation to my new location. What wonderful people would I meet? What would the surroundings be like? And, finally, the departure point would be blurred by the thoughts of the destination.

The point of no return can be found in this story of my career. It occurred when I finally knew where I wanted to go. The past dimmed as I set my goals on new horizons. We only look back to be sure we are still on the right track.

There are people who wander aimlessly during their lifetime. They have no goals, no touch with the past or future. There are others who know where they want to go and what they want to do.

When they have made that decision they have passed the point of no return, and from that point they are not diverted from their destinations.

Starting this book was a most difficult task. It took me a long time, even under pressure for many years, before I had the audacity to sit down and begin. Somewhere after getting started I passed the point of no return; there was no way I could stop until it was completed. I got caught up in the excitement of reliving my experiences and remembering the people involved. There was no way I could turn around and go back.

1

Background
to an
Aviation
Career

OX-5 Travel Air that provided my first trip off the ground in 1928.
Courtesy Beech Aircraft Corp.

Looking north over the town square of Le Grand, Iowa, 1929. Pilot John Paul, OX-5 Travel Air 2000. Courtesy Dean Gaunt.

Monarch Foods Ford Trimotor, near Marshalltown, 1930.

Bud Kramer and me with a Piper Cub, Mason City, fall 1938.

The arrival of the Hampton Flying Club plane with some of its members. Left to right: Lawrence Burwell, Roy Muhlenbrook, me, Roy Schaefer, Bill Long, Bob Grove (front); Bob Pickard and Johnny Allen (back).

Farm Boy

My earliest recollections of being transported include the sound of a horse's hooves clip-clopping along a country road. Then came my father's new 1919 Chevrolet touring car with its distinctive sounds and the rich smells of leather and new paint. That was the same year I saw my first airplane. We lived on a farm five miles west of Dodge Center, Minnesota, and I had seen pictures of airplanes in magazines that carried stories of action in the World War (World War I was a name not coined until World War II was underway). From those pictures I knew what to expect, but as a six-year-old I was not quite prepared for the sound of the whirring propeller or the shock of seeing an object so big flying in the air. I first heard the sound and looked for a car. I finally located the sound coming right across the field southeast of our house.

The pilot was making his way from somewhere down in Iowa to Clarmont for the Fourth of July celebration. I saw the machine up close the next day and was awed by seeing one of our neighbors climb out of it after flying over the countryside. I thought he was pretty brave and the pilot must be very close to being God.

The impressions left by that first airplane have been deeply etched in my memory. What to many people was an ugly assemblage of canvas and wires was about the most beautiful and exciting thing I could imagine. Probably nobody has been more impressed since some young lad a century before watched from a sandy beach while a fully rigged schooner scudded along with the wind until out of sight over the horizon. As I have crisscrossed this country, I have often wondered how many people have been awed by the sound or sight of one of the airplanes I was flying or stared at the white contrail left against the deep blue sky as I sped along in a jet at thirty-nine thousand feet and five hundred miles per hour.

Many airplanes have come into and passed from my view since

that first one, but none has been more important. With the first sight I was hooked. Later, after we had moved to an Iowa farm and I was older, many times my horses got a rest in the fields as I stopped to watch a passing aircraft until it was only a speck on the horizon.

From early 1921 until the spring of 1929 my family lived west of Le Grand, Iowa, on a stretch called Quaker Lane. This was part of the Lincoln Highway, the first transcontinental highway, later to be known as U.S. 30. Willie, Clyde, and Walter Hoover, cousins of President Hoover, lived west of us. Other neighboring families included the Knudsons, Emilys, Swensons, Perishos, and Keens.

In midsummer 1923 we all gathered at the railroad crossing between the Keen farm and Le Grand and watched President Harding's funeral train come through from Seattle on its way to Washington, D.C. Things like that were easily remembered because not too many exciting things happened to us. There was no television, and only the Knudsons had a radio. None of us lacked for entertainment however; we were good at making our own.

After an all-night rain, Monday morning arrived with even more thunderstorms and gully-washing rains. My cousin had spent the night with us, and when we saw the condition of the usually dry creek just east of our barnyard, we both got the idea that it would be most suitable for some swimming. Off we went wearing just overalls instead of swimming suits. If it had not been for the proximity of the highway, we would have foregone the formality of overalls. The creek was overflowing and rushing along at a good pace, heavily laden with mud from the adjoining fields. This was no deterrent to us. We were anxious to get into water deep enough to swim with our primitive dog-paddle strokes.

We entered the torrent upstream a little but in no time found ourselves near the huge culvert that went under the highway. It looked navigable to us, so we stayed with the current and came out the other side in the Emilys' pasture. Along the way we had encountered a batch of Spanish needles, a nasty weed that clings to clothing and irritates the skin. Since there had been few cars passing by, we felt secure in ridding ourselves of these needles by removing the overalls. Back in the water we went and had a great time. Suddenly it occurred to us that we had floated quite a way from our "swimming suits," so back we skittered to retrieve the garments. We got there to find the water had risen even more and they were gone! There we were on the wrong side of the Lincoln Highway with no clothes! Swimming against the current coming through the culvert was impossible, so it occurred to me the only solution was to get into the cornfield just west of the Emilys' house and dash for the safety of the grove of trees on the home side of the highway. This I hoped would be accomplished with no detection from prying eyes. Who needed the task of explaining how we got into this predicament? It worked. I was finally safely in the privacy of our own washhouse, where I quickly donned another pair of overalls and with a spare pair returned in the open to where my cousin lurked in the cornfield. Properly clad, we confidently crossed the highway and headed home.

By the next Sunday, the incident had all but been forgotten — or so I thought. However, after church, right in front of my mother, Mrs. Emily asked me what I had been doing in her cornfield the day it rained — with no clothes on. Here I thought we had gone unseen, while the truth was she had watched the entire episode from the moment we had first decided to shed the overalls. There is no embarrassment like that of a ten-year-old.

The colt arrived standing in the back of our 1919 Chevrolet touring car. Dad had removed the rear seat and tied her to the robe rail on the back of the front seat. She was little, scared, and away from her mother for the first time. She was black and beautiful. We called her Beauty. In less than twenty-four hours this four-month-colt was to become my friend.

Dad had bought her at an auction for thirty-two dollars, which had been saved for my sister and me in the form of Liberty bonds during the war. She was put in a large box stall where I worked with her the rest of the afternoon. I fed her oats, hay, and an apple now and then. Gradually she calmed and by midafternoon the next day she followed me out of the box stall as a dog follows its master. We were seldom apart for the next several years.

Not many weeks had passed when I became ill. In order to make it easier on those caring for me I was put in the downstairs bedroom. I could not see out onto the front porch, but every few hours I would hear the clatter of little hooves as the pony came looking for me. When she whinnied I would respond by calling her name, which seemed to satisfy her and she would leave the porch to graze on the grass in the front lawn. This, more than medication, hurried my recovery.

In summer Beauty had a short sleek coat. She was built like a little horse with a long tail and mane, which made her a thing of beauty indeed. By early September her coat began to grow in preparation for the cold winter months; by late October she was shaggy with long fetlocks and no longer looked like a little horse, but just like the shaggy Shetland pony that she was.

My cousin Gail came one summer for a week, and we constructed a cart from bits and pieces of old buggies and a harness from scraps of leather. Beauty was broken to drive, or so we thought. We had her out on the highway for a short jaunt, but when we turned around to come back we found she was making better time than we preferred. All efforts to slow her failed and we had to admit we had a runaway in progress. Gail rolled off, but I stayed on, trying to protect our property. Her hooves beating a tattoo on my shins and feet finally forced me off too, and I followed her to the barn, where she stood in what was left of the harness, with the cart in small pieces behind her. No more cart rides that summer.

The next summer Gail and I restored the cart, repaired the harness, and tried again. This time we seemed to be more successful, so after Gail left I took my little sister, Alice, for a ride through the walnut grove. All was going well when suddenly a shaft broke, the cart fell against Beauty's hind legs, and she bolted. I grabbed for Alice as I rolled off the cart, but I missed. She stayed on long enough to have a hoof planted against her forehead. She was bleeding profusely as I gathered her up and rushed her to the house, where Mom treated her with cold wet towels. I left on Babe, our riding mare, and went for Dad, who was working on the back fencerow cutting weeds. He left on Babe at a gallop and took Alice to Dr. Southwick in Le Grand for stitches and bandages. I walked the half mile back to the house feeling the pain of guilt all the way. We never tried to drive the pony again.

Beauty was a natural cow pony. In no time she knew which cows to round up for milking and which ones to leave. I would give her the reins and she would do the rest, nipping any recalcitrant critters on the rump.

I was somewhat shocked to find she liked to swim, for she would shy at every little puddle or stream. We were at the pasture on the Iowa River right after a cloudburst that put the river out of its banks, leaving some of our cattle on the wrong side. We had to get them back. Beauty entered the swollen stream with no hesitation. We crossed over, rounded up the cattle, and swam them back to the right side of the stream. Thereafter, every trip to the river pasture included a short swim.

We had a couple of bad falls. Once after a heavy snow, while riding pell-mell through the orchard, a hidden tree limb tripped Beauty and we skidded for yards in the deep snow, packing cold, wet snow into my collar and blinding me. It stunned us both. Upon finding her reins free Beauty would ordinarily take off for the barn at a gallop. Not so this time. I found her nudging me to see if I was hurt. Another instance was while riding at a fast pace along the walnut trees. I chose to turn in between two trees, but she did not get the message in time and turned in at the next one. I hit the walnut tree and was knocked cold. When I came around Beauty was again standing over me. Hurting all over, I climbed on and we returned to the barn at a normal walk.

Unfortunately I grew and duties elsewhere took me away. At every opportunity when I was home I would visit with Beauty. I had only to call her name and she would come and nuzzle my hand for an apple or a lump of sugar. In 1941 I left for the war. That same year, Dad sold the farm and all the livestock except Beauty, who went to live on the farm operated by my sister and her husband. When Beauty became too old and arthritic to find her way to the water tank, they finally had to put her to sleep. I have many warm memories of that little creature who took me as her friend when she was lonely. We had fun growing up together.

From the time I was ten I read every story about flying I could find. I read about airplanes, flying schools, racing planes, airmail routes, and all the trivia available. When the excitement of Lindbergh's great feat overshadowed all news stories, I was completely swept away and vowed that I would replace the plow and other farm machinery with a machine I could love.

I was sixteen years old in 1928. I could drive a car and I had my first date. But best of all, I managed to borrow two dollars and fifty cents from a friend and I took my first airplane ride.

Marshall County was having its seventy-fifth anniversary, and there were activities galore. I took part in the historical pageant,

Hotel Tallcorn opened, a parade of young women from each of the communities in the county vied for the queen's title, there were band concerts and football games — and airplanes arrived from all directions. A field out on Marietta Road that was smooth enough and somewhat free of obstructions was selected as a make-do airport. Standard Oil's Ford Trimotor was there; it was called the *Stanolind*. There was a Stinson Detroiter, which we learned was used to smuggle bootlegged alcohol in for the celebrants. There was a new OX-5 Travel Air flown in by the Lorenzen brothers from the factory in St. Louis. The biplane was painted blue with yellow wings, and it took my eye immediately as the Horne brothers and I arrived at this ex-hayfield airport.

Orville Thurston and his younger brother, Lawrence, were just getting out of the plane after their first ride when we came on the scene. The Hornes were ready both spiritually and financially for a ride. I was prepared with nothing but boldness. I asked Orville for a loan and was honored. He later became a banker and I a pilot. I have often wondered if he was as impressed with making his first loan as I was that day with airplanes. All three of us fit into the front cockpit. I am sure Alan Shepherd felt no greater thrill than I as the ground fell away.

After a couple of days' work on a neighboring farm, I had earned the money to repay Orville. Only then did I have the nerve to tell my parents about the business deal and my first airplane ride.

Other unexpected thrills awaited me at airshows. In October 1929 I skipped school with four of my senior classmates — Max Adair, Donny Hines, Dale Keen, and Russ Hibbs — and attended the city of Grinnell's Diamond Jubilee. We watched open-mouthed at the races and aerobatics, and trembled at the terrific sound of those straining engines.

The Automatic Washer Company of Newton brought in their new Travel Air monoplane named *Smilin' Thru*. Aboard was Harry Ogg, the president of the company; Gary Cooper, a budding movie star who had attended Grinnell College for a few terms; and the pilot, Wilford Gerbracht. Max got autographs from Gary Cooper for each of us. Twenty-three years later, Gary Cooper and I sat down together and discussed that day.

The day's activities were marked by a mishap suffered by Roy Ligget from South Dakota. Roy had entered his Cessna in one of the races and was doing fairly well until he hit an electric line on a low pass between pylons. His carburetor caught fire and he landed immediately. He snuffed out the fire and went back to turn off the fuel, which was still pouring into the carburetor. I can still see him walking back around the airplane to get to the door. By the time he had circled the airplane, it had gone up in smoke. In those days there was no such thing as fire-resistant material such as Monsanto's Skydrol, which eventually became standard hydrolic fluid on all of the Boeing and Douglas airliners. Following the Lindbergh frenzy came a great interest and development in aviation. Movies such as *Lilac Time, Wings, Hell's Angels, Dawn Patrol,* and many others were produced. Sound effects were introduced in *Lilac Time* and that was followed by talking pictures, but almost as fast as developments were made in aviation, the Great Depression made its drain on the economy and aviation's rosy future.

Being on a farm, we lived well enough as far as food was concerned, but cash was hard to come by. There was only one thing for me to do. I had to get an education as soon as possible. My first two years of college were at Marshalltown Junior College, where I could live at home, work on the farm, and attend school. My tuition was obtained by selling oats, and I earned my keep by doing chores in the morning and evening and all day Fridays and Saturdays. There was scarcely enough money, even with all that work, to keep the car in gasoline and tires to travel the eight miles to classes.

I played basketball as hard as my ability would permit, with an eye on going to Iowa State Teachers College (ISTC) in Cedar Falls for the last two years. My junior college coach, Warren Dickenson, had a brother, Art, who coached the ISTC team. With Warren's encouragement, plus a loan, I finished the last two years at Cedar Falls majoring in physical education and making the basketball team my final year. I made the track team the first year under Paul Bender and lettered in the half-mile. I was green about track and field events, but majoring in physical education, I felt I should participate as much as possible.

Teacher

My first teaching position was in Hansell, Iowa, and I was lucky to get the job. I was the first physical education major for over two years to be so successful, and, in a way, the job came looking for me.

Wayne Shaw, superintendent of schools at Hansell, came to Cedar Falls with Carney Baker, another ISTC alumnus, to see a Monday night basketball game. They were looking for a physical education teacher and coach who would be graduating in the spring. My name came up when they visited my fraternity house before game time and we had a short chat. They watched me play basketball — I was a starter at that time — and then invited me to come to Hansell in early March to meet the board. "You have the job if everything goes as it has before," Wayne said. "The school board has always followed my recommendations." I was glad I had played a good game that night.

When I met the board in March, to my surprise no one asked much about how I would run a classroom or handle a sports team. The board members were much more interested in how the corn crop had been in Marshall County. Since my father still lived on the farm near Albion, I was familiar with the corn production problems and prices. That knowledge got me the job!

I was hired to coach the boys' basketball team, teach five different subjects, handle the entire physical education program in junior high and the boys' physical education in high school, and be principal of the high school. The pay was for ten months at the rate of sixty-nine dollars per month. I lived in the teacherage, which was a small house run by the Wayne Shaw family. They had a bedroom downstairs. Two bedrooms were upstairs, one occupied by me and the other by two female teachers. We took our meals across the road in a private home for a dollar a day. If we were to be in town over the weekend we had to reserve our meals ahead of time.

Once basketball season had started it became obvious that the new girls' coach couldn't handle the job. After the loss of their first game, the players complained persuasively to the superintendent, their former coach, who then asked me to share the coaching duties with him. I agreed and took the defense while he coached the

12

offense. We made a good coaching team, each substituting freely regardless of the other. We won all the rest of the games in the league and went into the district tournament before being defeated. It is incidental that the little girls in junior high physical education classes that year were the same big girls to win the state championship six years later. I was proud of that since it was I who threw them the first basketball and taught them the fundamentals.

My boys' team also won all of the games in the league and were defeated only by Hampton in the county tournament and New Hartford in the finals of the sectional tournament.

I don't remember suffering for lack of money that year because I never had time to spend it. My reputation in the county was well established and I was offered a job at New Hartford. There was a sizable pay increase involved, but it was an error for me to have taken the first job that came along because within a few weeks after signing with New Hartford I was offered a job in the junior high school at Hampton. The Hampton job would allow me to be head track coach, assistant football coach, and boys' physical education teacher in junior and senior high schools. In addition I was to teach five classes a day in social studies. It was understood that the head basketball coach, with two years to go on his contract, would not be offered a renewal and I was to be groomed for that job. With a lot of finesse and cooperation I was able to get released from my New Hartford contract and I signed with Hampton.

I will never forget the great friendships and experiences that were part of my stay at Hansell. The Missildines were farmers who became second parents to me. Their two children were in high school: Hubert was a star basketball player and Myrna was a guard on the girls' team. They both were active in church and school activities and were without a doubt the pillars of the community.

During the winter the Missildines invited the teachers out one Sunday night for supper and bridge. About ten o'clock someone looked out and was amazed to see the amount of snow that had fallen. We scurried around and made the first mistake of the day: we left for town. The road to the first corner a half mile away was easy. We turned the corner to go west for the next two miles and went less than two hundred yards before bogging down in a snowdrift. There were two cars of us, so with some pushing and shoving we got them both through the first drift, but the next one was too much and both cars became stranded in the blowing snow.

13

Someone noted we were less than a quarter of a mile from the Wells' farmhouse and we struggled through the drifts and roused the family. I will never forget the welcome they gave us, nor will I ever forget the most uncomfortable night I ever spent in my life. The wood stove in the living room, where we stayed, would burn any part of us facing it, while our backsides would be freezing. This little room with ten teachers and most of Wells family was somewhat overcrowded to say the least. Sleep was out of the question and dawn was a long time coming. When it did, the sun was brilliant against the new snow, it was twenty degrees below zero, and the wind was blowing at least thirty miles per hour.

Mrs. Wells had started cooking breakfast long before daylight and was at it for at least two hours trying to feed this extra group of hungry people. Eventually we started out for Hansell again, this time with a team of horses and a bobsled. The wind was breathtaking and the cold was unbelievable. We finally got to town and into somewhat more comfortable conditions.

The cars were drifted in for several days; they were not needed for there was no place to go. All the major highways were closed, the train did not go through town for a week, there was no mail delivery, and the little grocery store's shelves were almost bare before outside supplies could be brought in.

There are few people who have grown up in Iowa who have not had similar experiences. Crippling blizzards and temperatures of fifteen degrees below zero would remain for a week or more; then a "warm spell" would bring the temperature up to about zero. It never failed, like dawn follows darkness. Eventually the thaws would come and it would be basketball tournament time. Spring days grew longer and teachers would begin looking forward to getting away from school for a few weeks and into something more lucrative.

During the summer of 1937, I worked at the Hutchinson Ice Cream plant in Marshalltown. I lived at home on the farm near Albion and drove the eight miles to work each morning, seven days a week, arriving at the job by five o'clock. By the Fourth of July, I felt fed up, tired, and underpaid at fifteen dollars a week, so I quit and did what I really did not like to do: I went to work on the threshing crew at the Sanford Collins Farm. It was not too bad; my team was hitched to a bundle wagon each morning and somebody put the horses away at night.

Like the others I would go to the field and load the bundles of oats on the wagon until it was piled high. A pitcher was on the ground, and he would toss the bundles up to one of us on the wagon. On one toss I jabbed my pitchfork at a bundle which fell too close to my feet and spiked the tine six inches down along the side of my shin bone. I headed to Liscomb to see Dr. Marble the old country doctor who had brought me into this world. I still hurt as I recall how it felt for him to punch that silver probe down into the hole made by the pitchfork tine, topped by the agony of raw iodine being poured into that tunnel of pain—all without the benefit of Novocain.

I do not remember whether the pitchfork business preceded or followed another threshing episode. The wagons with the bundles would line up on each side of the threshing machine. When it was clear, they would move ahead to the feeder, where the bundles were unloaded into the threshing machine. On one occasion a wagon came in slightly out of balance, and making the turn to line up with the feeder, it careened over onto the Farmall Tractor that was providing the power to run the thresher. The dry bundles fell on the exhaust stack of the tractor and soon we had a pretty good fire going. I jumped off my load and ran over to assist others in pulling the bundles away from the tractor. As fast as we pulled them away more would slide down on the tractor, and the fire was quickly out of control. Surrounded by fire, I looked around to find I had been abandoned by the others. Here I was alone trying to keep up with the sliding bundles, but I was rapidly losing ground. When I saw I was alone and would not be able to cope, I jumped off and started to get away from the heat when the whole thing blew up. Black clouds filled with angry red flames soared into the sky. Had I not jumped when I did I would have been a charred statistic. I don't know if I have ever had any closer call in aviation; if so I don't want to know.

It was 1937 before I could do anything about a dream that had been spawned on that farm north of Marshalltown. In the fall, Vern Schroedermeier, Lynn Evans, and I drove from Hampton to a football game at Iowa City. We stopped at the little grass airport east of Waterloo and I took my first flying lesson at the school operated by Bite Livingston, who was joined by his brother John in the spring of 1938.

I had earned the money to pay for the lessons by officiating basketball games. Without a basketball team to coach during the 1935–36 school year, I began to officiate two or three games per week, and I put away the extra money for flying lessons. You could say that I blew my way into aviation with a whistle and a striped shirt.

Learning to fly was all I had dreamed it to be, and my lessons continued from that moment on. Winter set in but that had no influence on my zeal. I just continued learning to fly, even though the season of heavy snows required skis. It was the only way to keep the airport open for traffic. Most of my landing and takeoff practice was on a little ski-equipped, forty-horsepower Taylorcraft. It is easy for me to remember how cold it can get in a canvas-covered airplane in the middle of the winter. No wonder the instructors groaned when they saw me arrive on a Saturday morning for my hour lesson—an hour instead of a half-hour because I had to drive sixty miles and I wanted to make the most of the effort. I had cash in my pocket from officiating a game the night before.

On a clear, cold day in January 1938 Ron Kendall sent me out to solo. I still remember each takeoff and landing and the stark loneliness in the cockpit without an instructor in sight. I made three circuits of the pattern and three passable landings before Ron stopped me. He then crawled in grinning from ear to ear for he knew how I felt about this accomplishment. After soloing in January I tried to build up time as fast as possible in order to qualify for a private license.

Sylvan Hueglin and Bud Kramer had a Piper Cub based at Mason City and about once a week they brought it to Hampton where several of us were in the same boat—building up time. Also, while visiting the folks one weekend I got acquainted with Glen Neiderhauser in Marshalltown. Glen had been flying for several years and had an airstrip on his father's farm on the Marietta Road. I felt quite a sense of power in being able to fly airplanes at three different places. It was Glen's Cub which I first landed on Dad's farm east of Albion. Later in the summer I landed there in a Taylorcraft while building up the necessary cross-country for my private license. When I landed, I was accosted by the family collie, who was usually friendly. This was different; I had not come home in the usual manner. I never heard a dog bark more severely than Prince did that day. When he finally realized I was someone he knew, I never saw a dog apologize more eloquently than he did.

It was a beautiful sunny day in July and the grain was beginning to turn. The landscape was about the most attractive it would be all year. I mentioned this to my dad and asked him if he would like to go for a ride; he was in the airplane almost before I could settle myself. I will never forget how much he was impressed by the view — a view few people at that time had ever seen. It was his first ride, and I think he was struck with the colors and the patchwork designs in greens and yellows and clover colors. He was my first passenger.

Early in the summer of 1939 John and Bite Livingston influenced my new career. They talked me into starting a flying club at Hampton, since there were almost a dozen others there who were at various stages of learning to fly. We formed the club and bought a fifty-horsepower Taylorcraft from the Livingstons. I was made manager of the club and given practically free flying time, which was what I wanted.

By the summer of 1940 I had enough time to look toward a commercial license. I took my written exam in the spring before school was out, so I was ready, with some brushing up, to take the flight test early in the summer. In July I had the ticket, and again John and Bite showed me the way to progress still further. They said I should take the government instructors' training course at Des Moines. This was free but they had to recommend who went from their area. I told them I had a teaching contract the next year and was not too sure I should leave the profession just then. They explained to me that I would make more money than I could possibly make teaching school. They insisted that flying was for me. It was a hard decision, made only because of the extreme pressure they put on me one evening after all the airplanes were put away. As we sat in John's gray Buick Century sedan, which to me epitomized opulence, I passed the point of no return as they convinced me to pursue a career in aviation.

The Hampton Flying Club

In June 1939 the Hampton Flying Club was formed. We purchased an airplane and moved a T hangar onto the forty-acre field we leased northwest of town and south of Beeds Lake.

The members were a cross section of the population of Hampton. There were the Hobbies, Les the father and Bill the son, who owned an automobile repair shop. Roy Schaffer operated a machine shop and told stories about his experiences as a pilot in World War I. He discovered that the fifty-horsepower Franklin engine in the airplane had the same cylinders that were in the engine of a Franklin car. Ken Penaluna, a trucking firm operator, belonged and flew regularly. Frank Long, the proprietor of the International Harvester implement business, and his son Bill were both members. Roy Muhlenbruck, a farmer from Latimer, had owned a biplane many years before. Earl Groves, from Coulter, was the proprietor of the Standard Oil bulk plant. He got us eighty-octane aircraft fuel on a regular basis and at a decent price. Lawrence Burwell farmed near Chapin. I was the high school basketball coach and the tenth member of the motley group.

Our first argument was in regard to the purchase of an aircraft. Muhlenbruck had his head set on an Aeronca, while most of the rest of us were in favor of the faster and more docile Taylorcraft. The majority won, and the Livingstons sold us a fifty-horsepower Taylorcraft demonstrator for a thousand dollars. So with an investment of a hundred dollars per member and an assessment of another ten dollars each we were in business with a flying club and a hangar. We took delivery June 9, 1939. The location of our airstrip was only a few yards from the newly filled Beeds Lake. It was only coincidental that our approaches were right over the bathhouses, neither of which had roofs.

The club had an arrangement with Bill Clifton of Sheffield to come down in the evenings to give flying lessons. Bill had been a pilot for many years and flew out of Spirit Lake with Stanley Fuller, an aviation pioneer who had one of the first Lockheed Vegas. I had met Bill during my first year at Hansell when our basketball teams played each other. When I moved to Hampton he was at a football game as the referee, and during half-time for some reason the topic of airplanes came up. It was then I learned that he was an experienced pilot. In fact, he had been the pilot for "Bat Man" Roland Kumzak, whom I had seen jump at the Iowa State Fair that fall. Bill told me then that he had been the one to take the Bat Man up to ten thousand feet every day in a Curtis Challenger. The Bat Man had sewn webs of canvas between his coverall legs and under his arms, and this was supposed to provide a certain amount of soaring ability. Perhaps there was some, but mostly it was straight down until he popped his parachute.

The club also had an arrangement with Bob Pickard, high school senior and relative of the Livingstons who came to the airport with me every day. Bob kept the airplane and the hangar area immaculate. He cleaned the airplane daily; there were always bugs on the windshield and wings or mud on the belly after a rain. In return for his work, all Bob wanted was a few free rides—where he did all the flying. Whether it was legal or not was not the issue. He soloed the day he started his senior year.

To augment my meager salary as the high school coach during this summer, I found a pleasant way to earn a few extra bucks. I rented a sixteen-millimeter projector and a different film every week. The movies were not necessarily new releases, but in most cases they were new to the small town viewers. I made friends with the lumberyard dealer. I would set up the portable screen and by placing concrete blocks and planks in an orderly fashion we made seating arrangements for the audience in the lumberyard. When it came time to change reels, we had a drawing for free tickets for an ice cream cone or some merchandise. I gave plenty of publicity to those who donated to the cause. It enticed people to come in and try their luck as well as see a full-length movie for twenty-five cents for adults and a dime for the youngsters.

It was a terrific summer and I accumulated a great deal of flying time, which was exactly what I needed. On Saturday night I was usually at the Surf Ballroom in Clear Lake dancing to the big band sounds of Glenn Miller and the other great bands of that time. They all came to the Surf; in fact, Lawrence Welk made his debut there. Glenn Miller's "Sunrise Serenade" and "The Angels Sing" were the hits that summer.

We tried many things during that summer. One was night flying. Our plane was not equipped with navigation lights, but since nobody else would be out flying in that area at night, it was not too important that we were not properly equipped. We flew passengers, too. To attract a crowd to the airport more than to legalize our night flying, we did fasten a flashlight to each wing strut so it would shine up under the wing. I was told it made quite a startling effect as we circled the courthouse on each flight. We sold rides for two dollars each. Sometimes we used a fusee on the top of a fence post to locate the end of the runway. Other times the moonlight was as good as daylight. We flew as late as four in the morning and often got complaints from those trying to sleep.

It was also during this summer of 1939 that I learned to do passable aerobatics. I did all but slow rolls and still did not put a strain on that remarkable little plane at any time.

Dwight Dinsmore was the new English teacher at Latimer, starting in the fall of 1939. He was a member of a small group in northern Iowa who owned a forty-horsepower Taylorcraft. He brought it down one weekend, and we tried formation flying for the first time. I could never understand why he was constantly rising and sinking in relation to my airplane. "Funny," he said, "that's what I thought you were doing." We soon found that formation flying was not as easy as it appeared to be from the ground.

During that winter of 1939–40, Dinsmore and I planned a trip to Florida. The Gulf Oil Company had sponsored such a trip in 1938 and found it was a great advertising tool and a very successful effort.

Up to that point I had used ordinary road maps to get around the state of Iowa, which is laid out in perfect grids. Iowa's roads, with few exceptions, run north and south or east and west. To navigate, all a pilot had to do was cross each road at the same angle and ultimately arrive at the destination. Simple. I had a difficult time understanding why Dinny wanted to buy sectional maps for forty cents each, spending several dollars to provide enough maps to get us to Miami. We did both agree to buy a compass from the famous Karl Ort catalogue, which had all the goodies anyone would want to be a well-equipped airman. We got the compass at the goodly price of three dollars and fifty cents.

The tour was to start at various places throughout the Midwest, but the one closest to Hampton was South Bend, Indiana. We made plans for Dinny to join me there after leaving his sister's home in Columbus, Ohio, where he was spending Christmas. The day after Christmas I made the trip from Hampton to South Bend, arriving just at dark. I considered landing in a field off the airport rather than run the risk of landing an unlighted plane after dark. Upon making a few passes at what looked to be a likely field I gave up, for I kept seeing what I thought looked like rocks in the fields. They were, indeed, I learned later. So I took the chance and landed short on a long runway far from the tower. As I taxied in toward the lights in front of the closest hangar, someone came out with a light and began frantically to wave the lantern crossways. I decided he wanted me to stop. He then came up to the airplane and shouted in the window that I was about to taxi off a four-foot drop onto the ramp. Boy, that was a close one!

Our first day out of South Bend took us to Indianapolis and then an overnight in Louisville, where for the first time in years the Ohio River had frozen over.

The next morning I knew our investment for the compass had been a complete waste. None of the section lines coincided at all with the instrument and I thought it had gone bad. But I was soon to find out that in northern Kentucky the river was used as a reference point, and since the river was not straight, neither were the section lines. They ignored north, south, east, and west. Before we got to Nashville we became lost and had to land to determine our location. It was misting, almost in the form of sleet, when we stopped in a large hilly pasture to learn the way to Nashville. We were sure that our compass was bad, and the roads were running in every direction. We asked a local fellow to point to where he thought Nashville would be. He swung his arm around to point and said, "It's right over yon hill." Over yon hill we went, and in time we did find Nashville. We began to believe that Karl Ort put out some pretty good equipment after all and had no trouble thereafter believing that little gem we had stuck up near the windshield. We were learning.

We were delayed most of the next day getting out of Nashville because of low clouds blocking out the little town of Eagle Mountain, which was on the highest ridge between Nashville and Chattanooga. We finally got off in time to reach Chattanooga before dark. We came in, as I remember, right over famous Lookout Mountain, which had been pictured in the history books I had read in school.

Our first stop the next day was Atlanta. Not only had the common terrain changed from the flatlands of Iowa to hills and ridges of some magnitude, but the color of the soil had gone to brick red. In Iowa we called soil that color clay and considered it worthless. In Albany, Georgia, our overnight stop, we saw our first palm trees and realized we were finally getting into warmer climates.

With two more stops for fuel we were finally at Orlando, where we spent New Year's Eve as guests of the local country club. The hospitality along the way had been fantastic. It was the first time so many airplanes had ever assembled in one group, so as a goodwill gesture almost every town pulled out all stops to outdo the others with parties and banquets. We made a lot of friends in the traveling group, as well as in the host cities.

One more stop for fuel at Vero Beach and we finally reached our destination, Miami. We landed at a field not far from the Thirty-sixth Street Airport.

Being teachers, both Dinny and I had only a limited time that we could expect substitutes to take over for us, so we made the best of the few days we had and saw all the sights possible in Miami and points nearby. Reluctantly, we started back on the afternoon of January 4 and spent the night in Orlando.

The fifth dawned with a typical southern fog. In Iowa when a fog is on hand in the morning it is usually gone by ten o'clock. Not so in Florida. We took off when we saw the first break in the fog, only to find it did not keep breaking up. We had gone only a few miles when the fog closed in under us. We returned to Orlando.

We took off again after a couple of hours. Once again we got out of the Orlando area and into more trouble. To keep visual contact with the ground we had to descend again, but this time we were over a broad area of tall grass. We could see only a short distance ahead, so we decided we should land, but each time as I began to level off Dinny said, " I have water on my side." After two such reports it was obvious we had made the wrong choice of where to land. The fog lifted just enough for us to spy an orange grove, which meant higher ground, so we headed for it. Luck was with us. There was a clearing large enough to get our little plane in without hitting trees. Down we went onto the soft sandy soil. It was very moist, which helped keep our wheels from being buried and causing a nose over, and we came to a stop with room to spare.

On the sixth we made stops at Valdosta, Macon, Atlanta, Chattanooga, Nashville, and Louisville. It was a long day. The next would be just as long.

The seventh presented some problems. It was snowing fairly hard when we left Louisville. We stayed low. Dinny watched the map as we followed the railroad, mentioning from time to time when we should expect to pull up as we went over viaducts. We were right down on top of the telegraph poles the entire distance to Indianapolis and again on the way to Joliet. Nothing much fazed us as we had to get home that day or have a lot of people angry with us. Our stops were now down to just Dubuque and Waterloo before our final landing at Hampton.

Somewhere between Joliet and Dubuque the weather began to improve and after leaving Dubuque we were out in the clear. We were at four thousand feet when the carburetor suddenly swallowed a bit of water and the engine coughed. We looked at each other and laughed while simultaneously we said, "Let her quit." We were over friendly terrain, Iowa, where almost anywhere is a good safe place to land. We made Hampton just before dark. We had left on the trip being underexperienced to say the least, but we had learned a lot. We came back veterans of cross-country flying. There has never been a winter since that I felt I was experienced enough to undertake such a long journey with such limited equipment. I believe in the compass and I believe in sectional charts. I believe in radio navigation and I believe in instrument flying. To try to make such a trip with anything less than that type of equipment and experience is nothing short of idiocy.

On the following Sunday Dinny borrowed the plane to go to Ottumwa to see his parents. He looked down to see what appeared to be a light dusting of snow. But upon landing at Ottumwa he was surprised to find they had about two feet of snow on the airport. It took four men and two scoop shovels to get the plane pulled out of the deep snow. He paid his visit, and when he was ready to leave, the Iowa Highway patrol was on hand. They stopped traffic while Dinny taxied up onto a viaduct on the highway near the airport. From that point his takeoff was easy and so was his trip home. He circled the town to alert me that he was back and I rushed to the airport. I got there just as he was making his approach. He landed in good shape, then rolled into the only snow drift on the field! The wheels stopped, the nose went down, the tail went up, and a prop tip flew off as the engine stopped. Dinny was one disgusted pilot. After twenty-four hundred miles of risky conditions and a landing on the snow-choked airport at Ottumwa, he had hit the only snowdrift in Franklin County. The prop replacement was about thirty-five dollars, but the damage to Dinny's ego was priceless.

I left the flying club in February 1940 to finish the year teaching at Boone, selling my share of the club for what I had in it. I had accomplished a lot more in way of experience than I had thought possible, so it was a good investment. Not everyone has the privilege of living through such a variety of activities while learning to fly.

The club was still in existence in 1987. There is probably not a member today that is aware of what went on forty-eight years ago in that little Hampton Flying Club.

John Livingston

I first saw John Livingston sitting in the cockpit of his taperwing Waco at the 1929 Iowa Airplane Tour, as it stopped at Wayne Robinson's newly mowed hayfield north of Marshalltown. My dad and I were driving a team of horses hitched to a hayrack, pulling a hayloader we had just purchased from a neighbor, when the first of the cavalcade of aircraft began to land in the field right next to us. We tied the team to a fence post and stayed to watch the activity. I knew John was to be there, so I worked my way to his airplane. Shortly afterward he started the engine and immediately made his takeoff run crosswind. This was something that even I knew was not done by cautious pilots. Moreover, as soon as he was airborne he rolled the aircraft upside down and continued the climb in a circle around the field while inverted. This was pretty impressive to a farm boy.

I learned later from John that he accomplished this by installing an extra carburetor on the top of the engine that was fed from a tank hidden in the faring of the left landing gear strut. When the aircraft was rolled inverted there would be slight cutout of the engine, then the flow from the landing gear tank would take over and feed the carburetor which was installed on top of the engine, now at the lowest spot on the airplane and thus fed fuel by gravity for sustained inverted flight. Often this was done while in tight formation. Today such a problem is easily solved by the use of fuel injection, which was not available then.

Driving the team home that afternoon, I thought about my future and I could see nothing that included the view of the aft end of a team of horses. During the next ten years in particular, and during the rest of my life, John Livingston and his brother, Bite, were to have great influence on my destiny.

During the early thirties the Baby Ruth aerobatic team flew at air shows. This team consisted of John Livingston, Art Chester, and Art Davis all flying taperwing Wacos. They were among the first to fly a series of formation aerobatics. Everyone today has seen the Thunderbirds and the Blue Angels and is impressed with their precision flying while in tight formation. The Baby Ruth team did it all while being tied together at the wing struts by heavy hay rope. One mistake by anyone would jeopardize the entire group.

Another of the things I learned from John was the story about Benny Howard's aircraft, the Howard DGA. John had been in Cleveland for the air races and was packing up to fly back to Aurora, Illinois, which was his base at the time. Benny Howard, a friend of his, showed up and asked if he could hitch a ride back to Midway Airport in Chicago.

John rearranged his toolbox, dirty coveralls, and tie-downs to make room for Benny to sit on the collection. This was the Monocoupe on which John had clipped the wings, so there was very little left outboard of the struts. He had averaged some good times for a 145-horsepower engine, and in fact had swept the class in every race. Benny Howard was no amateur himself and recognized the performance of the little airplane even as heavily loaded as it was on this short flight from Cleveland to Chicago. He was so impressed he said to John, "If I enlarged the dimensions of this airplane to accommodate four or five passengers it should be a damned good airplane." Those who know airplanes will remember the Howard DGA. It was indeed just a Monocoupe enlarged to a regular-sized aircraft in the category with the stagger-winged Beech and the Stinson Reliant. It was used in several of the Bendix trophy races and made a name for itself well before World War II.

John was in his prime when air racing was at its peak. He had one ability that he carried to his grave. He could get a lot out of little horsepower. He was the one to beat at any of the races. He had discovered some sort of technique unknown to any of the other pilots; he could gain speed and altitude on a pylon turn. He asked me once if I would be interested in learning that technique, but by that time I was well past the stage of getting into racing. He may have offered it to others, but to my knowledge none were given the secret.

Not only was John able to get the best out of an airplane, but he never stopped trying to perfect the streamlining of his racers. He would leave an airplane sitting in the hangar gathering dust until a summer shower came along. Out would come the airplane and John would take off and dart into the rain hanging under the cloud. Back in after the landing he would fill in the spots still covered with dust behind each and every rivet on the plane. This way he eliminated burble and drag behind every little knob or interruption to a smooth airflow. Each little bit helped gain a little more speed. It was this sort of striving for perfection that caught the attention of Richard Bach, who wrote the best-seller, *Jonathan Livingston Seagull.* When I read the book I had no doubt who Bach had in mind. He dedicated the book to John saying, "What everyone has been trying to learn, you have known all along."

When I heard about the book on the "Today" show I called John at his home in Pompano Beach, Florida, and asked him if he knew that he was now even more famous since the book was out. He said he had met Bach a few times as he hung around the hangars out at Executive Airport. He was not aware that Bach had been using him for the philosophy well depicted in the book.

John was interested in airplanes until the day he died. Each time I brought a new airplane anywhere near where he was, I would have John fly it awhile. That included the twin Beech, DC-3, Convair, and finally the Sabreliner. Some of the later models were a little out of his realm, as he was a seat-of-the-pants pilot and never did make the transition to instrument flying, but he would have been good at that too.

He was testing a small aerobatics airplane one day at Executive Airport when he called the tower and said, "I am in trouble." They asked if he needed the emergency equipment, he said he was not feeling well, and he was quickly cleared to land. He got out of the plane and collapsed. They got him onto a sofa in a nearby trailer and he soon began to recover. Some suggested they take him to the hospital, but he said he was all right and would drive over to his doctor himself. As he arose to go he collapsed again and died.

A huge cottonwood tree shaded almost a half acre of ground

where cars were parked. A flawlessly symmetrical hard maple tree cast shadows from the afternoon sun on the grave site. As people slowly and sadly moved back toward the parked cars after the service, the sound of aircraft grew in the East. Looking up we saw a loose formation of biplanes heading west over the new grave. Pilots, friends, and admirers said their last good-byes, each in a special way, to one of the world's greatest airmen, John H. Livingston. That afternoon, as the biplanes passed overhead, I realized the end of an era had come. He was one of the last of the men who could eyeball a biplane and tell what was needed to get it properly rigged. He was a master of many facets of aviation and carried many secrets to his grave. He was able to pass on many other bits of knowledge. I received enough to have kept me alive on many occasions when otherwise I might not have come through. I am proud to have known one of the greatest of pioneer airmen.

The Summer of '40

During the early weeks of the summer I started fixed-base operator experience in Waterloo. My chores started shortly after daylight when we pushed the school airplanes, which had been refueled the night before, out of the hangar in a row on the flight line.

Cleaning out the hangar was an almost endless job. There was always some thoughtless goon who would taxi up to the flight line and swing around, blowing sand and dust into the hanger. When all the regular chores were done, we found engines to clean, airplanes to wash, and bugs to remove from windshields. Trimming and mowing grass around the hangar and the clubhouse were at least weekly chores.

I am glad I had the experience because it has given me a much better understanding of those who never would be lucky enough to rise above that level. I knew, and so did everyone there, that I would not be staying on as a line boy.

It was not long until I was put in charge of the parts department, mostly because I could type the invoices. Daily I would handle the filing and billing of mail orders. It was important for me to remember this was not necessarily a white-collar job, and no one felt any qualms about pulling me from the typewriter to gas an airplane or help unload a few cases of oil.

There were two of us that summer going through the same apprenticeship which was to culminate in our commercial licenses. Dick Kraschel was my partner, and every time we had a chance, we would take a plane up to practice on the maneuvers we expected in our flight test. I had taken my written test during the spring. The tests were a lot different back then. I sat across the table from Les Orcutt in the Des Moines office of the Civil Aeronautics Administration (CAA). I wrote for eight hours one Saturday and four more hours the next. I received good grades, but I sometimes wondered how much of the longhand answers Les could actually read.

Dick's father had been governor of Iowa for a couple of terms, and Dick had a brother who was rapidly becoming a well-known lawyer. Dick, still in his early twenties, was having a difficult time adjusting to the real world, especially the one his predecessors expected him to enter. We stayed at a little motel down on the corner, but the cabins where we slept were not modern. To get to the modern part, we had to walk to the main building to shave, shower, and prepare for the day.

We worked seven days a week and envied Bite and John Livingston, who each took a day off during the week. Being one of the pilots able to haul passengers, I got some breaks from menial tasks and had a taste of what commercial flying was all about. There was a Stinson 105 used for passenger flights, but like most Stinsons, it was underpowered. It was a special privilege to fly it on Saturdays and Sundays when people arrived from northeast Iowa. They came to watch airplanes land and take off, and there were always a few who would gather enough courage to take a ride.

The little Stinson carried two passengers if they were not too big. It was well insulated, and the engine was rubber mounted. About all it needed to be a first class airplane was a 225-horse-power engine instead of the feeble 90-horse Continental, a problem that was corrected in later years.

We took off with about ten degrees of flaps; after getting airborne we gently retracted the flaps as the airspeed and altitude increased. Once we leveled off, the flight became a very pleasant experience. The soft gear almost guaranteed a smooth landing.

Another extra duty coming my way was trips to the factory in

Alliance, Ohio, for new planes. Dick Kraschel and I would depart from the Waterloo railroad station at about four thirty in the afternoon, eat in the diner, and then retire to berths, although I could never sleep on a train. The arrival the next morning in Alliance was usually about daybreak. We took a cab to the factory and found the planes and papers ready. The night watchman would sign us out and we would take off for Waterloo.

The early part of the flight was the best. The sun was at our backs and the air was smooth and cool. We watched the day on a farm unfold as the farmers drove cows into the barn for milking, while others fed livestock and later headed to the fields with their farm machinery. Our first stop for fuel was usually Findlay, Ohio; then Lafayette, Indiana; Joliet, Illinois; and Dubuque, Iowa. From Dubuque to Waterloo was the worst part of the trip. The sun was in our faces and the air had become rough and hot. Clouds began to form, and it was not uncommon to have to dodge a few thunderstorms and rain. In that last leg we found very little to sustain the romance and interest in flying. We were always glad to get out of the little plane after so many hours. The windshield, wings, and struts were covered with bugs, and the airplane needed a wash job before being put on display the next day.

We were on duty every day until the last plane was put away, which in summer was after nine o'clock. We would barely make it to the motel for a light supper before being ready for bed. On rare occasions when neither of us was ready for sleep we would just sit in front of our cabins and look up at the stars and think and talk about the universe or any other topic that came to mind. We both enjoyed that part of the day.

Anything that broke the monotony at the airport was welcome, and one Sunday Dick and I found a way to do just that. There was an early model Cub parked in the back part of the hangar that we brought out when things were a little dull. Both side windows and doors were off. Dick got in the front seat and I in the back. We took off and made a trip around behind the hangar and then down in front of the crowd that had gathered in the shade of the hangar. We had changed seats. Next trip we had changed again. Finally on one of our passes some kids ran around to the back of the hangar and found one of us climbing out on the strut while the other moved into the vacant seat. The one on the strut took the other seat before our pass before the crowd in front of the hangar. It created just the amount of interest needed. As soon as we landed, we were swamped with requests to ride in the little Cub. Other planes picked up the slack and we had a good afternoon going for us.

Several interesting things happened that summer. A Fairchild 24, obviously owned by a very wealthy lady and flown by a commercial pilot, arrived for refueling. It looked like a pretty nice job to have from my standpoint as a line boy. Each month Ralph Hall would arrive in the Texaco Northrop Gamma, which looked even better to me than the Fairchild job.

The Inman Brothers Flying Circus came through on a barnstorming tour, flying a trimotor Stinson formerly owned and operated by American Airlines. Its three fixed pitch props on those Lycoming engines really roared and could be heard for miles around. They also brought along an antiaircraft searchlight, playing it around the night sky to draw crowds of curious onlookers.

One night while Art Inman was out with a load of passengers, a sudden squall came up. People scampered to their cars, the wind began to blow, and rain came down in sheets. The operator of the light did what I thought he should do. He doused the light to keep the cold rain from breaking the lens. That was not too popular with Art Inman, who was trying to land ahead of the storm. Everybody did something wrong that night. Art should have waited out the storm. According to Art the light operator should not have turned out the light as that was the only way Art could see the field in the dark. All ended well, but we heard a great deal of swearing and ranting before the storm passed on and silence took over. Needless to say, that ended the day's activities, for those who ran to their cars kept going. The parking lot was soon empty and we were alone.

One of the regular tenants that summer was a heavy Fairchild with a Pratt and Whitney 450 Wasp on the front, used by an aerial mapping firm. When it was not flying it was kept in the hangar. They could fly only when there were no clouds anywhere within miles, so they flew about once or twice a week. When they did go up they flew only until noon because the air got too choppy to continue after that. We had no tow tractor to move heavy equipment, so this big bird had to be pushed by hand in and out of the hangar. It took all of us to move the monster, which we called the "Hangar Queen," "Hernia Hattie," and other endearments not fit for tender ears.

Dick and I left together for Des Moines after getting our commercial licenses. Our government instructions' training was scheduled with the Iowa Airplane Company operated by F. C. Anderson and Leo Brennan. My instructor was Charlie Butler.

The Piper family had close friends in Des Moines by the name of Earl and Zoe Merrill. Earl worked for the *Des Moines Register.* When a new radio announcer was brought in from Davenport to work at WHO radio, Earl offered him a room until he could get settled. The room Dick and I shared in the Merrill home was the same room that had been used by the announcer, a guy by the name of Ronald ("Dutch") Reagan.

I absorbed the ground school like a sponge takes on water. The flying came at me and was digested just as fast for I had made up my mind a few nights earlier sitting in John's Buick.

My oral and written were long and searching tests, but having been a teacher gave me an advantage over most applicants. The flight test was flown with inspector George Ireland sitting in the left seat. I was in the right and acted as the instructor throughout the test.

He gave me the works — stalls, power on and power off; pylon eights, around and on; lazy eights, large and small; Chandelles, left and right; steep turns; vertical reversements; and finally spot landings. We could not slip or use the throttle once the glide had been established. To hit a spot no more than twenty feet in diameter was not easy with an inspector in the seat right next to the applicant. It all worked out.

I completed all of the two-week course in seven days. I returned to Waterloo through Boone, where I saw Principal Larry Evans and had my contract nullified. I left Dick in Des Moines. He was taking things a lot less seriously than I was, for he had not yet decided where he was going. Whether he finished the course or not, I never did know. I heard later that he went to Bell Aircraft in Buffalo as a test pilot. I lost track then until I reached Romulus in 1943.

CPT

After returning from Des Moines, I became deeply engrossed in training Civilian Pilot Training (CPT) students. I am sure I learned almost as much as they during the first few weeks.

CPT was a program started in late 1939 and early 1940 by the then-administrator of the CAA (Civil Aeronautics Administration), Grove Webster with consulting service from George Haddaway. We were not at war and any effort too obvious to aid the Allies would have jeopardized our neutrality. The program was designed to build up a backlog of pilots to a stage whereby the transition to military flying would take minimum time. Having been personally involved with both CPT and army air corps primary training, I found a great deal of similarity.

To build a backlog of pilots there had to be instructors. Webster appointed a team of experts to travel through the country rerating instructors. The licensed instructors who could grasp the standardization program with ease were rerated. Some could not make the change, and those along with instructors-to-be, were sent to an instructor school where, with more time, they could learn the new way of instruction and standardization. CPT schools and instructor schools sprang up in each state.

After the primary course was well underway a secondary course, primarily featuring aerobatics, was offered. It was followed by the cross-country course featuring navigational training. Pilots completing all three courses often found commercial jobs and continued as professionals. Many found their way to the primary training bases for the air corps and became instructors. The fruits of CPT programs were obvious long before we went to war in late 1941. Those efforts plus the military training program contributed to the largest air force ever assembled in just a few short years.

I flew all day, seven days a week. Usually there was a student who did not mind early hours, and I would schedule him for a half hour before daylight. We would do air work until it was light enough to make landings. He would be leaving when the next student arrived at sunup.

If there was an advanced student, we would stay out until well after dark. After things on the horizon were no longer visible, we would orient ourselves by the lights on the bridge crossing the Cedar River in downtown Waterloo. Often we would get engrossed in lazy eights and stay out an hour after sunset. It was always a busy day when we came to the cross-country stage in the student curriculum. Again we were airborne before sunup. We had enough light to land at the first stop, which was Canfield, near Cedar Falls. The second leg was to Glenn Neiderhauser's airport at Marshalltown and the final leg was back to Chapman field. After the first trip was completed, the student was given a breather while I prepared the second airplane and student for the next dual ride. The first student was ready for his solo cross-country. After he took off, making the same circuit as before, we followed behind just far enough so he could not see us. So it went all day for ten students. We never lost one, and we knew at all times where they were. While changing students, I had time to critique the solo flights for the students before they left the airport for the day.

We had one student who was the sales manager for International Harvester for the northeast part of Iowa. By previous arrangement I would fly him first in the morning, landing just at daylight. He would return in the late afternoon for his second session of the day. We landed every night by the light from the hangar shining out on the runway. Ten days after he started the course, he had passed his final private license check ride with flying colors, a record that has seldom been topped.

Knowing I would be going into heavier trainers with more horsepower, I was anxious to get as much experience as possible. When things were dull and we were between classes, I would get Dale Madsen, the pilot-mechanic, to help me get out the Travel Air with a Warner 145 in the nose. We would start it up, but for some time the engine would quit every time I got the tail up for the takeoff run. It finally dawned on me that the float in the carburetor was sticking, and even after we took the bowl off and worked it over the problem persisted. It was early winter when I finally got the monster airborne. I had learned that if I let the tail up very slowly, the engine would not quit.

My impressions of that airplane were not too complimentary. It had the most resistant aileron movement imaginable and it was grossly underpowered, even with the big engine in the nose.

2
The War Years

Instructor for the Air Corps, Cuero, Texas, February 1941.

Me in the cockpit of a Stearman shortly after
the acceptance flight, 1941.

My first *basha* mates in front of The Town House, Tezpur, 1944.
Left to right: me, Baker, and Warren.

View of the quadrangle of *bashas* from The Town House.

Looking out the copilot window of a C-87 while crossing the Hump, somewhere in China, 1944.

Me receiving the Distinguished Flying Cross from Lt. Col. Steele, March 1945.

Cuero, Texas

The day after Christmas 1940 I drove to St. Louis from Albion, Iowa. I had received information by telegram that Brayton Flying Service of St. Louis would be needing instructors to staff a new flight school, which would probably be located near Waco, Texas. This was an army contract school to provide primary training to air corps cadets using Stearman trainers. Teaching at such a school was what I wanted.

Early on the morning of the twenty-seventh I went to Brayton Flying Service headquarters at Lambert Field and found it buzzing with army brass and important-looking people. The secretary suggested I talk to Art Soper, the chief pilot. Soper was very receptive and took my name and credentials. He seemed pleased with my qualifications despite the fact I had a rather limited background of eight hundred hours. Perhaps he was pleased because of the two CPT classes I had completed. I returned to Waterloo to await the call which I hoped would arrive soon. Little did I know what would transpire before the next Christmas.

Early in January I received a wire requesting that I report to the Brayton Flying Service headquarters at Cuero, Texas. My reaction was, "Where the hell is Cuero, Texas?" I got out a map and looked and looked before I found it, south of Austin. I had hoped for Waco, but wanting to get into a new operation, I left my friends in Waterloo for Albion, where I gathered my few worldly goods and headed for Texas.

Leaving home was somewhat traumatic. My dad was having a closing-out farm sale in February, since he had bought a produce business in Marshalltown. After many years of hardships trying to eke out a living during the depression and numerous other setbacks, he had decided a change was necessary. I knew he would have stayed on the farm indefinitely had I shown the interest he

39

would have liked. So in a way I felt somewhat responsible for his being upset at facing an entirely new life. Mom was exceptionally quiet and seemed more deeply disturbed than I had expected. It was later that winter before I was to know why. As I look back on that moment, I am sure she never expected to see me again, but she held it all back except for a few reluctant tears.

I stopped in Ames to see some of my friends about joining me later if all turned out as I expected in Texas. They were instructing on secondary CPT in Waco UPFs, and an open cockpit in winter in Iowa did have some drawbacks. Since none were able to leave at the time, I continued alone and made it to Ft. Scott, Kansas, the first night. The next forenoon I stopped to visit some friends at the Spartan School in Tulsa where primary training was also being done. Doc Brown and Millard Gossman both were already accepted there and about to be assigned students. Both had instructed with me during the summer and fall of 1940 for Livingston Airways. Their vivid accounts of their acceptance rides did not help my confidence any, but I continued on my way, staying in Austin for the night.

I arrived in Cuero the next day in the rain, and after inquiring for directions, found the airport northwest of town. What I found was more of an idea than a reality—piles of lumber, an old wooden windmill tower, and a lot of mud. I had driven eleven hundred miles for this?

The land had been a rice field one-half mile wide and a mile long. It had irrigation ditches along each side and was surrounded by the ubiquitous mesquite trees. Kos Morgan, a rancher, owned the land and had offered it to the city of Cuero for the duration. This provided the means for the city to make the offer to Brayton Flying Service. I soon learned there were other Brayton people in town.

Brayton's headquarters were cramped in a small upstairs office on Main Street, presided over by Elaine Jones, a beautiful woman with long red hair. I learned I would have to take a physical that afternoon, but otherwise I was another newly registered arrival on the pilot staff. During lunch I got acquainted with those already on hand. There was Art Soper, from the St. Louis Brayton Flying Service, Charlie Daley, Charlie Severin, Jack Shelton, and Bill Kraft from St. Louis. Bob Sexton and Monty Lane were the only two at the time from Texas. Ed Hensley and Joe Hamilton were from Oklahoma, and Dick Elsey arrived from Kansas later. We were the nucleus of what was to be over 150 flight instructors.

Also in the early arrivals was Buck Taylor, who had been instructing at a primary school in Dallas and was designated director of flying. Prior to that he had been the test pilot and demo pilot for the Guiberson Diesel airplane—the only one that ever existed as far as I know. Another key man was general manager Gordon Mathews, who had been with an airline at one time and more recently with the CAA. He was a good choice, as he handled the hundreds of start-up problems connected with a project of such magnitude.

Brayton had to have some financing to get the project off the ground. Sam Weill appeared among the early arrivals, and although we could never quite understand his status, we knew him to be wealthy and suspected he may have come to watch his investment. He was friendly, well educated, and a talented musician, who had a great interest in flying from an amateur standpoint.

At the many group meetings, as we went through our ground training, we were often told the supervisory jobs were all wide open and they would be filled as talent showed up. Gordon Mathews evaluated the talent on hand and almost daily urged anyone chosen not to try to wiggle out of the responsibility. The decision was based on flight training as well as how well we did in ground school. There were openings for the flight commander for each of the two classes, which were to be conducted simultaneously, and check pilots were to be chosen as assistants to the flight commanders.

It was from some of these group sessions and through some personal conversations with Gordon Mathews that I began to suspect I was being seriously considered for one of the top jobs. With my lack of experience I felt the need for at least one class under my belt before taking on management responsibilities, and I told Gordon that. Art Soper and Ed Hensley were selected to head the first two classes.

Ground school was almost over when the first Stearman arrived at our muddy airport. It was followed closely by the second. No buildings were up at this point, so we worked out of our cars parked alongside of what was to become the main runway. Elwood Scott had arrived and was to be the parachute rigger. Scotty's background was strictly army and he had many tales to tell of early days in the air corps. He was a good rigger and he made us feel secure, even though none of us were anxious to test his product.

Buck Taylor took me out for my first indoctrination flight, which was my acceptance ride. It was one of the most memorable flights I had ever had. While managing the flying club in Hampton in the summer of 1939, I was able to experiment a lot. I had done some loops in a Cub and several in the Taylorcraft prior to the club's formation. That summer I attended the Iowa State Fair and watched Dick Grenier, a well-known stunt pilot, and his son do a team act with straight Cubs. They did it all, which gave me some confidence. After careful planning on the ground with the aid of a model airplane, I would then take off and try some of the things I had seen them do. I heard from several people at Livingston Airways that we should not try slow rolls with the Taylorcraft for fear the wing struts might buckle. They were strong enough for stress but we were not too sure about compression. If one buckled so would the wing. I learned to do passable snap rolls and Cuban eights, but I had a little trouble with the Immelmans. It seemed that at the top, where I was to roll out, I continually ended up ninety degrees off my intended heading. After many attempts and going through the maneuver again and again with the model, I finally discovered my problem. I was not putting enough forward pressure on the stick as I rolled out. The elevators were acting like a rudder and letting the aircraft turn ninety degrees on top. I corrected that and finally could do a satisfactory Immelman holding the direction throughout the maneuver. So although I arrived at Cuero with a limited amount of experience, I did have the fundamentals of all aerobatics except the slow roll. The fact that I had been doing these maneuvers without the security of a chute made me execute the maneuvers with the least amount of pressure. Once I got my hands on the controls of a Stearman, I had little trouble in learning the rest of the aerobatic basics. Everyone knew a Stearman was built like a truck, so with it and a chute under me for the first time I felt secure and ready.

As the flight began, Buck did a series of stalls, power on and off, and I did some. He did a loop and I did a loop. He did a couple of snaps and I did one each way. Then he did a slow roll pivoting the nose on a point slightly above the horizon. This was the first time I had really had to hang in the belt upside down; looking up I saw the mesquite covered landscape. After a couple of tries I got the feel of that maneuver also. He did precision spins and I did two each way. We used the last fifteen minutes of the hour learning about the approved traffic pattern and the normal glide to landing. After the hour was up Buck crawled out of the front seat with his parachute, buckled the front seat belt, and said, "Take it up and have some fun running through the maneuvers we have just done."

The next hour was spent rolling and spinning and having the time of my life without fear of buckling struts or losing a wing. I can still remember the smell of the new airplane and the exhaust. The sound of the beautiful new engine on that Stearman was music to my ears. After some few hours of dual and solo practice I was ready for my final ride.

Captain Price was a regular army noncom who gave a try at flight school and made it. He rose rapidly from sergeant to captain and was certainly the right man to send to Cuero to establish standards for the new school. He was an absolute perfectionist and was quoted as saying, "See that fence post? There is a nail on the top of that. I want you to use the head of it for your point around which to make your pylon eights!"

He was also noted for shaking the stick at some point during takeoff to determine just how tense the student in the back seat was on the controls. We could see confirmation of such dynamic action on almost every takeoff. When we saw the ailerons wobble and the rudder flutter, we knew that Captain Price had another frightened pilot in the back seat.

Lieutenant Fitzgerald was a West Pointer whose background was vastly different from Captain Price's. He was second-in-command at this new post and also acted as an instructor and check pilot. He was as thorough as Price, but very mild mannered and shy.

Guess which one I drew for my final check ride? After getting seated and buckled in the aircraft, Captain Price told me what he wanted me to do. It was the entire routine. We were judged from the moment we started the engine until we returned to the parking line, a grueling forty or fifty minutes. At takeoff I was ready for the stick shaking and booting of the rudder. Since Price felt no resistance, I never felt him on the controls again. Apparently I did all right for I remember no comment except, "Okay, go to the next." I had passed the final hurdle to becoming a full-fledged instructor for the U.S. Army Air Corps.

Another fond memory of those early days in Cuero was the warm reception we received from the townspeople. Without fail, people opened the doors to let us in. Homes otherwise considered very private were made available to roomers. Some homes were vacated for lesser surroundings by the owners to make them available to Brayton families. The mayor's home was no exception— airport people roomed there, too! My room was in the home of Caroline and Bill Ferguson, a popular young couple who ran the main variety store in town.

This feeling of warmth was in complete contrast to what I knew was an innate dislike for anything with a Yankee connotation. We, from the Midwest, were somewhat unaware of the depth of feelings that were present all over the South as a result of those despicable days of the Yankee carpetbaggers. We were all the more flattered by the welcome when these feelings became known to us during our getting-acquainted period. Our fondness for those people and theirs for us grew with time. Many adjusted to life in Cuero and never left. Several instructors married local women and some stayed in business in the town. It may have been like this in most towns where primary training was done, but I do know that Cuero was outstanding.

I cannot remember what my room rented for, but by midspring, the house that Lieutenant Fitzgerald and Captain Price shared became available when Fitzgerald got married and Price was transferred. Dinny, Scotty, and I took over the cottage. It was a furnished house with two bedrooms, living room, kitchen, dinette, plus an attached garage—all for forty dollars per month. We also employed the maid that Price and Fitzgerald had hired. She came in every afternoon, cleaned the house, made beds, and prepared our dinner. We gave her money to buy groceries for the next evening as she left, so when she came to work through town she picked up the groceries. We paid her scale as the local people were afraid we would have a tendency to spoil the help by overpaying. She received two dollars and toting privileges—any leftovers that did not look as if they would last until tomorrow were hers for the taking. Needless to say we always had fresh food for every meal.

For awhile we took turns being house manager—planning the evening meal, paying the utility bills, taking the laundry on Monday and picking up on Tuesday, and paying the maid and providing her money for groceries. It was soon evident that only one of us was domestically inclined. When bills went unpaid for two months, laundry started to pile up, and the food got pretty bad, I decided something would have to be done. I offered to take over all those little chores for free rent and my roommates accepted gratefully. They preferred paying a little more and getting the service to taking any of the responsibility.

The little house soon became home, not only for us but for many of our former cadets who went on to San Antonio for further training. They had made many friends in Cuero during their cadet days, and on weekends they migrated back to Cuero and made our cottage their headquarters, dropping off their shaving kits and changes of clothes. Usually we did not see much of them until Sunday afternoon when they would begin to drag back to pick up their clothes and depart just in time to make the retreat parade in San Antonio. What a gang they were! Even after leaving advanced training many kept in touch with us while they scattered to the various parts of the globe. What a blow it was when we heard that, one after another, they had become another war statistic.

After about a year Scotty moved on to another base and Dinny got married, so I shared the cottage with Larry MacDonald, one of the supervisors in the maintenance department, until I left Cuero.

The first class of cadets arrived in late February and assignments were made. I ended up with five cadets—five of the most wonderful guys I have ever met. There was Marty Boswell from Roswell, New Mexico, an all-American football player from Iowa State; Bob Johnson, an aeronautical engineer from the University of Minnesota; and Al Sorenson, another graduate engineer. All three had had some CPT training, so they were easily started. Jim Talbot and Dick Carlton were green, but they learned fast and kept up pretty well with the upper three. When they took their final check ride they all passed with flying colors. It is sad to have to comment that cadets in that first class were washed out because of a stupid percentage quota requirement stating that so many in each class must fail. Those who washed out could have been outstanding students in the classes a year later. Even through advanced training and a few times after I left Cuero, I would hear from one or another of that first class. I was able to locate only Marty Boswell after the war, but I will always remember each of them as a prime example of American manhood and the pride of this wonderful country.

The last three months of that first class were something of a nightmare in my personal life. I had scarcely gotten the class underway when I received word from home that when the folks had completed the move to Marshalltown and Mom had hung the lace curtains, she had walked downtown to see Dr. Hansen to get a checkup. Apparently she was not surprised at the findings. She had cancer of the left breast. This explained her quietness when I had departed for the unknown. She had been scared, but she did not want her fear to show lest it deter me from my plans for the future. Looking back I am sure she thought she was saying goodbye to me for the last time.

It was not until my class graduated in June that I was able to get away. I rushed back to Iowa and was relieved to see her well on the way to recovery after a mastectomy. Old Dr. Hansen must have done everything right, for Mom lived another forty-one years. On my last Sunday at home, I was the best man when my sister Alice married Don Renaud. I had to rush away from the reception as I was due back in Cuero for my second class on Tuesday.

Halfway through our first class, the second class of cadets arrived and were assigned to the second echelon of instructors. In that group of instructors was a large contingent from Iowa: from Des Moines Bob Browne, Ernie Britton, Johnny Strauss, Ross White, Johnny Trett, and Phil Greer; from Ames Bob Nolan, Chuck Kennedy, and Marion Wearth; from Nevada Bill Oliver and Ernie Thoreson; from Ft. Dodge Glen Rohrer and Phil McCarty; from Waterloo Bruce Edge, Spider Eiler, and Ron Stark; from Decorah Charlie Buecher; from Davenport Ed Buergle; from Forest City Dick Thurston; and from Mason City Bill Evans.

Even Forrest O'Brine of the Jackson–O'Brine endurance team showed up. O'Brine had been flying for a new little airline called Chicago and Southern. He had received very little training as background in his career, which began to show up as he was taught the precision maneuvers. We found he had little sense of coordination, which was noted, and he was sent up for an army check ride where he failed and was released from the class. He was later killed when the plane he was delivering while in the ferry command crashed into a mountain in New Mexico.

I had my class at the stage of solo when I was pulled for check pilot duties. My class was broken up and distributed among other instructors, who by this time had vacancies from washouts. I retained one student who needed some special attention. One day he flew like a veteran and the next day like he had forgotten all he was supposed to have learned. I accused him of having learned to fly prior to joining the service. One noon when all the planes were out of the air I took him down to the home field traffic T and crawled out, telling him to make a couple of landings and we would go in for lunch.

The T was in the center of the field in order to conduct traffic patterns both right and left simultaneously. He took off in the right traffic pattern, proceeded successfully around the pattern and landed, bouncing over the T and me and landing finally on the left side. He took off again and negotiated the left traffic pattern as if nothing had happened. When he tried to land again, he bounced, recovered, and went around about three more times before I could stop him. This was one of his poor days. I was getting hungry and was concerned about having to shoot him down. He finally landed and came to a stop, so we finished the day. Later I was invited to his graduation ceremonies when he had completed the course at Ellington Field. I arrived too late to see the ceremony but had the honor of pinning on his new gold bars. Again I accused him of faking, but he still denied it.

Our first fatality occurred just before Christmas 1941. A weird contest had been going on for some time without our knowledge. The goal was to see how many turns could be accomplished during a spin in the Stearman. It apparently was up to about six or seven when we first heard about it, and then one of the daring young men set the record of eight. The problem was that after five turns a Stearman really starts to wrap up and it takes a special amount of technique — as well as a lot of altitude — to stop the spin. On this tragic day the spins started at about five thousand feet and ended at a minus three feet.

In the aftermath of the crash something happened that shaped my attitude as a check pilot from that time on. The day after the fatal spin I was conducting a routine check ride on one of Monty Lane's students. He was found to be far below proficiency level for the amount of time that he had. I was surprised he was not up for a washout ride. I made note of his many failing maneuvers. He was particularly bad at comprehending what a normal glide was supposed to be and was exceptionally rough and erratic on control use. At the end of the flight I told him I wanted to talk to his instructor before he went out solo again. Tears filled his eyes as he pleaded with me and told me how much it meant to him just to get through the early part of the course. He was sure he could make it from there. I relented and allowed him to go solo, but I warned him of things he should not do and what he should work on. I still wanted to talk to his instructor.

He checked out an airplane from the dispatcher and flew to a point near the site of the previous day's accident. When he suddenly discovered he was too close to another aircraft doing S turns along the road, he reacted with rough use of controls and snap rolled right into the ground within a few feet of where the accident had occurred the day before. We learned from other cadets that he had been watching while his friend was trying to set the spin record, and the crash seemed to bother him a great deal. For some sordid reason he chose that area to go to for practice that day. Up to that time I had prided myself as being easy to ride with. I tried to get students to relax so I could evaluate their ability rather than get the results of a frightened student who was tense and not producing up to par. After that, every time a student began to work on my sentiments I saw that boy with tears in his eyes pleading with me to let him get by. His death was on my conscience, but never another, for I remained fair and unrelenting when it came to ability to fly safely.

On the morning of December 7, 1941, I went to church in Cuero. After church, as I drove to the Morgan ranch for Sunday dinner, I heard on the car radio some confusing comments about a place called Pearl Harbor but could not make much of what it was all about. When I arrived at the ranch, they were all talking about the Japanese attack on Pearl Harbor. Like many others, I asked, "Where is Pearl Harbor?"

On Monday morning about ten of us unmarried pilots were standing in line awaiting the arrival of the commanding officer, who would commission us in the army. When he arrived at his office a wire was there. It was from the Gulf Coast Training Command and it stated that all instructors were frozen in present status until further notice. That ended that.

After Pearl Harbor and the two fatalities in our school, I welcomed the long weekend we had at Christmas. Dinny and I and a couple of friends made plans to go with the newlyweds, Elaine and Dick Thurston, to Monterrey, Mexico. Due to the war we had to obtain special releases to leave the country even for that short time. We picked up that bit of paperwork in San Antonio and proceeded toward the border at Laredo on Friday afternoon. Without difficulty we passed into Mexico and arrived in Monterrey after midnight.

That little outing is well remembered as it was the first time any of us had been away from home at Christmas, but it was only a forerunner of the many other Christmas holidays we would miss before the war was over.

We had all day Saturday to do nothing but sightsee. Being aviation minded, we included a visit to the local airport on our agenda. Here we found two almost obsolete airplanes, the best of which was an early model Stearman. An officer of questionable rank finally showed up, and upon learning we were instructors for the United States Army Air Corps, he offered each of us a commission of full colonel in the Mexican army if we would stay and take over the training. We were looking at the entire flying stock of the Mexican Air Force. I have often wondered what would have happened if we had been more dyed-in-the-wool soldiers of fortune, because before the war was over, Mexico had a sizable and impressive air force.

My first Christmas away from home gave me cause to wonder about the local customs. I had never heard firecrackers at Christmas. The plaza with promenading people was also new, the music was plaintive and beautifully strange to our ears, and the smells and sights were definitely alien to us. It was a weekend we had needed. When we returned, the unpleasant memories of the previous week had been somewhat dimmed but were never entirely gone.

The school went through many changes as it grew. Gordon Mathews, having completed the original start-up chores, found a better challenge in a similar position in South Carolina. Frank Altman, ostensibly a maintenance manager from Spartan School of Aeronautics in Tulsa, was hired to run the maintenance and the flight line. By January, Buck Taylor, Charlie Severin, and Jack Shelton had left for the newly established Air Transport Command (ATC) base at Love Field.

My check pilot duties ended and the responsibilities of the

instructors' school became mine in early January 1942. This meant full days at both ground and flight training, and the duties included the acceptance rides to determine if the candidates had the proper aptitudes to make it through the course. Some did not pass the initial ride due to lack of experience, a deficient background in the art of instructing, or the improper use of controls. During this tenure, which lasted a month, I successfully produced seventeen new instructors with a washout record of only two.

The day I was relieved of the instructors' school duties I was asked to pack my bag for a week and make a tour of all primary bases in the general area. The mission was to see if we were ahead or behind in procedures. I traveled to San Antonio, Uvalde, Corsicana, and several places in between, finding little if anything new. I returned to Cuero and made my report. At that point I was told that I was due for my annual check ride from Captain Fitzgerald. Apparently that went well; as soon as it was completed I was told that by complete agreement between the school and the military I was the new director of flying. This announcement came one year almost to the day after my acceptance ride at the school.

It was a little difficult to believe that in one year I had come from an eight hundred-hour applicant to the director of flying with thirteen hundred hours. I was now in charge of 50 instructors and 250 students. The school continued to grow, and by the time my release came through in June 1943 there were 150 instructors and 500 students.

I felt that my proficiency had grown with the growth of the school. I had always believed that any pilot should have some instruction experience. When I first acquired my instructor rating back in Des Moines, I thought I just about had it all. I didn't realize how wrong I was until I put through my first class; that is when I finally learned what it was all about.

With dozens of check rides per week I was soon able to predict the type of ride I would get before we had even taken off. Often I would write on the back of the grading sheet what I thought the grade would be. We would then go ahead with each maneuver and I would grade the execution before going to the next. It was amazing how many times I totaled a student's score and found it was exactly the same as the one I had recorded before takeoff. When weather interrupted our flight schedule and put us about ten hours behind in the program with only a week to go, everybody had to do double duty, including the cadets. On many occasions I would have a dozen or fifteen check rides per day.

It was a great shock to me to find some who really wanted to be washed out. One cadet who wanted out nearly killed us both during his progress check ride at about solo stage. As usual, I told the cadet what I wanted him to do in the flight. All was passable through taxiing out and leaving the ground. He made the first turn at two hundred feet, which is low, but it was necessary to get the planes taking off out of the way of planes that follow. However, when this cadet started the turn with insufficient airspeed, I knew we were in trouble. I took over just in time, as we went into a bad slip at treetop level. I shouted through the Gosport tube that I had it and told him not to touch the controls again. I flew it around the pattern and landed. I taxied in and parked, shut down the engine, and then turned around and said, "What were you trying to do out there, kill us both?" His reply was most astounding. He told me that the only way he could get out of the horrible tropics, where he had been assigned previously, was to put in for flight training. He did not want to fly and had no intention of ever soloing. He wanted to be washed out and reassigned.

I said, "You sure picked a suicidal way to do it." This being the first of such startling events, I personally escorted him to the commanding officer's office, where the story was repeated. Within fifteen minutes he was off the base and gone forever from flight. Needless to say we watched for future cases so we would not be caught in jeopardy on the first turn. What bothered me most was the fact we had some cadets who were pleading for another chance to stay with tears in their eyes.

With any new job come new responsibilities and duties. As director of flying one of my new duties was to go out and pick up planes that had been landed off the airport. Most often the planes were there because the student had concentrated on his practicing and forgot to keep his position in mind in reference to the home field. When he learned that he was lost he would notice too that he did not have enough gas to spend much time looking for home. As a precaution, the students would pick a likely field and set the plane down. When we got a call we would keep the cadet on the phone until we had a very definite location. I would put a thumbtack on the wall map, pack up ten gallons of gas and my parachute, and drive with a mechanic to where we thought the plane was located. Often it would be more than a two-hour drive. When I left Cuero in June I had sixty-five pins on the wall map.

One day we got a call from a farmer just west of our field. He said that an airplane had crashed but he had seen a parachute before the plane hit. We located the wreckage site on the map and started out to gather up a cadet. We had not gone far when along the side of the road we found a red-faced cadet carrying a bundle of parachute silk. We asked him how he got there because according to our directions he should have been about five miles farther west. "Oh," he said, "that's another one. I saw him as I was coming down. My airplane, or what is left of it, is right over the hill." We quickly got out and went to look for the wreck and there it was. With the engine about three feet in the ground, the entire wreckage could have been covered with a ten-foot tarp. It went straight in, and the plywood wing had burst into a million small pieces upon impact. With one down and another to find we loaded the cadet and his silk aboard and proceeded to the locale of the original call-in.

This was the stage after solo when each student is given a routine to follow during solo flight. They start off with stalls, both power on and power off. To recover from either one takes a certain technique which includes quite a forceful forward movement of the stick. This forward movement was just enough to catapult a careless cadet straight out of the airplane. That day neither had remembered to fasten his seat belt before taking off, although that is not what we were told had happened. "I must have caught my sleeve on the belt release during my stall recovery" seemed a better answer than admitting negligence. Chalk off two PT-19s in less than two minutes.

I took my vacation in the summer of 1942 and flew a Luscombe home from Cuero. I rented the airplane from Arley Simmons and took advantage of the easy transportation to visit all the friends I had left at Waterloo and Hampton. I enjoyed the week a great deal. The day before I was to leave I jokingly asked my dad if he would like to fly down to Texas with me and come back by train. At that point he had traveled only in each of the states bordering Iowa. "I'll go!" he said quickly. I am glad I asked him, for he talked about that trip until the day he died. We overnighted in a small town in Oklahoma, dodged a few rainstorms the next morning, and arrived over Cuero by midafternoon. I let the little Luscombe merge with the military traffic, flew the pattern, and landed. Dad had made his longest journey ever so easily that it was hard for him to believe we were over a thousand miles from Iowa and home.

Mac and I took a day off during the next week to take Dad to San Antonio to see the Alamo, the zoo, and the beautiful parks of the city. He was impressed with that and the cotton fields in between. We even took him out to visit Richie Taylor's plantation, where he was treated to a wonderful luncheon. It was like dumping him into the midst of *Gone with the Wind* and he was no less impressed.

After almost a week of new sights and sounds he was ready to return to reality, and I think he looked forward to the train ride home, for it was something he could understand.

Although we were busy at Cuero and we worked hard, we still had time for some extracurricular activities. My favorite was basketball, which had had a great influence on my development. It all started in the eighth grade and ended in 1943. When we were seniors in high school Max Adair was center, Russ Hibbs and Don Hines were the forwards, while Alvin Rosedale and I were guards. We won the county and sectional tournaments but finally were ousted in the district finals just prior to going to the state tournament.

I made the starting lineup during my first year in junior college under Coach Warren Dickenson. Players were Gil Collison at center, Don Taylor and Red Akers at forward, and Don Ulmer and I at guard. My playing on the varsity at Iowa State Teachers College led to my first job as coach and teacher at Hansell. The real kicker was that I earned the money for flight training by officiating both boys and girls basketball games.

While at Hampton I played against the original Globe Trotters on two occasions. During my last year at Boone I was on a team that won an industrial league tournament. The team consisted of Wayne Hill, the high school basketball coach; Bucky O'Connor, a former Drake star and later the University of Iowa coach; Donald Knight; Mike Martin; Walter Hagaleen; Ed Yegge; and me.

At Cuero we had a very good team made up of flight instructors, most of whom had come from the north since basketball was not a major sport in the south at that time. I think we brought the first fast-break type of basketball that had been seen in those parts.

We did all right against local teams but stepped out of our class when we took on the air corps team from Victoria. That group had a bunch of ringers, all of whom had played college ball. They were younger, bigger, and faster than we were, and we were barely able to keep from being routed.

Basketball kept me in shape and added to my ability to handle the rugged schedules we would fly later while I was based in India. There is no doubt in my mind that the years of basketball and my college courses in tumbling made it much easier for me to accept aerobatics than it was for those who had not had the experience.

Romulus

Charles Kennedy came to Cuero from Ames, Iowa, with the third tier of instructors and was one of those obtaining a release early in 1943. He went to Romulus, Michigan, west of Detroit, and wrote back about the need for pilots at that Air Transport Command (ATC) base. So when my release looked imminent I sent an application to Romulus and was accepted, pending passing the board of review, a flight test, and a physical.

By this time I had about all the single-engine time needed to make a balanced background. I was looking to the future and felt that when the war ended there would be a need for transport pilots; therefore, I wanted all the multiengine time I could get as soon as possible. Going to Romulus seemed to be the best way to do that. Romulus pilots were chiefly engaged in ferrying B-24s, the Liberator bombers, out of the nearby Willow Run factory. I did not have high altitude training or training on large engines, controllable-pitch propellers, retractable landing gear, hydraulic systems, electrical systems, and many other facets of flight, such as radio communications and navigation. The three years of intensive single-engine time at Cuero was a meager background for the type of flying I was about to encounter.

Leaving Cuero was sad because I was leaving good friends made during the previous three years. My memories are still rich with the moonlight dancing at River Tavern; the music from that jukebox was almost as good as if Helen O'Connell had been right there singing "Amapola," "Green Eyes," and "San Antonio Rose." The parties, especially those sumptuous barbecues out at Richie Taylor's, with ribs and chicken and goat all bathed in succulent sauces plus the camaraderie of genial friends, provided memories I carried on my way to Romulus. Somewhere along that northward route I began to subdue the thoughts of Cuero and to look forward to what was going to happen when I arrived at my destination. I had passed the point of no return.

I spent a few days at home in Marshalltown, and on June 7, 1943, I pushed on toward Michigan on old U.S. 30, past Chicago and within a few miles of Romulus. On the morning of June 8 I was at the gate, the threshold of one of the largest steps I would take in aviation.

The acceptance board was the most awesome hurdle to me, since it was an unknown factor. The board was made up of Major House, Captain Bright, and a third member whose name I have since forgotten. The board was to determine my suitability to be commissioned as an officer in the U.S. Army Air Corps. I was interrogated at some length and felt all was going well until they brought up a topic for which I was not prepared.

A few weeks before I left Cuero we had to fire one of the instructors who had put his student out of the plane at one of the auxiliary fields and replaced him with his young bride for an airplane ride. Of course the student's time went on but he was not getting his training. Some others saw the incident, and the student had to verify what happened. This same instructor had applied for acceptance at Romulus just a few days before my arrival. How the board learned about this incident I will never know, but they had and they wanted confirmation from me. They also asked for my opinion about the matter.

I didn't know exactly how to answer all those questions. I was not too interested in any of the past details. I just wanted to get in and be free of such matters. How could I answer without jeopardizing my position or his? Possibly I was being interrogated to see how loyal I would be or how much I could be trusted. I resented the position I was put in. Finally they asked me how I would like to fly with him as copilot or have him as mine. I said that I would rather not do either. It seemed to be what they wanted to know. I was accepted and he was not. I felt bad about it, but after all, I did not create the awkward situation — he did. I understood later he went to Canada and was well situated soon after leaving Romulus. That ended that problem.

Before the day was over I had successfully met the board, spent an hour in the back seat of an AT-6, and taken the physical. The next day was spent signing in on the base, which seemed an endless task. I did not know until much later that the board recommended that I be commissioned a first lieutenant instead of a second, one of the last such commissions to be given out at Romulus.

I was assigned to the Fifth Squadron and reported for duty, which consisted of letting them know I was there and then sitting in the ready room for an assignment. I was assigned to the copilot's seat in a C-60 Lockheed Lodestar. What I knew about a C-60 you could put in your eye and never feel it. The pilot, however, a Lieutenant Young, was most considerate and had this type of problem almost every day. He was helpful and before we got back from the seven hour flight I had a little knowledge of how to call the tower and tune in the radios for navigation. I had learned just enough on that first flight to know how much more I had to learn in a hurry.

My next assignment was as copilot on a B-25, North American's twin-engine Mitchell medium bomber. It was a great experience but I learned very little on that flight, for there was only a single-pilot cockpit on that version and my radio work was about the only help anyone could give the pilot. There was another C-60 flight with Lieutenant Young, and four days later I was given a PT-26 for delivery to Bowden, Canada. The other pilot was Lieutenant Breithaupt, formerly with Reading Air Service, and later to be the chief owner. Our route took us up across the Dakotas and Montana. While in Great Falls for lunch, we noticed a group of Russian pilots. They were there to pick up a flight of P-39s our pilots had delivered from Buffalo. The Russians refused to allow anyone to fly into their territory. They were obviously a rugged lot.

From Great Falls we flew to Lethbridge, Calgary, and finally to Bowden. We were rudely surprised upon our arrival to find the instructors were very much against the changeover from their beloved DeHavilland Moths to this new design, although one would think that the enclosed cockpit would have had some attraction in that climate. They had heard some bad reports about the spin characteristics of this new trainer, but there was no basis whatsoever for such rumors. No airplane ever recovered from spins any easier than the PT-19 series. We offered to give demonstrations but they were not receptive, so we left somewhat nonplussed by their attitude.

It was a long trip back. We had to stay in the little town until about midnight to catch a train to Calgary. It was worth the wait however, as it was Saturday night and all the country folks were in town, just like "Little Town," USA. The noticeable difference was that every woman had a long, heavy fur coat. Before the sun had gone far over the horizon I could understand why. It got very cold, even though it was July. Following the train ride to Calgary our flight on Trans Canada Airlines took us to Kapuskasing, and late at night across the area north of the Great Lakes and into Detroit. I saw northern lights from the plane — we were in them. In the moonlight one could see for miles in all directions — nothing but water and trees and endless space.

Going out on a delivery, I was soon to discover, was the best first-class transportation one would get during the entire round trip. We had no priority and had to return with the available transportation, which was often a local train with its milk cars, no diners, and certainly no sleepers. We would arrive back at our base dirty, tired, and somewhat disillusioned about the so-called glamour of flying during wartime.

I had another trip on an L-2 out of the Taylorcraft factory in Alliance, Ohio, to Mobile, Alabama. This took us out over the Fourth of July and again we experienced a horrible train ride back from the deep South.

When I checked in at the squadron the Monday after the Fourth of July, I found I was enrolled in pursuit school. This meant a lot of time in the back seat of an AT-6 in order to get the feel of landings without seeing too well. We were to get the P-40 first, then the Bell P-39 AirCobra. I had checked out in the AT-6 and was about to get my first indoctrination in the P-40 when I got another call. I had been enrolled in officers' training school (OTS), which was a six-week course.

I never got back to pursuit school and actually never regretted it, since I was hoping to get all the multiengine time I could muster. As soon as I graduated from OTS, Lieutenant Russ Hopf and I were selected to head the training of the next class. Our immediate superior was Captain Flo, a very exacting officer who had experience as a mail pilot during the fiasco when Roosevelt felt that military pilots could do a better job than civilian pilots. The military pilots were trained in military tactics, but what they knew about instrument flight at that time was nil. Consequently many innocent pilots hit the mountains in the night and during bad weather, and were losers in both the battles.

Flo survived. He had had some medical problems, and while awaiting reinstatement as a pilot, he had been given the assignment of ground training, which included officers and boot training. He spotted Russ and me and asked us to be his assistants.

It was about this time that I underwent a heartbreaking episode. I saw a lot of my friend Chuck Kennedy after I arrived at Romulus. He gave me the aid of his experience, since he had been there about a month. While I was in officers' training, he went on with pursuit transition and by the time I had graduated from OTS he was building up time on the Curtiss P-40 Fighter. No one knows what caused it, but his P-40 caught fire. He tried to get it on the ground as soon as possible, since he was too low to jump, and the smoke prevented his being able to see enough to land on the highway north of the field. The plane went in and Chuck was killed instantly. My first duty as a commissioned officer was to accompany his body back to his home in Ames, Iowa.

It was an uncomfortable duty. What could I tell his mother and sister? How could I soften the blow? I left Detroit on the train about four thirty in the afternoon following the accident. The train was due in Ames the next morning. Out of Chicago, I had just completed my morning's refreshment and had come back to my car when I ran across Glen Smaha and Russ Hibbs from Marshalltown. They had been in Chicago the day before to see a Cubs game. I was glad to see someone from home, and they helped me keep my mind off the ordeal ahead for some time.

I don't know how or what I said, but the family made it as easy as possible for me, and I did the best I could to do the same for them. Just being there as a friend, I think, was most important to them.

Although it was to be expected during the war, facing death head-on never became any easier. Two of my close acquaintances who had graduated from OTS with me were on a delivery in west Texas. They were apparently flying close formation when an unexpected gust caused a collision; neither could get out before they crashed in a heap. On another occasion, I had just completed my checkout in the Lockheed 60 when a new crew took the aircraft out for landing practice at a field near Toledo. No one ever found out why, but it stalled and crashed on the downwind leg, taking the instructor and two pilot trainees to their deaths. One of my new acquaintances at Romulus was Lou Stumbaugh, who had been a test pilot at Bell with my friend Dick Krachel. Lou told me about Dick's accident. He was doing tumbling tests in the dangerous P-39. Things went wrong and Dick got out too late. Another friend was gone. These catastrophes and others kept me from ever relaxing or thinking that I had it made.

Going through officers' training precluded my flying from July 10 to September 2. Having some status now on the base, I was able to pull some strings and get into transition for training in my spare time. They put me in the Curtiss AT-9, which was a good twin-engine trainer; if you could fly it you could fly almost anything else. If you had five hundred feet of altitude over the end of the runway and chopped the throttles, you would land almost under the spot. Its glide ratio was just about zero. It had a big cockpit with the same layout as the Curtiss C-46.

I earned my first multiengine rating in the AT-9 and following that came the UC-78, a most docile airplane in comparison. The Lockheed Hudson bomber was a British design. It was known as the A-29 and had controls only for the pilot. Ours was a special dual-control trainer, on hand for transition. I had about four hours of that training and was considered checked out.

The C-47 came next. I had had a copilot trip with Russ Hopf to Montreal before taking any training myself. Russ had checked out in the C-47 while I was working on the A-29. I finally got assigned to get my checkout in the C-47 destined for Montreal as part of a group of planes. Lou Ramey was my instructor. We made one trip around the traffic pattern and had to land due to overheated oil on the right engine. It was almost noon, so while it was being corrected we went to lunch. When we returned we found departing was to be expedited due to freezing rain predicted in Detroit and along the route. I scurried around to find Lieutenant Ramey, who also had an airplane to deliver. He said, "You are checked out — get going!" So, with less than ten minutes in the air in the left seat, I was on my way. My copilot was Curly Gullet, whom I knew while in officers' training. I also knew he was a pursuit pilot and did not necessarily care about big airplanes.

At this point I did not have an instrument rating, which was not too startling since very few others did either. We were off and en route with this new airplane loaded with freight for England. It had British markings and was part of the big push before D day, a date which at that point was unheard of. By the time we got to Toronto, the clouds had lowered and we were beginning to pick up ice, so we aborted the flight and landed. The C-47, the civilian version of which is the DC-3, has a big rudder, much like a big barn door. The wind was gusting at Toronto and the landing was passable, but pretty scary to a pursuit pilot who was used to landing by dragging his tail on the ground.

When I leveled off to land, Curly almost came out of the cockpit thinking I would be stalling any second. The wheels started rolling on the runway much to his and my relief. In the crosswind, while taxiing in, Curly had to help me on the rudder, because it was about to push me out of the seat at every gust of wind. When we finally got parked, Curly tried to get out of his seat and almost fell down because he had worn out his one leg trying to hold the rudder steady for me. He was not impressed with flying big airplanes and said he would much rather never see one again. Curly was soon transferred to another base and later to India. (It is ironic that he was killed in a Curtiss C-46 commando, with Charlie Gatchet, a pilot I had known in Iowa, who had for many years flown the *Des Moines Register and Tribune* planes. On a test flight an engine caught fire and burned the wing off, dumping them in the ocean off Karachi Air Base.)

The next morning dawned clear and cold in Canada and we delivered our planes to Montreal. What a sight it was. The center of the field had been rolled to pack the snow. The runways were kept clear but the snow kept piling up in the infield. Hundreds of planes were parked there awaiting suitable weather to make the Atlantic crossing. There were B-17s, C-47s, B-25s, and C-46s — all loaded with freight and supplies of all kinds for the big push, which we knew was bound to come sometime. It took supplies and backup to win a war, and what I saw was most encouraging. Planes landing went out of sight to watchers on the infield because of the high packed snow. It was difficult to get back to Detroit by train, so we were routed through New York by air then back to Detroit by train.

By Christmas Russ and I had the ground school under control and we took delivery flights any time we could work them in without interfering with our primary duties. I made three deliveries to Newark before Christmas: a British PT-26 plus two Stinson Re-

60

liants, also destined for the British. The Stinson was known as the AT-19 and was filled with sophisticated radio equipment, perhaps to serve as an observation platform in a combat zone. They were dismantled at Newark and shipped by sea to their destinations.

Russ Hopf and I spent many hours working out the training program, and when we got bored we would go over to operations and check out an airplane. It was a good arrangement and we were getting the experience we needed. We had similar backgrounds and were commissioned side by side in July while in officers' training.

Once we found ourselves involved with the ground school we were ready to try some new steps. We were both struck by the lack of organization in the ground school each time we had to attend a session. Since we had the responsibility dumped in our laps, we got our heads together and did something about it. It took several weeks and a lot of cajoling with the brass above us to get a go-ahead. We developed a ground school course commensurate with the flight training. For example, pilots who were new took an indoctrination course, and if they were flying visual flight rules (VFR) we saw to it they knew map reading and the pertinent rules and regulations. Advanced pilots took courses related to instrument flying. No longer were we to hear complaints from pilots who were delivering B-24s to Europe about having to take map reading courses. Instead, we gave them what they needed—high altitude flight, long-range fuel economy, radio navigation, and other related subjects. It made sense to us and eventually to the powers that be. We implemented our system, and one-by-one the pilots upgraded themselves in logical order from Phase I through Phase IV. Hearing about our new system, people came up from headquarters in Cincinnati to study the procedures. We learned later it was adopted at all bases in the ferry division of ATC. (We should have had a promotion!) Everybody benefited and that meant something to us.

It was many months later when I went to Reno that I learned that I had made an error. Since I had done all I could with ground training I made the mistake of asking to be assigned to transition in order to build up flight experience. One does not ask for a transfer. It did not occur to me that moving sideways, such as this, under the same colonel who was in charge of both ground and flight training, would be a black mark against me. Apparently he used that as an excuse to give me a "very satisfactory" rather than an "excellent" rating. It also struck me that he was getting even with me for a bad call I made at first base during a softball game in which I had served as umpire. His squadron was playing in the game and I remember he got pretty hot about the call which I tried to forget. Apparently he did not. At any rate, I did not get my promotion until I had served six more months—after receiving an "excellent" rating in India. I had heard of worse cases of injustice so I did not complain too much.

Before Christmas of 1943 I was serving on the same acceptance board that had screened my own application. It was an honor and yet a sorrowful experience to turn down applicants with three to four thousand hours because the pilot pool was up to saturation point. Had they applied earlier they would have been accepted. As it was, great pilots went back to being privates in the walking army. What a waste of talent! Injustices were rife during those tumultuous years.

My transfer to transition worked out the way I wanted, as I was instructing on the C-47 and building up time on the B-24 until I was qualified in that bomber. I also acquired my instrument rating during the spring months and had an opportunity to use the skills many times. From June 1943 to June 1944 I had accumulated more experience than in any other year since my first solo.

Reno Bound

By early July 1944 I was an experienced instructor in the transition department. I had instructed on the UC-78, C-47, and all the single-engine aircraft including the C-64 Norseman.

One morning I was killing time before I was to go on the afternoon schedule and fly until midnight. I got to the airport a little early and found they had been trying to get in touch with me all morning. I learned I had been transferred to Reno and was to leave that night. Checking off a base is an all-day job and here I had only a few hours until I was to be airborne for Reno. It was a frantic time. No one had bothered to relieve me of the responsibility for equipment in the ground school. It seemed I was the "owner" of several mock-up cockpits, a lot of radio equipment, office equipment, and supplies. Had it not been for a kindly WAC who was high-up in the supply division I would still be there. Even then I was barely able to get an overnight bag packed and make the departure from Romulus at five o'clock.

The C-47 was loaded with pilots, most of whom I knew. The command pilot was also a friend of mine, Paul Engard. The first stop was in Des Moines, another in North Platte, and a third in Cheyenne, plus one more in Salt Lake City where we had a lousy breakfast at the line shack. The final leg into Reno was rough and hot. We had been unable to get anything but catnaps all night and were dirty and tired when we were unloaded like a bunch of cattle at the Reno Air Base. That trip was only an introduction to the rough six weeks which were to come.

We spent most of the first day checking in and getting equipment we would need for the course. I now realize what we were getting was the equivalent of an airline transport course of instruction. In fact the school was operated to a great extent by Pan American personnel. The flight instructors were former Hump pilots, but most of the ground school was conducted by civilians on the Pan Am payroll. It was rugged.

Our schedules started out with a full day of ground school, with scarcely time to grab a sandwich between classes. Then we had the Link trainer well into the night. My first closeup look at the massive Curtiss C-46 was at midnight. On the preflight inspection when I looked up into that gaping hole which was the wheel well, I wondered how anybody could learn to handle such a monster.

Each instructor was assigned two pilots. My flying mate was Lieutenant Peterson, who had been at Long Beach ATC. Our instructor was Stanley Janeczko, who had been based at Sookertang in Assam prior to returning to the States. We were his first students. Our first flight took us from midnight until noon the next day. We flew over to Sacramento and shot landings for several hours. And then when it was daylight we went through all the air maneuvers such as stalls, multiengine procedures, and other projects to get us acquainted with the airplane and its flying characteristics. We were through at noon and had no more activity scheduled until noon the next day. So it went — twenty-four hours on and twelve off. We could not understand such a rigorous schedule until we got overseas and found that that was a way of life on the front line.

Reno Air Base was located north of the city. Approaches were made on the low frequency range station located near the down-town airport. From there it was another ten miles by automatic direction finder (ADF) to the air base, all of which had to be done under-the-hood with precision.

During our time off we took advantage of the entertainment in downtown Reno. We became acquainted with the dealers and the casino owners, one of whom was a special friend of pilots. On one occasion he took a couple of us into his office and showed us a spindle full of checks. They were post dated checks from pilots who needed some extra money, and he had loaned them what they needed. He said he had yet to lose a dime.

We all had special haunts. Mine was the Town House. There was an organist there and a friendly bartender. I remember it was there that I first heard the song, "I'll Walk Alone." It seemed a very appropriate tune. Even though we were together, each of us knew it was up to only one person to see the thing through.

The day for the final check ride came. Ground school was over, the cantankerous Link trainer was subdued, and off we went for the final test flight. Mine was with Big John Payne, who had been in India. In fact, he was mentioned in Robert Scott's book, *God Is My Copilot-pilot.* John was there when they needed to evacuate a bunch of Burmese from an airstrip in northern Burma. According to the account the strip was only about eighteen hundred feet long. Burmese are small in stature, granted, but there were something like thirty-five of them to take out in the C-47 or leave to the invading Japanese. He landed at Chabua with thirty-six, as one of the passengers chose to have her baby during the flight.

I don't remember much detail about our check ride. It was a repeat of all we had been practicing for six weeks, and apparently we passed. Having four hours to go on our required time we took a plane on a sightseeing trip, because all this time we seldom could see our surroundings as we were under the hood or too busy to notice.

We took off and headed for Mount Shasta. We had seen it at a distance from time to time but had never come close to its beautiful snowcapped conical peak. Circling, we discovered it had a small active volcanic cone near its base. Upon further observation we could tell that the big peak itself was of volcanic origin. From there we wandered on down over Sacramento and saw it for the first time in the daylight. Flying over the ridge to Tahoe and Donner

Summit, we were reminded of the stories of early pioneers who were marooned there in the winter of 1846–47.

While at Reno I finally got to be a believer in use of oxygen. We were flying one night between Reno and Salt Lake City at fifteen thousand feet and I felt pretty good. Up to this point the instructor had said little about the use of our oxygen mask. He was using me as an experiment. Suddenly the instrument panel began to blur and dance before my eyes. I could not understand what was happening. Things got dim and I was unable to concentrate on anything. Stan said, "Put your oxygen mask on and turn it on to pure oxygen." I did. Suddenly the lights flared to brilliant white, the instrument panel settled down, and so did I. I was at the brink of passing out for lack of oxygen. Our procedure from that point on was to go on oxygen at nine thousand feet and leave it on throughout the landing no matter what the altitude of the landing site. Since the many hours of oxygen use, I cannot fly above nine thousand feet without it.

Nashville and Beyond

After our four-hour joy ride in the C-46 we had just enough time to make one more visit to our casino friends in Reno. I heard "I'll Walk Alone" once again at the Town House.

All of our class were en route to the pilot pool at Nashville. After a short stay of two days in Marshalltown, I checked in at the ATC base at Nashville early in September.

We reported each morning for roll call, and if orders did not concern us, we were free until the next day's roll call. We spent time at the commercial terminal building watching the world go by; we spent time at the officers' club and wherever a person could kill time. We were bored most of the time.

At one point we went to the firing range for weapons qualification. Someone got the idea that even flying officers should know how to handle a gun. First it was the Colt automatic. This .45-caliber handgun was designed during the Spanish-American War, ostensibly for use in the Philippines to kill or stop the frenzied

Moros, who seemed to thrive on facing gunfire head-on while running at full speed. The .45 carried such a wallop with its huge slug that it was supposed to fell a Moro if you hit him anywhere above the knees. It was also unpredictable. About ten feet was the maximum range you could depend upon hitting anything with such a gun.

Before the shooting even started, I got lucky. The gun I drew had a hair trigger and always fired before I expected it to. My record for the rounds before lunch was ninety-six out of one hundred bull's-eyes. Naturally I marked the gun so I could use it in the afternoon session. I found the little gem after lunch, used it for the bobbing target event, and made eight out of ten of those. The bobbing target was about the size of a man's torso and bobbed between a full front view and a side view the thickness of the target only.

My eight out of ten, plus the morning score, qualified me for the designation of Expert, which is the marksman medal with a wreath around it. The range master was so impressed he took his own medal off and gave it to me, saying that by the time the scores were processed and the medal returned I would perhaps be long gone. I appreciated that and told him about the gun I had used, for it was special.

Proof that .45s differ was demonstrated one day at West Palm Beach. We were awaiting orders to proceed with our trip overseas when my navigator, copilot, and I decided to go to the range and sight in our newly assigned sidearms. I found that I was lucky to hit the clay bank behind the target. The gun kicked like a mule and the trigger pull was rough and difficult, but I did not turn it in for another because another may have been even worse. All I did was accept the fact that I had a typical .45 and pray that my life would never depend upon my shooting something with it.

We were at Nashville almost a month when some of us got orders to go to Buffalo and move some C-46s from there to Romulus and Memphis. Lieutenant Peterson, my flying buddy at Reno, was on the same orders as I. We rode to Buffalo in the bowels of a B-17. We delivered C-46s to Romulus and had lunch there at my old officers' club, where I saw many friends.

It was while we were there that I heard about McCaffery. Red was in OTS with me and was commissioned a first lieutenant shortly after I was. When I asked for transfer to transition he took over my place as head of the ground school. He was soon promoted to captain. He had finished a PBY delivery to Honolulu; while standing on a street corner on the air base, he was hit by a drunken sergeant in a jeep and killed on the spot.

After lunch we returned to Buffalo and picked up the second bunch of C-46s destined for Memphis. Peterson got tail number 6789 and mine was 6787. They were eager for us to depart Buffalo just for their record, so ten aircraft left there and went as far as Columbus, Ohio, and there spent the night.

The following day we flew to Memphis via St. Louis. I remember how difficult it was to see Lambert Field from twelve thousand feet through all the haze. It appeared, from that height, that Lambert was in a bowl. We delivered the airplanes to Memphis and were flown back to Nashville for more waiting.

A few days later we were back in Memphis for staging. Here pilots-in-command were appointed and crew members and planes assigned. Surprisingly I got the aircraft that Lieutenant Peterson brought in from Buffalo and he got mine. We flew together on almost all of the overseas delivery. My copilot was Lieutenant Joe Farrel. We were assigned a navigator whose name I have lost. There was also a crew chief aboard to take care of maintenance problems. Each airplane was equipped with a dome for celestial sightings by the navigator.

While we were in Memphis we were also issued clothing and equipment. We got gas masks, oxygen masks, mosquito netting, warm underwear, and rough GI shoes and socks. From such an assortment of clothing and equipment much speculation was made as to our destination. There was never any doubt in my mind where we were going. However, they did need airplanes and crews along the route to move equipment and people, and there was always that chance you might get something less than the Hump. The C-46 was often called the "Music Box"—open the door and you hear "Song of India."

We left Memphis at eight o'clock with an empty airplane the morning after arriving there. Our destination was West Palm Beach, where we were to pick up part of our cargo load. The flight took only four hours and fifty minutes. En route I located the spot near Opopka where in 1939 I had made a forced landing among the orange groves due to heavy fog conditions.

We also noticed that both fuel quantity gauges were inoperative. We could not go on without those important instruments, and it took ten days to have them replaced. While at West Palm all we could do was spend the time at the officers' club pool and talk to the local ladies who came out from town to keep us company. The nights were typical of southern Florida, with low cumulus clouds, moonlight enhanced by the white sandy soil, and the silhouette of palm trees everywhere. It was hard to take and harder to leave.

Our trip to Miami was only a forty-minute hop to the Thirty-sixth Street Airport. Here the plane was loaded for its final dispatch for overseas. It took all day October 12 to accomplish the task. We had two Allison engines, several spare tires, and tool kits aboard, which just about filled the cavernous interior of the cargo area. Belly compartments were also well filled but with enough room for our personal duffel.

On the morning of Friday, October 13, we left the Thirty-sixth Street Airport and climbed out over the Caribbean, with orders sealed until one hour out of the country. It was dark when we left and we had most of our nine thousand feet of altitude before we began to see daylight. The navigator had made several trips similar to this so we were leaning on him to keep us informed on what to expect.

It is a good thing I am not superstitious, for there we were at nine thousand feet between layers of clouds on Friday the thirteenth, and when the sun began to appear we saw rain from the upper level clouds falling into those below. I was curious about a rainbow that formed a perfect circle around the tail of the airplane. Another fateful phrase struck my mind. As a child I had learned a variation of the saying "Red sky in morning, sailor take warning . . . " that went "Rainbow in morning, sailors take warning; rainbow at night, sailors' delight." How many more omens did I need before panic set in?

An hour out we opened our sealed orders and were not surprised to find the plane and contents were destined for Calcutta. I was to report to the ATC headquarters at Hasting Mill in Calcutta for further assignment.

Our destination the first day was Borinquen Field, located on the western coast of Puerto Rico. It was an uneventful six-hour flight from Miami to our destination. The air base was surrounded by tropical vegetation, lots of palm trees, and acres of banana plants. I had never seen anything like this before, yet I sensed that I had been there. Déjà vu. Our bachelor officers' quarters (BOQ) were on a high bluff overlooking the Atlantic to the north and the huge valley of tropical growth to the south. A breeze off the blue sea kept the comfort level ideal and bugs and flies were not present. We got another surprise at the officers' club that night. Before dinner we ordered the ever-popular daiquiris. They were served in huge fishbowl glasses for fifteen cents. After the first two or three we didn't seem to care if we were going overseas or not.

With a destination of Georgetown, Guiana, we left at dawn and made a stop at Bean Field on Trinidad. From that base we were given vectors to fly toward our destination of Atkinson Field because some aircraft had gone down in the jungles and had not been located. Each plane was given a different heading to fly in an attempt to locate the wreckage before finally leaving the search. Then we flew direct to Atkinson.

On Sunday morning, October 15, we left Atkinson on time, destination Belém, Brazil, This is a little spot almost on the equator. Again we were on the alert for lost aircraft in a dense jungle for as far as we could see to the west. Seldom was there a rise in the flat, endless terrain. To our left was the Atlantic. We finally crossed the wide Amazon mouth—almost a hundred miles of water, islands, and more water. Then Belém.

Here we had another new experience. Since the trip was only five and a half hours long, we were on the ground well before nightfall. We went in the BOQ in broad daylight, cleaned up, and when we stepped out a few minutes later it was completely dark. There is no twilight in the tropics. When I looked at a globe I understood. It is the same principle that causes twilight to last almost all night in the far north in the summer months.

The next day's destination was Natal, Brazil. Natal is located on the easternmost tip of South America and was chosen by the Pan American pioneers as a good jumping-off place for the African continent. Again, we were thoroughly surprised at the results of the bar offerings. Just one bottle of Brazilian beer and we were out of touch with the world. It seems they did not have the restriction of 3.2 percent beer which prevailed in the States. It took little to go a long way under those circumstances.

Our schedule called for us to be on the flight line for the longest leg of our journey early the next morning. The crew was on hand and the airplane was ready, but operations would not clear us for the flight because pilots had been coming in from Ascension Island in record time. Since the report indicated that we would not have the favorable winds necessary to reach Ascension Island with fuel reserves, we were able to enjoy an unexpected day on the beaches of Natal, where I could barely walk out to hip-deep water without being toppled by the crashing waves. A few bottles of Brazil's favorite beverage kept our minds off swimming and off the fact that we would have to face the day's navigational problem all over again. The next morning found us at the flight line ready to go again. This time wind reports showed that it was possible for us to make Ascension with fifteen minutes of spare fuel. Ascension Island is an eight-hour trip under ideal conditions. We had only a little over eight hours of fuel available. We were cleared to depart by the dispatchers, so off we went without too much confidence about where we were going to land.

Usually the time aboard was spent playing poker. On this leg, however, I noticed the navigator was taking sun shots almost every hour. We knew we were on track out of Natal because of its powerful nondirectional beacon. The navigator's readings told us how far out on the track we were. It was a boring flight except for our strong doubt about making it. I spent my time reading *The Robe,* resetting the autopilot from time to time, and trying to see submarines and report their locations. We saw nothing but water, water, and more water. When the eighth hour arrived the poker game was over and four pairs of eyes were searching for the dark shadow which we hoped would be the barren island of Ascension. Ascension was a lava mass scarcely a mile wide, only a few miles long. It was perhaps the most important bit of land in the world at one time or another for thousands of pilots in our position.

Finally, there it was—the most delightful sight I can remember. At eight hours and fifteen minutes we were on the ground and parked. Our fuel endurance was to have been eight hours and twenty minutes when we left Natal, but the plans proved to be incorrect. We did not have even five minutes of fuel in those tanks.

Ascension Island is bleak, beset with winds and rough seas day and night. It is a lonely place at best. That night we had dinner at the officers' mess and sat outdoors for the movie *Wuthering Heights.* The setting on the moors was complete with mists and darkness. Our own environment was in a misty rain, in the wind and darkness on a godforsaken island in the middle of the Atlantic Ocean.

We were up and about well before dawn for another eight-hour trip to Accra. Somehow it did not seem quite so serious as we had the entire coast of Africa as a target. It was on this takeoff that

I suffered my first case of vertigo. I had heard about it but did not believe it was possible until that morning.

Since it was pitch dark at takeoff time and there was no horizon with lights in the distance, I had to depend upon the instruments for orientation. My landing lights covered the runway to the end. We were airborne suddenly and the lights did nothing for us, as there was nothing for them to contact but unlimited darkness. As they retracted back into the wings my last touch with the outside was distorted. It took all the power I had to keep from diving the airplane into the black Atlantic. I kept checking my set of flight instruments with those on the copilot's side and even then fought a terrific urge to turn left and down. I felt I was climbing to the right and too steeply. After several minutes the horrible sensation left me and I was a believing instrument pilot. We leveled off at cruising altitude, the crew started a new game of poker, and I opened the book and continued to read *The Robe*.

Lunchtime came. Our in-flight lunch every day for the entire trip was the same—a dry sandwich, an apple, and a couple of cookies. It got so we would almost have preferred the cardboard box the lunch came in rather than the lunch itself. In time the coast emerged out of the haze on the horizon, and we landed before dark.

The next day's six-hour trip to Madugri took us into the heart of Africa. All of the bases we used on this entire trip were the possessions of Pan American Airlines. What a job they had done in pioneering commercial aviation! Little did they know at the time they surveyed the routes that these many airports would be the lifeline for ATC to the Orient.

The half-day flight to Khartoum on the twenty-first was a routine trip except for our first encounter with sandstorms. We could scarcely see the ground during the entire flight due to these storms and haze. Occasionally we could make out native villages of grass shacks, fenced-in compounds, and dry rivers called *wadis*. Due to poor visibility our approach to Khartoum was on instruments almost all the way to touchdown.

Our BOQ that night was the famous Kitchener's Barracks on the Nile. The facilities were as comfortable as mahogany furniture can make it. Each stop gave us more of the primitive; we had long ago seen our last regular bed and mattress. Now it was a wooden bedstead with ropes to support the thin mattress, rough sheets, and no protection from the insects except netting supported by bamboo poles. I slept fitfully amid the ghosts of Kitchener and his men.

October 22. My birthday. Our destination was Aden, Arabia, on the tip of land just across the Red Sea. We were glad to leave the dust storms and get out toward clear water. I had finished *The Robe* and was contemplating all that I had been reading when I looked up and saw the Red Sea. It was a unique experience suddenly to be in the environment depicted in the book. After landing at Aden, we saw the Islam religion in action; the faithful were being called to prayer at noon. From everywhere appeared rugs and men kneeling in prayer while facing Mecca. I remember that birthday well.

We skirted the coast of Arabia on the next day's flight to Misera Island, a bleak desert land with no interesting sights. At that point little was known of the oil under that desolate land.

That night we were housed close to the water and took advantage of it before darkness fell. The surf was high and we were in fairly shallow water. My navigator was diving off our shoulders into the waves when one gave way just before he hit. He landed in shallow water and sprained his wrist. The pain increased by the hour all night until we all believed he had broken some bones.

We arrived too late in Karachi the next day to get the navigator into the dispensary. They told us to come back in the morning. Meanwhile his pain was still increasing. When we were called the next morning for flight we informed the Charge of Quarters (CQ) that we had a date at the dispensary and would not be taking off on time. Apparently there was some kind of penalty for operations to miss getting every airplane off on time—to hell with the reason why. We were accosted by armed MPs and escorted to the flight line. No breakfast, not even coffee, and certainly no sympathy for my navigator and his excruciating pain.

The all-day trip to Calcutta on the twenty-fifth included a stop in Agra to off-load some freight and pick up more. No aircraft moved in that theater without having every inch of space utilized. We lunched in Agra with an officer returning to the States from China, and his tales of the food shortage and conditions did little to enhance our expectations.

After lunch we were airborne. Even from our height and through the haze that prevailed over most of India at that time of the year, the famous Taj Mahal was beautiful and awe-inspiring. Finally our navigator brought us into Calcutta on time. His job was done, but he still needed medical help because by this time he was in absolute agony. Again the dispensaries were closed and he had to wait until morning for an appointment.

That night we dined, to use the term loosely, at the Great Eastern Hotel, a famous spot in Calcutta. This was my first view of squalor. I never dreamed human beings could live under such conditions. The stench and the sights were all my midwestern upbringing could cope with. Hordes of people lived in deplorable conditions. Beggars were everywhere; cadaverous beings slept on the street or in the gutters. Enough was enough. We scurried back to the BOQ at Barrackpore to spend the night. Sometime before morning I was struck by dysentery — a red-hot sword going through my intestines. I don't have any idea what the culprit was, but I had it bad.

We breakfasted at the officers' club between my trips to the men's room. The first person I saw there was a Colonel Cochran, made famous by his cartoonist friend Milton Caniff, who called him Colonel Corkin. We were in the land of "Terry and the Pirates" for sure.

This was the day we had to go to Hastings Mill for my new assignment. Hastings Mill is located on an island in the Hoogley River. The whole crew went as they, too, had to be assigned to new stations. We rode over in one of the sampan-type boats poled by native Hindus dressed in their smelly muslin. Upon checking in at headquarters I was asked what I was doing in a C-46. I told them that I had been assigned to bring it over. They replied that they were in need of four-engine pilots and since I was qualified they were assigning me to Tezpur, a four-engine base. I was to deliver the freight to Chabua and the airplane to Deragon, and proceed under orders from there to Jorhat, the nearest base, and from there to Tezpur. All this time I was suffering unmercifully from the tourist tantrums.

We had a smooth trip from Calcutta to Chabua even though it was my first flight without the navigator. He finally got medical help in Calcutta and was scheduled for return to the States before we left for Assam. It was difficult to see him leave us, for now we were really on our own, without benefit of any previous experience. Finally we arrived at Deragon, a new base which was to use C-46s. I was a little sorry to leave the airplane at this time, as I thought that getting in on a new base would enhance my chances of promotion. How wrong I was! It was much later while flying above the mountains in the four-engine C-87s and C-109s that I looked down and watched C-46s struggling at fifteen thousand feet amid peaks much higher. Then I knew that fate had been kind to me.

By bus and by shuttle flight, I finally arrived at Tezpur, dysentery and all. The dispensary provided medication that did the job — too well, in fact. For the next week I fought constipation, and it took a month to get regular.

My copilot and engineer stayed with the C-46 at Deragon. I saw the airplane once in China and the copilot once still later, but then I lost track of both.

The long trek was over and I was finally at Tezpur. I found my way to the living area, which was a mile and a half from the flight line. I checked in with the CQ to get my quarters assignment. The officers' quarters were located in a large quadrangle of *bashas,* the Indian term for hut or cabin. Housing three or four persons each, they were made of bamboo poles and concrete, with a thatched roof of palm fronds and a small front porch. The bath facilities were on the opposite side of the area from our *basha.*

By this time my spirits were a little low. My navigator had left for the States, we had become separated from Lieutenant Peterson and his crew after leaving Khartoum, my crew was left at Deragon, and I was alone. I received the *basha* number from the CQ and lugged my duffel bag and all my possessions toward my new home. I found it, and right there on the front, in bold Old English letters, was its name: The Town House. I started humming "I'll Walk Alone."

The Hump

The Hump was a term given that portion of the Himalayas which lies between India and China.

Japan had occupied eastern and southern China as well as most of Burma for many months. The surface routes between India and China had been severed. The Burma and Lido Roads had not been completed because of damage inflicted by the Japanese and by the outlaw tribes in Burma and China. Adverse weather had

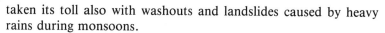

taken its toll also with washouts and landslides caused by heavy rains during monsoons.

The American Volunteer Group headed by General Claire Chennault had been operating out of Kunming and had been doing a fairly good job of holding the Japanese advances to a minimum. Supplies were vital to them and their success. The only way to supply the Flying Tigers, as they were called, was over the north portion of the Hump where fewer Japanese were encountered.

Eventually the Flying Tigers were absorbed by the Fourteenth Air Force and ATC continued to strengthen the lifeline between India and China with more frequent flights over more routes. Bomber bases were established in Chentu and Luliang as well as Kunming and other sites while fighter wings continued to fly cover for their bombing missions. Gasoline and bombs were priority cargo for ATC transports to move into those bases in central and North China.

Supplies came to Assam via river and railroad from seaports in Calcutta and Dacca. ATC bases were numerous. In Assam there were bases at Misamari, Tezpur, Jorhat, Chabua, Sookertaang, and Mohanbari. In Bengal there were Tezgon, Kurmitola, Shamshinager, and others in Calcutta dispatching flights day and night and in all kinds of weather.

A glance at the route charts will show why the Hump became known as the most challenging obstacle. The most powerful factors along the Hump were the high altitudes necessary to clear the terrain and the weather. The extremely cold, high pressure atmospheric systems generated in the mountains and plateaus of Tibet mixed with the moisture-laden air masses moving in from the India and China seas. This mixing occurred right on the Hump routes. The meeting of these two opposite air masses was a collision of such magnitude that the 25 percent losses of transports along the route was a higher casualty rate than that of combat groups. Chilling stories of encounters with this weather phenomenon contributed to the mystique of the Hump.

Without the support of the Hump operation, China would have fallen; the Japanese would have had access to unlimited supplies and might have been able to continue the war for many more years. So the China-Burma-India theater (CBI) and the Hump became known as that strange battlefield never experienced before or since WW II.

The C-87 started out to be a B-24 but got sidetracked. It was the same airplane with the same systems and power as the B-24, but from the wing back it was a cargo plane rather than a bomber. Instead of turrets in the nose and tail there was a large cargo space in the nose and a regular tail cone. The other two turrets were also absent.

The B-24 flew for the first time in 1939. It was initially nick-named the "Banana Boat," but later came to be known as the "Liberator." The design improved on the performance of the B-17 "Flying Fortress." With its Davis Wing — a long wing with a rela-

Map of Assam-Bengal-China air routes. Courtesy of Hump Pilots #1.

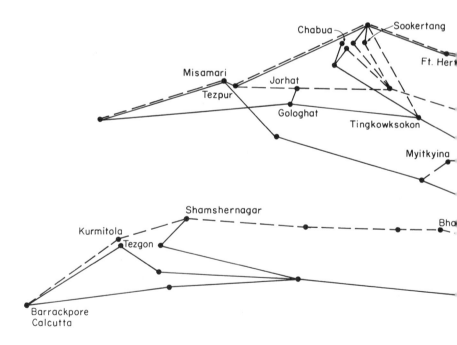

tively short chord — the B-24 would fly higher and faster than the Flying Fortress. The Fortress was designed to carry a bomb load on a round-trip mission of a thousand to fourteen hundred miles; the B-24 Liberator could go out twelve hundred miles with a bomb load of five thousand pounds and still return.

With the same characteristics as the B-24, the C-87 was a natural for the Hump. The wing would carry fifteen hundred gallons of fuel while the cargo compartment would carry about fifteen barrels of fifty gallons each. This made it possible to leave a sizable amount of fuel in China. Even so there were many times when we

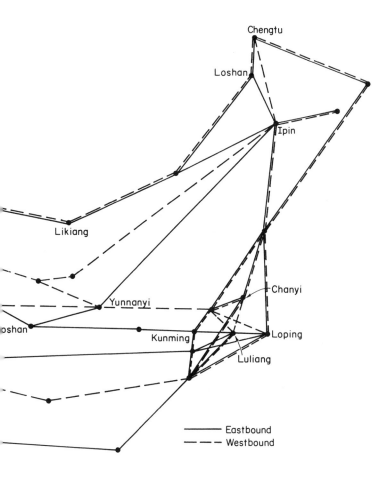

had to take on more fuel to get back than we could leave in China. Those flights should never have been started.

Another advantage of the Liberator over the Fortress was the fact the Pratt and Whitneys on the Liberator were turbocharged and much higher altitudes were possible. These turbocharged engines had Honeywell controls, a complicated system in which one knob would control all four engines after they had been properly adjusted. When more altitude was needed you just turned the control knob another turn and there was more manifold pressure. There was a limit, however. It was well known that if too much boost was used at high altitude, the turbo blades had a tendency to leave due to centrifugal force. When the blades started to go they usually took other important parts of the engine with them, so we flew at high altitudes with a certain amount of trepidation.

Those of us who flew the C-87s had a great amount of confidence in them. They were rugged, and not once was there a report of one of them breaking up in the worst of thunderstorms. The Davis Wing had a great amount of flexibility, which gave it more strength under turbulent conditions. The wing was so flexible that the pilot could not see the number one or number four engines from the cockpit on the ground; while airborne the upper halves of the nacelles of each outboard engine were visible above the inboard engines.

Why all the publicity regarding the Hump only mentions the C-46 is a mystery. There were five bases using the C-87s — Jorhat, Tezpur, Kurmitola, Tezgon, and Shamshinager. The C-46s were based at Mohanbari, Misamari, Sookertang, and Chabua in Assam. There were a few aircraft based in the Calcutta area, but ton for ton the C-87s probably carried as much if not more than any other type plane.

There was also another version of the B-24 called the C-109. This was a real bastard in that it was neither a B-24 nor a C-87. It was close to a B-24 with the turrets out and the bomb bay tanks installed. Each tank carried several hundred gallons. The good news about the C-109 was that the tanks could be jettisoned in a hurry, but the bad news was there was no time to do so, as they were prone to blowing up in the air. The slightest leak and a faulty electrical system, and there was a volatile bomb. These were nicknamed the "C One O Booms."

At our base we had a choice of load — either hundred-octane

gasoline or high fragmentation bombs. The bombs were in crates and hard to move, so they were not necessarily preferable to gasoline. Gasoline was in barrels and easily rolled to the door when dumping the load was necessary.

It was routine for us to fly the loaded C-87s over the Hump at eighteen thousand five hundred feet and return empty at twenty-one thousand five hundred feet. This left the lower altitudes to the C-46s and the C-47s, which had to remain well down at or below the fifteen thousand foot levels. This necessitated careful navigation, for most of the peaks exceeded fifteen thousand feet.

My *basha* mates were Lieutenant Warren and Flight Officer Baker. Baker was a permanent copilot and flew almost every day. He was close to having enough time to go home. Lieutenant Warren was a check pilot and also high on time. We lived together for approximately a month, when they finished and left for Uncle Sugar. The first replacement was John Ayala, whom I had known in Romulus. John was also a flight officer. However, he was ambitious and finally got his service pilot wings changed to the military wings in order to become a second lieutenant. This was done by proving he could fly a military AT-6 from the back seat. It mattered not that he had been flying military aircraft over the Hump for some time.

John and I had both checked out and had several pilot-in-command trips under our belt before Gus Keiser arrived. Gus had been an instructor on B-24 aircraft at Liberal, Kansas. As bleak as Liberal may have seemed to him, it was a Garden of Eden compared to where he was now. Each of us made several trips together. Between trips, a permanent hearts game was in progress, interspersed with volleyball at its roughest.

I checked in at Tezpur on October 30 and was on my first trip the very next day. After the first trip in daylight to Chenyi, all the rest were to Chentu. After a dozen trips I was deemed thoroughly indoctrinated, and I was sent to Gaya for special training prior to checking out as pilot-in-command.

Gaya is a town situated near the foot of Mount Everest, which we saw almost every day. It was also known as the birthplace of Buddha, and shrines were everywhere. I spent Thanksgiving Day flying and that night had one of the best meals during my entire stay in India. We had turkey, which had been canned; potatoes, which had been brought to life again after having been dried;

canned sweet potatoes; homemade bread; and a selection of canned vegetables. Nothing was fresh, there was no milk, and the water was so heavily mixed with chlorine it was difficult to drink without gagging; but it was still the best meal of my entire stay. I finally finished the twenty hours of instruction there and was sent back to Tezpur for the final checking out.

I had one check ride with Lieutenant Czark, the chief pilot, and the final from my *basha* mate, Lieutenant Warren. My first trip as pilot-in-command was on December 8.

On my fourth trip as pilot-in-command I had barely reached the first ridge of the Naga Hills and was still climbing when I lost the number two engine. Oil was spewing back along the side of the fuselage, so I had to feather the prop while there was still enough oil to do so. It seemed foolhardy to try to go on over into China with a sick airplane and, in fact, I was not too sure we could have taken the load to a safe altitude on the remaining three engines. We had not yet reached the point of no return, so it was my decision to make. I turned around and told the crew chief and radio operator to toss off barrels to lighten the load. We didn't have to empty the cargo compartment completely; I could tell we were going to get back to the valley with plenty of altitude. I had in mind going back to Jorhat, which was also a four-engine base, where we could have received maintenance service. But when we reached Jorhat we had altitude to spare, so I decided to go on back to our own base.

I was questioned later by one of the operations officers as to why I did not take the load to Myitkyina in Burma, because I would not have had to climb to get there. First of all I did not know if that was one of the days the Allies had Myitkyina or if it was a day when it was in the hands of the Japanese. They had been fighting over that strip ever since I had arrived in India. We could see the lobbing of shells back and forth from one end of the runway to the other every night we flew near the place. It never occurred to me to go there. It seems that if I had unloaded there our base would have been credited with tonnage for the month delivered into combat zone. It was then that I realized my welfare and the safety of equipment were secondary to the record they were trying to make to impress the brass in Calcutta.

I flew twelve trips in December; my total time was 129 hours and 40 minutes. Eighteen hours were on actual instruments and over half the hours were at night. I was indoctrinated.

Often we would receive invitations from the tea plantation owners to attend dances at their club, which was located about fifteen miles northwest of our base. The trip was not difficult and the road was elevated so that it would stay passable during the monsoons.

The clubhouse was stark compared to what one would expect in the States. The furnishings were obviously cast-offs from some home—worn sofas, austere and uncomfortable chairs not meant for complete relaxation. Most of the walls were taken up with windows to take advantage of the occasional breeze; pictures and other wall decorations were at a minimum.

Our hosts were quite cordial and in their own way tried to make us feel welcome. The music was supplied by a dinky record player wound by hand at frequent intervals. The selection of records dated back to World War I. We danced with their wives and girlfriends, as there were none for us to bring.

There was one thing that happened every night about ten o'clock. Without an obvious signal, everything stopped, even the music. The wives would produce a little tin box and take their husbands to a corner by themselves to have little sandwiches and tea. We were never invited to join them. It was a private ritual for each couple; the couples did not even join each other. We soon learned that this was not a snub, but just one of the peculiar customs that had been practiced for generations.

I will never forget my last trip to their social gathering. It was a moonlit night and we were on the way home in a jeep. Our only protection was the .45s we always carried. Suddenly, we were looking at a beautiful tiger standing in the middle of the road. When he realized he was among strangers he took a giant leap into the tall grass on the side of the road. We stopped and listened as he kept on leaping through the undergrowth, putting distance between us. The jeep with no top and our .45s seemed a little puny to us all of a sudden.

We had seen other tigers during the winter, when there was less food available for them and the odors coming from the post bakery attracted the big cats. Several were shot during my stay at Tezpur. They were considered too dangerous to be allowed to roam in such highly populated areas.

It was not unusual to find tigers near us; Frank "Bring-'em-back-alive" Buck's original camp was only a few miles east of our base. It was located there due to the proximity of abundant wildlife.

In more recent years Tezpur has been the city known for providing refuge to the Dalai Lama on his escape from Tibet ahead of the Red Chinese invaders, but no one could have been in Tezpur without being aware of a lesser claim to fame — the bats. Right in the middle of the town square were several huge trees filled with mammoth hanging fruit bats. With wing spans of eight inches to a foot each and weighing over a pound, they hung there all day complaining to each other and dirtying the streets under the trees. They were a repulsive sight, but were accepted by the populace as a part of their existence. Perhaps other areas had the same collection of hideous creatures, but I remember those in Tezpur.

China Flight

It was one o'clock in the morning India Standard Time. I vaguely remembered having signed the call sheet, but I became slowly aware of a strong light in my eyes and that I was cold, sitting on the edge of the cot. Slowly it dawned on me that another trip over the Hump awaited my pleasure.

I arose and dressed while still half asleep and checked my parachute bag for necessary items — oxygen mask, electric flying suit, flight cap, gloves, heavy winter flying boots, flight jacket with the CBI insignia on the shoulders and the American and Chinese flags across the back, my .45 automatic, two extra clips of ammo, my belt with trench knife, and first aid kit. Everything seemed to be in order.

Shouldering my bag and with flashlight in hand, I turned off the light over the one table in the *basha* and stumbled out into the dark, chilly, damp night, heading for the shuttle bus stop. I saw bouncing lights coming from elsewhere in the area as other crews approached the bus stop. The bus finally appeared and ground to a stop. I crawled on and with a jerk started the jostling ride a mile and a half to the flight line.

At last I was awake and thoroughly ready for the task at hand.

"China Flight" originally appeared in *China Airlift — The Hump*. Reprinted with permission.

I left the bus, parked my parachute bag, checked in at operations, and was notified of my destination. Next I went to the briefing room to fill out my flight plan, picked up my briefing folder with maps, an E-6-B computer, and instrument letdown manual. I synchronized my watch with the navigator's chronograph on the counter and proceeded to the weather office. I read weather reports brought from China by pilots who had landed in the past few hours. I got the weather officer's signature on my clearance, then went back to the operations desk to sign the manifest. My copilot showed up, having caught a later bus, and I found it would be a short wait before the plane was ready. I stepped over to the line mess for some GI coffee.

Finally I was notified that the plane was ready, so I picked up my parachute with the jungle kit attached and a money belt I hoped would never be needed to buy my way out of China, and crawled into another truck which took us to the revetment area.

As the truck drove up to the airplane, the crew chief and radio operator emerged from the dark interior and helped lift the gear aboard and onto the flight deck. With flashlights, my copilot and I inspected the exterior of the airplane: cowling fasteners, tires, landing gear struts, props, turbos, hydraulic fittings, brakes, and all other checkpoints. Everything seemed to be in place, so I crawled up into the cargo compartment and on the way to the flight deck I inspected the cargo for leakages and proper tie-downs. In the cockpit I read Form One. The plane was OK. A quick but thorough cockpit check and I was ready to start the engines. The auxiliary power unit was connected and started. The master switches were turned on, mag on number three, the booster pump on number three, accelerate starter on number three. The starter wound up, reached a high pitch, and we engaged number three starter. She coughed and sputtered to life. I caught it with the mixture control and watched manifold pressure, RPMs, fuel and oil pressure gauges of number three engine flicker to life and hold steady on the green arc of the instruments. I repeated the process for number four, then number two, and number one. I signaled to disengage the auxiliary power unit, and the little flickering of the lights gave the clue that it had been pulled out of the way.

The radio was turned on and checked. We listened to the taxi instructions from the tower. I set the altimeter and got another time check from the tower operator. The navigation and landing lights were turned on and we taxied to the warm-up circle at the end of the runway for the run-up and engine check.

After the engine check, I used a checklist again to see that all was in readiness for the heavy-loaded takeoff. The crew was ready, the radio operator had contact with the tower and was receiving our ATC clearance. We were cleared on the Easy route, to TK boundary to cross TV at twelve thousand feet to cruise at eighteen thousand five hundred feet. We were cleared into position for takeoff. Flaps were set at twenty degrees, trim tabs set, turbos on, props high RPM, mixtures rich, booster pumps on, cowling coming to trail position, gyros and instruments checked and all were in the green. All set. Now that we were ready for takeoff some of the tension seemed to be released, as I realized that we were about to get to the task at hand. I held the brakes on while pointed straight down the runway. I moved the throttles on up rapidly to the forty-seven-inch marking, then released the brakes. As the ponderous mass gathered momentum and sped down the dark runway, I let the copilot take over and hold the throttles, as I needed both hands on the control wheel to pry the nose wheel off the runway and up to an angle for takeoff. I began to feel the lift, bounces became lighter and lighter, and finally I had a liftoff. "Gear up," I called as I touched the brakes to stop the spinning wheels.

As the last dim runway light disappeared in a blur under the nose we concentrated entirely on our instruments to maintain a steady climb and heading. I called for the first power reduction for the climb, and as we gained altitude I gradually turned to the heading for the Hump. The copilot adjusted the prop controls to synchronize the four roaring engines. They responded by settling into a steady reassuring drone. I watched the altimeter slowly wind to fifteen hundred feet, two thousand, twenty-five hundred, three thousand. I made more power adjustments by setting the manifold pressure at thirty-seven inches and RPM at 2,300 for the long climb. Finally I could breathe a normal breath again. I could feel the tension of the entire crew relax, knowing that the overloaded airplane was at a safe altitude. It had taken a terrific mental and physical effort to get the plane on course and in a normal climb from a dead standstill on the runway. I noticed I was covered with perspiration, and I remembered the night those friends of mine did not get off in time and hit the trees. I can still see the terrific fire and remember how quickly it happened. That is why I took a deep breath and why I was soaking wet.

At eight thousand feet I turned the controls over to the copilot and stepped out of the seat to crawl into my electric flying suit. I fit the oxygen mask to the flight cap. After donning the heavy flight boots I went back to the seat and plugged in my electric flying suit. The oxygen mask and its built-in microphone were hooked to the proper attachments. I snapped on my oxygen mask and tested the indicator. All set. I took over from the copilot as he had to go through the same procedure.

At twenty-eight minutes from takeoff I noticed a flickering of the radio compass needle. It swung down on the dial to 180 degrees, which meant we had passed over the first checkpoint. I called the radio operator on the intercom and told him my time over the checkpoint, twelve thousand feet, on course. "Roger" was his reply, and I switched to liaison position on the radio jack box, to hear him contact the ground station and give our position.

The copilot crawled clumsily back up into the seat and made the necessary adjustments. When he seemed ready, I turned it back to him and took another look at the charts. I tuned in the next station and watched the compass needle swing into line. I checked the engine instruments, altitude, and heading. A slight adjustment here and there and I finally realized that we were out over the Hump. We had climbed up through the scattered clouds into a clear sky. The temperature had dropped from thirty degrees Centigrade on the ground to minus ten degrees Centigrade at this altitude. We were finally leveling off at eighteen thousand five hundred feet. I pulled the power back to thirty-two inches of mercury and 2,150 RPM. Mixtures were lean, more trim adjustments were made, and we heard the engines settle into their steady beat for the long, arduous journey ahead.

At last I could look outside and down into the gloom below— the Hump. I could see tiny dots of lights and make out a snakelike formation. Those were the trucks crawling along the Lido Road. They were moving army supplies up to the China-Burma fronts. I pitied those poor fellows down there. They could look up and see our dim navigation lights and the red and blue exhaust flames from the four droning engines, and they probably felt the same about us.

Checkpoint after checkpoint slid by beneath us in the dark. I began to feel the chill of the high altitude and the night air creeping into my bones and I gave the rheostat on the heated suit another twist. I wondered what the folks were doing back home. I glanced at the clock and realized it was about time for them to be heading home after the day's work. An evening of radio, reading, perhaps a show, the neighbors dropping in for a chat, were all a far cry from my existence. But all in all, I would not trade, because there was a job to be done. Thousands of others were over here, too. Every trip was like a drop in a bucket toward getting through with the job. I hoped it would soon be full so I could leave this strange life of broken sleep, missed meals, foreign chatter, strange sights and smells, all in a land so far away from those things natural to me.

Back from my reverie, I realized I was at the checkpoint near Mount Likiang, where I had to alter course to the northeast. Another hour and ten minutes and I took up a new heading to the final destination. I called the radio operator on the intercom and asked him to get the latest weather at our destination airstrip. Soon the report came from the radio operator. "Chentu contact, ceiling six thousand feet, sky overcast to fourteen thousand feet, altimeter setting 30.04, temperature ten degrees, dew point five."

I took over from the copilot and called for power reductions in preparation for the long descent to cloud tops. Gradually we descended at the rate of three hundred feet per minute. When over the station I called in for instrument letdown clearance. We were cleared number one for approach. We were required to report when leaving each thousand-foot level.

With ten degrees of flaps we started a five-hundred-feet-per-minute descent. At fourteen thousand feet the stars began to blink out. A red glow appeared as our passing light burned into the overcast and we were being swallowed into its cold, wet gloom. We concentrated entirely on our instruments: air speed, rate of descent, heading, and time out from the station. As we reached the three-minute point north of the station, we turned forty-five degrees to the left, and we aligned our airplane with the final approach heading. We checked and double-checked this with the radio compass needle and against the magnetic heading of the airplane. Constantly we watched our instruments as our radio operator called out our altitude to the tower operator below "thirteen thousand, twelve thousand, eleven thousand, ten thousand . . . "

I asked the copilot to keep a sharp lookout for lights below. Finally he reported contact, and I glanced out to see the runway lights dead ahead and below. We were at fifty-five hundred feet and continued to descend to five thousand feet, as I called for landing instructions. The answer was to land to the south; altimeter setting and wind velocity were also given. I was asked to call on the downwind leg. We swung a little to the right so we could see the runway and fly the length of it. We turned east for fifteen seconds and then turned downwind to the north. I called here for gear down, booster pumps on, mixture rich, 2,300 RPM, and the engineer came up to inform me that the gear was indeed down and locked. I asked for ten degrees more of flaps and notified the tower of my position on the downwind leg.

As the last runway approach light went by number one engine, I checked the time and gave myself forty-five seconds before turning on the base leg. On the base leg I checked the landing lights. I called for half flaps and turned onto the final approach. I kept lined up with the runway lights and called for full flaps, landing lights on. I eased off on the throttles as the landing lights began to pick up the runway surface. The boundary lights flashed by, I cut the throttles and held the back pressure on the control wheel just right, so the airplane hung just above the runway losing flying speed. Crunching gravel and a slight jar told us that wheels were rolling on China soil once more. We kept heading straight down the runway, gently tapping brakes as the great weight slowly decelerated to taxi speed. The copilot had been busy with cowl flaps, turbos, wing flaps, booster pumps, and answering the tower's taxi instructions. Following a jeep off the runway, we finally came to a stop in the revetment area. Switches were cut and we realized the toughest part of the trip was over at last. I picked up the necessary papers and started back to the cargo door. Already the plane was swarming with Chinese soldiers unloading our cargo and chattering in their native tongue. I occasionally recognized a *Ding Hao* and answered with the same statement, thumb uplifted as a grinning Chinese soldier appeared in the yellow lantern light.

At the operations office I turned over the papers and made a weather report, then walked to the line mess for a batch of "eggus," the Chinese pronunciation of eggs which we all used. Food never tasted so good. A side order of hard fried potatoes and some dry bread with hot tea, and my insides began to come alive.

Outside again, the gray dawn brought out the silhouette of nearby mountain ranges and the ghostlike outline of huge bombers dispersed in the revetment area. There is a set procedure for letting down between those mountain ranges and getting the cargo safely to the airstrip where these hungry bombers are based. The clearance signed, weather information from the valley, and we were jostling in a jeep back to the plane. Now unloaded and standing higher on its landing gear struts, it seemed eager to get started back across the wasteland to India.

In the cool air of the breaking day, we were warmed only by the excitement of another takeoff and climb for the trip back across the Hump. Engines started, we taxied out for the warm-up. Everything was all set, and we got the clearance from the tower and permission for immediate takeoff. We rolled onto the runway, eased the four throttles forward, and the empty ship leaped into life as it gathered speed down the runway. Being so light, it always was a surprise when it broke ground so soon and started a rapid climb into the gray overcast. On instruments at six thousand feet and up to fourteen thousand, we finally broke out into the blazing sunlight which poured out across the snow-white billowy clouds that rushed by beneath the plane. At twenty-one thousand feet I eased the power back to cruise setting. I leaned out the mixtures as the copilot synchronized the engines to a rhythmic purr. A few trim-tab adjustments and the journey homeward became a monotonous waiting and counting of checkpoints as they went by.

Now in the light of day we saw the tall, stately Three Sisters peaks on the right. Minutes later Mount Likiang in all its majestic glory rose high and silent above the cloud formation and the more inferior peaks pointed toward it with pride.

Passing this monarch of the Himalayas, we altered our course to the west and soon saw the deep gorge cut through the mountains by the raging Salween River as it tumbled its way through mountains and jungles to the China Sea. I noticed the mountainous terrain giving way to lower foothills and denser jungles. I realized then that we were over the Fort Hertz Valley in Burma with one more range to traverse.

This is the most impassable jungle in all Asia, but our four engines were still putting out their sleep-provoking beat. We saw the last ridge ahead so we started a gradual descent by reducing the power settings. Finally down to fourteen thousand feet, we crossed the last ridge, and the flat valley of the Brahmaputra River lay below in the province of Assam. We continued our descent and finally at eight thousand feet we found no more need for the cumbersome oxygen mask. The heat from the valley seeped into the frigid air of the cockpit. Toes and fingers began to tingle into life.

Turning the ship over to the copilot, I crawled out of the seat to remove my boots and the heavy flying suit. It was a beautiful day and life was good again. As our four engines sang their way idly down into the semitropical valley, I recaptured that thrill of flight that had almost been forgotten.

Following the broad, lazy, winding Brahmaputra down the valley, I finally spied the landing strip of our home base dead ahead. Further power reductions were made as the copilot called for landing instructions. On the downwind, base, and final approaches, we kept the tower informed of our position. Easing the huge, speeding plane to a landing on the strip, I finally braked her to a stop and turned off into one of the revetments where her ground crew was waiting to prepare her for another flight. As soon as the engines stopped, the crew was swarming over the plane, refueling, and reloading. Even before we could gather our gear and get out, the cargo compartment was half loaded.

I bumped my way back to operations, turned in the parachute, money belt, and briefing folder. At the debriefing desk I made my report and turned in the flying time. On the bottom of the report under "Remarks" I wrote "Routine trip—mission completed." In the back of my mind I was hoping the remainder of the sixty-five or seventy flights could be commented upon in the same manner.

A shot of free whiskey at the dispensary next door lightened my spirits after a hard grind. The world looked rosy. I returned to my *basha* and chalked up eleven hours on the going-home chart tacked on the back of the *basha* door.

I had made three trips to Chentu since January 1. On the sixth, I had been on the alert list all day. It was almost dark when I went to the officers' mess hoping to get some food before being called. While I was there several pilots came in with weird stories about what was going on over the Hump. They had just landed and were pretty excited about the violence of the weather. By the time I became concerned the word came out that all flights were canceled until morning. That was a new one!

Several months prior to this, some general, who shall go nameless here, made the statement that the Hump is never closed. He had made the trip on one of those rare days when the weather was not too hostile. Apparently the conditions had become much worse than ever before, and the losses had risen at such a rate that prudence took over and the Hump was indeed closed for the first time. At least we would be able to wrestle with the problems in daylight. But I was able to get little sleep and was on the line the next morning well before daylight.

My *basha* mate, John Ayala, was my copilot for this trip, and I was glad to have someone along whom I knew and could rely on. We got off early and had not even reached our assigned altitude of 18,500 feet when things began to happen. There were violent currents, lots of clouds, and icing. Unfortunately, our destination was the furthermost base northeast of Chentu, A-3. When we made the turn at Mount Likiang almost an hour early, we knew we had some terrific winds. The crab angle to Ipin indicated westerly winds of over a hundred miles an hour. When we arrived over A-3 we were held at ten thousand feet due to a lost C-47 below us. We held there for over an hour with reduced power, but icing became a problem. Not only were our wings picking up a lot of ice, but the inlets to the oil radiator and air intakes to the carburetors were gradually closing. It was only a matter of time before the engines would be choked out or overheating due to the uncooled oil. I finally declared an emergency, explaining we could not stay at holding altitude any longer regardless of an unreported plane below. We got our clearance and descended to minimum altitude. It was really a lousy day everywhere. We only had a few seconds after breaking out of the overcast before we saw the end of the runway in the fog and snow. It took some time to unload the barrels of hundred-octane fuel we had brought over and to remove the ice from the wings and the cowling intakes. John and I computed the winds and the time it would take us to make the return flight. It was discouraging to find we would need more fuel to go back than we had brought over. Under such conditions the flight had not been a very bright idea in the first place.

Our plans called for a flight of over five hours, so we put fuel on for a little over six. That was a mistake. We finally became airborne near dark. A C-87 with only wing fuel aboard will climb like a homesick angel. We were going through layer after layer of clouds until we arrived at our assigned altitude of twenty-one thousand feet. Cumulus buildups were everywhere, and in the clouds the vicious currents made it impossible to control the aircraft. We elected to stay out of the clouds wherever possible. We finally arrived at twenty-seven thousand feet, which topped most of the buildups, and we went around others. The problem then was the radios. All had arced out due to high altitude. The ADF made continuous circles, and no communications could be made with base stations. The inevitable St. Elmo's fire played on in balls and jagged lightning. We ground out the miles in frustrating fashion, with perhaps less than a hundred miles per hour of ground speed. We passed Mt. Likiang and the two sister peaks nearby, all covered with deep snow.

With all radios out, it was a welcome sight to see my friend Orion in the western sky. By keeping the nose of the plane lined up with that constellation, I knew I would be heading west; how far right or left of course I could not tell. If we were too far south, we were over the Japanese-held territory in Burma; if we were north of course, we would be over the unsurveyed peaks of Tibet! Hour after hour went by, and as the clock approached the five-and-a-half-hour mark, I calculated tanks and remaining fuel. We had no accurate gauges, so time was the only thing we could use. As we approached the six-hour mark, panic grew. I knew I should alert the crew to our predicament, but I was not too sure I could muster up a steady announcement about the situation. John Ayala was aware of the problem; I could see him spinning the computer and doing a lot of figuring. First he would say we would make it, then he would figure again and look at me with great doubt in his eyes. It was dark and bone-chilling cold; we were running out of fuel and did not know for sure where we were — we only hoped we were on course.

When six hours were up, I knew I had to make a statement, such as, "Buckle up your chutes and get back by the door because when these engines start to quit, we are going to have to leave the ship." I could not do it. Suddenly through a break in the clouds I thought I saw a green beacon. I did! I timed it, and it was definitely on an airport. I pushed the nose over into a steep dive, aiming directly at the light and hoping the clouds would not close in on my target. It stayed in place. When we went through fifteen thousand feet the radios began to come back into operation. The ADF picked a signal and steadied on a point near where the beacon was still shining. We had located Chabua, the first station in the valley. We never let the light go out of our vision.

The radio operator made contact with the Chabua tower and their booming response in our earphones was a most welcome sound. We positioned ourselves on the downwind leg at ten thousand feet, power at idle on all four engines. We turned onto the base leg at five thousand feet with gear out and flaps coming down, then turned final with everything hanging out and slipped onto the rain-covered runway still in idle power. We let the plane roll out onto a taxi strip and told the tower to come and get us! We were not going to taxi another inch! We both put our arms and heads on the glare shield and thanked God we were on the ground once more.

The ground crew came out and picked us up in a jeep. Just before we left for operations, I asked the crew chief to go out on the wings and check the tanks. He was back shortly with the news that two of the four cells were dry and the other two could have possibly supplied enough fuel to have made one circuit of the airport. We were exhausted both mentally and physically. At first I thought we would wait until daylight and then go on to Tezpur, another 150 miles. However, after some food, the first in over eight hours, we began to feel a little better. With the plane refueled, we all agreed to go on home. When we arrived at Tezpur we parked in the revetment area and went into the operations office for debriefing. We found our number on the board under a fresh erasure. Next to it was the remainder of a stark statement still clearly legible—"Missing." Because our radios had been out, they had not received a report from us since we left China more than twelve hours before. The ground communications were also out due to the storms, so Chabua could not report our arrival there. As we stood looking at the board, we felt like we had been given a reprieve and had just returned from the dead.

How bad was it? It was estimated that during the two nights of this horrible weather, fifty airplanes had been airborne when the notice came to close the Hump. Our crew was one of the few that made it back. It was my thirteenth trip!

Near the end of February I made a trip to Kunming, and with a tail wind of something like seventy miles per hour, I was over Kunming in less than three hours. A Japanese bomber had just finished laying eggs down the length of the runway, so we were unable to land.

No problem. We went just a little south to Chenkung and called the tower. They asked if we were "wet" or "dry," code names for gasoline or bombs. When we replied that we were "wet," their reply was that they were full and could take no more "wet" cargo.

So we proceeded another hundred miles to Luliang, where we were stacked at twenty-one thousand feet with a delay of unknown length. All traffic was beginning to pile up due to the Kunming shutdown. In an hour I had only gotten down to fourteen thousand feet, so I chose Yunanyi, another base back toward India. Ordinarily this base was closed to four-engine aircraft except in emergency, but this was becoming an emergency. We wanted to get down and get unloaded. When we arrived over Yunanyi the tower was swamped, so the landing instructions were to get in the pattern and call on base leg. In other words we were on our own, and be careful out there! It looked like a Christmas tree over that airport. There were planes circling everywhere. I got in behind the closest one and kept him in sight. When he was on final, I reported turning base.

The airport was closed to four-engine aircraft because of a mountain peak too near the end of the runway. Planes normally landed south and took off to the north. This night, due to heavy traffic, we had to land and take off in the same direction. Our departure included a nice smooth chandelle to the left, clearing the mountain with room to spare. We dodged our way up to altitude through the circling horde of planes and returned to Assam.

On June 18, I was on a trip to Chanyi in a C-54. I had been instructing on the C-87s and C-109s since arriving at Kurmitola, and this was my first trip as pilot-in-command on the wonderful C-54. In addition to that, the wing flying safety officer was aboard, so we were trying to do everything right. There were no problems en route, and we had made our letdown at Chanyi through clouds and rain and had been cleared by the tower to land. On the base leg I saw an airplane in position to take the runway, so kept him in mind. Sure enough, when we were on final and low enough to see his airplane in our landing lights, he pulled out on the runway and began his takeoff run! Continuing our approach would mean landing on his back. I did a lot of things in a hurry. I called for gear up and flaps up to one quarter. Meanwhile I had pushed the mixtures and props up to full takeoff power and followed rapidly with the throttles. I turned lest the aircraft taking off hit me from below. There was a hill at a point less than a mile from the end of the runway; only empty takeoffs were permitted in that direction. Furthermore, it was raining fairly hard, which restricted visibility. The good old C-54 gathered up her skirts and got out of there. I felt like I had lifted it and the entire load out of there myself. We finally landed and parked the airplane. The flying safety officer disappeared and only joined us as we were finishing our "eggus." I asked him where he had gone and he said, "The tower will be writing letters for some time." That was enough for me to know that I had not been blamed for the goof, and apparently our procedure in handling an aborted landing was satisfactory.

The terrible experience of January 7 was during the peak of the premonsoon season. Storms were more violent then than during the actual monsoons because there was a greater difference between the two air masses that were being blended. A look at the routes we flew shows something of the causes of bad weather. The high plateaus of Tibet produced intense high pressure centers, while the Indian Ocean produced moisture-laden air which flowed over Burma, China, and India. These two contrasting air masses collided right on our flight routes. Early in the year violent weather could be expected. Later, as the monsoons came, the air was more stabilized but heavy with moisture. It rained from March through July until everything was saturated. Then as quickly as it had started it quit, and the land became arid and barren. Vegetation died, the heat was sweltering, and dust and filth took over.

By March I had accumulated more than enough time to have earned the Air Medal. It was about that time that I was tapped to be an assistant operations' officer. I was told that I could continue putting in flight time during my days off. The shift schedule called for us to work from eight o'clock until four o'clock, followed by twenty-four hours off; then we would work the next shift from four and work until midnight, followed by another twenty-four hours off; followed by a shift from midnight to eight in the morning. That seemed like a fairly good schedule, especially the twenty-four hours off at each shift change.

It looked as if I could get in an extra trip after each shift, but it hardly turned out that way. By the time a shift was over it was time to get more sleep. I did get in some such trips but only about once per week, and that left me completely out-of-step with anything else. I could not adapt to the sleep schedule. I lost weight with the loss of sleep and found there was no way to improve the situation. To compensate for loss of time on the Hump, I did all the flying I could in the valley. Valley time was worth just half of what the Hump time was worth toward going home.

It was because of this arrangement that I made many trips to Calcutta and up and down the valley. A makeshift airline service was operated throughout the area on a semiregular schedule. It was our duty at Tezpur to take our turn each week on the shuttle. Thus I built up time flying the C-47 and slowly built up time toward the day I could head back to civilization.

The Air Service Group had a maintenance base on our field but had no assigned pilots. When they came looking for a pilot to do some test flying, I volunteered. This was another source of building up time and it broke the monotony of flying the same airplane all the time. I found a great variety in the group. There were B-25s, C-46s, and many different single-engine planes, among which was a Stearman. I asked why it was there, and they said it was for anybody to fly who wants to. So I checked out a helmet and goggles and proceeded to have a good time with aerobatics and spot landings. I found an abandoned fighter strip out in the country some distance from our field and told Les Pruitt, one of the chief operations' officers, about it. We went out there one day and had spot landing contests. I would go up and make a couple of 180 degree side approaches, then he would take it up and do the same.

We did 360s overhead, 180 overhead approaches, and had a marvelous time. We saw hundreds of curious natives coming out to the strip to watch our activities. We both enjoyed the opportunity to sharpen up on our aerobatics. It had been months since we had been able to just play and have fun with an airplane.

I did flight test work not only for the Air Service Command but also for our own group. Whenever there was an engine change or major maintenance work on the plane, it had to be test-flown and written off by a test pilot as being airworthy and ready to return to service on the Hump.

On one of the test flights for the Air Service Group I located a white rhino and an elephant herd. Near the elephant herd was a huge bull with a broken tusk. It looked as if it was broken close enough to his head to have been terribly painful. He was not allowed in the herd, and perhaps that is the way he wanted it. It was hard to see such a big animal in such obvious suffering. I also located crocodiles on the islands in the Brahmaputra, which ran along the south edge of Tezpur. When I told the people back at the Air Service base about all the wildlife they were interested and asked me to fly their photographer on a filming trip.

Two cameramen came aboard in the little UC-78, and in a short while I had relocated the elephants, the rhino, and had found scores of ten-foot crocs basking on the mud flats of the river. They got footage of all that we saw, even of the rhino charging our plane when we went down low to get good clear shots. It was rare footage.

I managed to take at least one trip per week across the Hump. The premonsoon weather was becoming somewhat more mild but it was not gone completely. I had a C-47 trip to Myitkyina to deliver an engine one nice day. I would get Hump time for that and looked forward to it as a *bakshees* (easy, free) trip. The weather on the way over was fairly calm with only a few buildups showing, and we made the delivery without a problem.

During the time it took us to unload, things changed in a hurry. After takeoff, we inadvertently stuck our nose right into the base of a violent thunderstorm while climbing to clear the first ridge. The minimum altitude was eleven thousand feet. I was leveling off when I was hit with a tremendous gust, and suddenly we were at fourteen thousand feet. Before I could get things back under control, ice and water had stalled my left engine. I got heat on as soon as possible but it was too late. Meanwhile the downdraft had taken effect, and nothing we could do would stem the downward plunge. Regardless of the minimum altitude of eleven thousand feet, we were at nine thousand and still going down when another gust hit us and up we climbed again. How close we came to the Naga Hills I will never know, as we were under complete instrument conditions. There was a lot of lightning, extreme turbulence, and heavy rain. We finally traversed the worst of it and could see through a break in the clouds that we were over the broad flat plains west of the hills. We let down and soon were below the storm. Even in the tropical climate it took several minutes for the ice to melt off the wings, props, and windshield. We finally got the left engine started again and headed for home. What started out to be a peaceful little trip to Myitkyina ended in the worst possible storm.

The routine continued until mid-May, when we learned that our base would be abandoned by ATC, and a B-24 bomb group would take over. We felt for them, as they were going to fly fuel over to China with their combat airplanes. All the armament added to the load and detracted from the amount of fuel they could lay down in China. I never did learn how they fared, but it looked like a loser to us.

In early June I was made Air Officer (AO) at Kurmitola for a twenty-four-hour period. I learned about the base, but I spent most of the time in the tower watching operations from the other side of the fence. While there, rather than call it a complete loss of time, I memorized Poe's tantalizingly beautiful "Annabel Lee." Sitting in the darkened tower and listening to call-ins from far away added to the atmosphere Poe was trying to create.

I also served as AO at Tezpur shortly after my arrival there. I had made a few trips, one of which was with a Lieutenant Butow. On the night of my duty I had a snack at the line mess with Lieutenant Butow and his crew, who were about to depart for China. I had just gone back to my bunk in a small area under the tower and listened to a departure. Minutes later I got a call from the tower telling me an aircraft had gone in on takeoff. I rushed out and found the dark night charged by a brilliant, fiery-red mass a half mile off the end of the runway. I got in the jeep with operations personnel and drove as close as the heat would allow. There was obviously nothing that could be done at this point. The wreckage was strewn over a quarter of a mile, with smoldering remains of an airplane, clothing, and parts of the crew. It was a horrible shock when just minutes before they were alive and jesting with me at the line mess. Lieutenant Butow had been a good pilot.

Our planes were loaded to full gross weight. The runway was only five thousand feet long, and on hot days it was not uncommon for the plane finally to become airborne as the wheels bounced off the little rise at the end, which was the road that crossed the runway. We all knew if an engine even so much as coughed our chances of becoming airborne were virtually gone. To make matters worse, there was no room to come to a stop if something did go wrong. Consequently I made every takeoff with that fiery scene vivid in my mind. My practice was to get as much speed and altitude as fast as possible so there would be a better chance of survival if something happened to cause us to lose power. I felt I could never handle a plane with a dead engine with less than two thousand feet of altitude.

Every takeoff was the same. There was complete concentration for the first five minutes while we struggled to gain enough altitude to be safe. I would be soaked completely and then have to climb into subzero temperatures at altitude. It was that way for more than fifty takeoffs. Once unloaded and with an empty airplane the trip was more than two-thirds over.

After the catastrophic ending to Lieutenant Butow's takeoff, I did a lot of pondering. We all knew the airplanes were loaded to the maximum, considering the length of the runway. We knew all four engines would have to be putting out full power on takeoff and the climb out, or the results could very well be fatal.

After that accident I took a little pause after the checklist and before calling the tower for takeoff clearance to say a short prayer. I could think of nothing more appropriate than the Lord's Prayer. As time went by, "deliver us from evil" took on a new and important meaning. After each prayer a certain feeling of serenity cloaked me and I calmly went about the task of getting all that mass off the ground and skyward bound.

With all the protocol instilled in the minds of military personnel, a camaraderie develops among crew members which transcends any rules. Crew members tend to become attached to one another. This is especially true after a crew has experienced a few hardships and dangerous situations together.

For security reasons none of us ever wore rank insignia while flying into China. It was difficult when we landed for anyone to tell the captain from the crew chief or radio operator. Certainly no one who flew regularly would even sport the Good Conduct ribbon.

This unwritten procedure led to some embarrassment one night in our officers' mess. It was the same night the Hump was closed for the first time. We had been joined at the hall by a major I had known as the adjutant at Romulus. He was forced to RON (remain overnight) at our rustic base due to a lack of available transportation to Kunming. He was en route to take over the position of CO on the ATC base.

The major did the right thing for the same situation in the States — he came to the officers' mess in official uniform. His choice was the short Eisenhower combat jacket, with each air corps insignia in its proper place, as were emblems of rank and the pre–Pearl Harbor and the American theater ribbons. He was a flying officer and a graduate of the West Point Military Academy. I respected that.

Regardless of propriety, he was out of uniform among the others in attendance that night. I looked around the hall and saw those I knew to be majors, captains, first or second lieutenants; all of them had earned at least an Air Medal if not the Distinguished Flying Cross. Yet there was not one sign of rank or decoration on the whole lot. It must have suddenly dawned on the major from the States that out at the end of the line, rank and protocol no longer demand the meticulous attention they receive elsewhere.

If a crew worked together for any length of time, confidence and respect for each other grew rapidly. Eventually each man felt his was the best crew in the air corps. This was the case with a crew of mine that had made several trips together. One day while we were having eggs together in Kunming the topic got around to where each of us originated. One was from Dubuque, one from Ottumwa, one from Pocahontas, and I was from Marshalltown—Iowans all. What a coincidence! Not only was it highly unlikely that four crew members would be together more than once but to be from the same state was rare indeed.

The major we met in Agra, who was returning from China to the States, had warned us about the food situation. He was in pretty bad shape and told us why. The food supply line was constantly being short stopped at all the bases along the route. By the time it got to India or China it was merely what no one else wanted. Consequently we had dried milk, dehydrated potatoes, canned vegetables, canned sauerkraut, canned wieners, canned or dried everything. The only thing about our supplies that was good was they were better than those rations that went on to China!

On our trips to China we always had breakfast, no matter what time of the day or night. That was about all they had in way of food supplies in the flight line mess. The eggs in China came from bantam hens or smaller. Even fried they would have a hard time covering a silver dollar. Those little "eggus" and greasy fried potatoes with some homemade, coarse bread constituted the menu, day and night. Believe me, nothing tasted better when we were cold and tired and had been without food for more than eight hours.

There was a certain ritual I did not fail to observe before

dining in China. When my plate was served and I was about to spread the toast or bread, I held it up to the light and looked carefully to see that there were no dark spots in it. The dark spots would be weevils baked in the bread. If the bread was clean I was lucky and ate in peace. If I found something in the bread I traded it in for a more sterile slice.

On one of my trips to Calcutta I had the first sergeant of the medical department as a passenger. He was also an experienced chef and an experienced scrounger. After landing in Calcutta he asked me about our departure time and said, "Be sure to wait for me if I happen to be a little bit late, for it will be worth your while!"

Before departure, as I was about to close the main cargo door, I saw a jeep speeding toward the ramp and homing in on our plane. When it got closer I recognized the sergeant. When the jeep screeched to a halt, he dived for something in the back and came out with a quarter of beef on his shoulder. He ran to the plane, heaved it up onto the loading deck, and said, "Take off! Quick!" Being late already, I spent no time getting squared away and was taxiing out when he came forward and said, "I made it!" He had spent his time loitering about the officers' club, where he had located the meat supply. He commandeered a jeep and driver through some devious method and timed his raid to coincide with our takeoff time as nearly as possible. By so doing, he cut down the time between when the alarm would go off and when he would become airborne. He said he had been followed part way by the MPs but shook them off in traffic.

I was not too sure what portion of the blame I would have to take for aiding and abetting, but I was willing to go along with it since I had not seen fresh meat since leaving the States. When we landed back at Tezpur he picked up his loot and headed for the compound but not before asking me where I lived. I told him and he told me not to eat until he got there.

We took him at his word and somewhat later, after dark, he appeared with a sizable chunk of meat. He brought with him a sharp butcher knife, some garlic cloves, and a bottle of Mazola oil. All *bashas* had a little stove not much bigger than a Bunsen burner, which our bearer used to heat water for tea each morning. He lit the stove and produced a mess kit, filled it half full of oil, and got it piping hot while he carved steak after steak from that fresh meat. Watching each piece seething away in the boiling oil was a beautiful sight, and the aroma was indescribable. My *basha* mates and I each had at least two huge steaks washed down with warm beer. It was the best meal I could remember eating in India.

Being curious, we asked him about his background and learned that prior to being caught up in the army he had been head chef at the Blackstone Hotel in Chicago. Needless to say I gave him space on any flight I made to Calcutta from that time on. He was a scrounger par excellence.

I had always wondered how assignments were made. Upon what basis is a pilot sent to one base or another? Finally, I was given the task of reassigning all flying personnel. It was the duty of operations to do this but only two of us actually worked on the job. We had two choices, Jorhat or Kurmitola. Jorhat was a four-engine base right up the valley. Kurmitola was in Bengal near Dacca and was also a four-engine base, but they had the advantage of being in the process of changing over from C-87s to C-54s. There was another advantage in choosing Kurmitola. Located in Bengal, they were a lot further south than we were in Assam. Thus, we could fly lower routes from India bases to China. By this time the Japanese were all but pushed out of Burma. Certainly they were south of any route we would take from Bengal to Kunming. The minimum altitude en route was twelve thousand feet. I presented the picture to my *basha* mates and many others whom I had known in Romulus or even before. They all wanted Kurmitola. My *basha* mates also appreciated the fact I was in operations, for I was assigned an aircraft to move us. We, therefore, did not have to worry about stripping our possessions to minimum but could take almost anything we wanted. This meant I could take my supply of beer.

It was routine after each trip and after debriefing to be given a chit at operations which was good at the dispensary next door for a shot of scotch or bourbon. This was supposed to relax the tired nerves and body, and, believe me, it did. After long hours on oxygen and in a state of fatigue, a straight shot of either would hit you so hard you almost thought it would be a good idea to go right back out again.

Now I had never been too fond of scotch as it usually gave me a headache, and I could barely stand bourbon, but when it was chased by a cup of Lister-bag water steeped in chlorine, it was too much and I would just plain gag. I still can't stand the smell of bourbon in any quantities. Being without refrigeration on the base at Tezpur, I had developed the habit of carrying a couple of cans of beer over the Hump in my duffel bag. When we got back, the beer was filled with ice crystals, and the end result was the same as if I had taken a shot of whiskey.

A lot of trading took place over there. Money was not much of a commodity, but those who had something to trade had takers. I let it be known I would trade my ration at the line for a six-pack of beer. Beer was doled out free each month to everybody, whether they wanted it or not. It did not take long for me to build up quite a supply of beer in cans; I would not take bottles as they were too difficult to carry over the Hump and the cans refrigerated quicker.

I stored the extra beer under my bunk. That area was soon filled, so in time my bunk was about six inches off the floor, being supported by beer cans rather than the legs of the bed. Had I been riding to Bengal on the shuttle this would have presented a major problem, but having assigned myself an airplane, the problem was minor.

May 29 was moving day and it took one four-by-four truck just to move our gear from our *basha* to the flight line where we loaded the huge C-87. We did not bother about weight and balance, but a short calculation made us aware of the fact that we may have been fairly close to maximum gross weight — just the three of us and our loot. It was the same at Kurmitola. A four-by-four was needed just to carry the load we brought in one airplane. I was a little chagrined to learn that I could not keep my beer with me but had to check it in at the officers' club. I found it would be refrigerated there, and all I had to do was have my card punched for each beer.

The officers' club was made of bamboo, with concrete flooring and a thatched palm roof. There was a huge bar, many dining tables, and, of all things, a grand piano in the dining area. This was the famous Raiders' Roost, named by the cartoonist Milton Caniff, whom everyone knew for his "Terry and the Pirates."

We spent most of our time between trips playing hearts and drinking warm beer in our tent. Why we did not spend more time at the club I will never know, as it was certainly much more comfortable than our English tent, with its dirt floor covered with tar paper. The flaps of our tent were held out by bamboo poles in an intricate framework. This let air flow through freely and also kept the eternal rain from flooding our bunks.

I inquired about the grand piano one evening while the mess sergeant was tuning it, which he did almost every day due to the heavy rainfall and high humidity. Finished with his tuning, he started to play. Having heard little if any music of quality for many months, I was most impressed. He played Debussy's "Clair De Lune" more beautifully than I had ever heard it. He played on and on. Everything he did was outstanding. I discovered he had been NBC's concert pianist before being caught up in the confusion. This was his only chance to keep up his proficiency, which he did as he entertained many of us who appreciated such magnificent music. Even today when I hear "Clair De Lune," I am back in Raiders' Roost, and the rain is pouring off the thatched roof and splattering on the flagstones below.

The Eager Beaver

I had only to follow the eyes of the new man to know the question about to be asked. In the revetment the big four-engine C-87 was being loaded with freight to be airlifted to China that dark, lonely night.

"How long do you ride as copilot around here before you check out as first pilot, Captain?" I stopped momentarily to confer with a soldier who had pulled up in a jeep. He handed me a message which I read casually in studied silence, the interlude giving me time to ponder.

"That's pretty much up to you," I ventured finally. "Depends a lot on how fast you can learn your airplane." (You keep right on doing that until the day you make your last flight in it, I reminded myself.) I patted a dingy pile of maps. "Then it takes time to learn the mountains and the routes, the minimum altitudes." I pointed to the puffy cumulus clouds over the Naga Hills. "Of course, there is always the weather. You'll want to know a lot about that." I stopped, suddenly looking up. I felt sorry for the kid in a strange way. Green! Yes! Just out of training; new gold bars gleaming in

---

"The Eager Beaver" originally appeared in *China Airlift—The Hump.* Reprinted with permission.

the moonlight and that fresh "Go-get-'em-tiger" look! For a second I felt like one of those old leather-like sheriffs in an old western trying to keep his new deputy from reaching for his gun! I kicked aimlessly at a loose pebble on the steel matting on the floor of the revetment. I had seen it all too many times.

This was the gist of the first of many conversations between such new pilots and me, acting instructor pilot on C-87s, C-109s, and C-54s. My job was briefing newcomers as best I could before their first trip over the Hump. Then I'd take them out on their first indoctrination flight before assigning them to a regular instructor for the remainder of their checkout. Keep in mind that to these new lads, the big airplanes were a lot of iron to check out in early. To be able to write home about such an accomplishment would add a great deal to the pile of material from which local heroes are made.

Our pretakeoff briefing let it be known that occasionally a stray Japanese bomber would sneak through the early warning net and make nuisance raids on the airstrips intended to be our destinations. It was no big deal; it was well known that we were ATC and supposedly did not enter combat zones. But, of course, we did enter combat zones daily. Our crews accepted this as a way of life! Was there an alternative?

After takeoff our trip was usually fairly routine—record checkpoints; check altitudes; adjust engine instruments; put on warm high-altitude gear; adjust and connect oxygen masks; sniff for gasoline leaks; double-check speed and position; and listen for possible weather problems ahead. Understandably, by the time we were in our approach area in China, there was a somewhat addled copilot in the right seat. As slow as we flew in those days, things were nevertheless happening a little too fast for the new arrival to digest.

Our descent from high altitudes, usually through an undercast of some depth, almost always brought the same results. The cold airplane meeting the moist cloud layer caused rime ice to cover the windshield and gather on the props and wings. Usually it was night and this was the first real instrument approach a new kid had ever experienced. The navigation lights reflecting off the clouds cast eerie shadows and made weird effects inside the cockpit. About the same time the eager beaver had figured out this phenomenon the props would start letting go bursts of ice against the fuselage, back of the copilot's head. It sounded just like machine gun fire in the latest war movie, which really brought him up and out of his seat. To look at those startled eyes peering out over the oxygen mask was a pathetic sight.

We always broke out, eventually landed, off-loaded cargo, and took off again for our return trip. Now the trip back was the reciprocal of the trip over. So was attitude. The eager beaver from the early part of the mission was then docile and terribly contemplative; he had little to say and seemed deep in thought. Back over India, we started our long, beautiful glide down into our tropical valley; warmth penetrated the supercold atmosphere in the plane, oxygen masks were hung, and the high-altitude gear was removed. Talk was resumed. Finally, the first mission looked as if it might be a success. Invariably the first question was, "Captain, what if you decide you do not want to check out — just stay copilot for the rest of your stay over here?"

That first trip soon became buried by the second, third, and fourth, but none would have any more lasting effect than the first trip for the eager beaver.

Flying out of Kurmitola was much different than flying the higher routes out of Tezpur. It was not long before I was in line to check out in the beautiful C-54s, the four-engine Douglas craft which, as the DC-4, would become the mainstay of the postwar commercial airlines. The same Lieutenant Ramey who had checked me out in a C-47 in less than five minutes of training checked me out in the C-54. I received a little more time here and went through a ground school session before my one transition trip over the Hump. My last ten trips were made on that airplane.

It was a great contrast to fly in a heated cockpit for a change, versus being bundled up in high-altitude gear or in the temperamental electric flying suits. One night my electric suit caught fire in the area of my left elbow. The insulation had deteriorated in the tropics and in time just plain rotted out. The bend of the elbow increased the concentration of heat and it erupted in flames. I pulled the plug immediately and put out the fire, but from there on I had only a light flight jacket to wear, and I suffered excruciating cold before the trip was over.

Not only were the cockpits of the C-54 heated and comfortable, but our routes were never over twelve thousand feet. On a rare clear day we could often fly back empty at altitudes below ten thousand feet without oxygen. Stateside flying could not have been any better than those last ten trips.

One morning while playing hearts with my tentmates, the CQ came along and informed me that I was to report to personnel with him. Upon my arrival I was greeted by *"Captain* Piper, congratulations!" Those were beautiful words and most deeply appreciated. Now I had earned two silver bars. I had waited a long time, but it was finally a reality.

While in Romulus I had become acquainted with a dentist, Monroe Levin. I had been at Tezpur for a few months when I heard my name being called out across the quadrangle. It was Monroe's way of looking for me. He was a captain by that time and pulled a few strings and got himself on the manifest for a trip to China with me. Before returning I think he sort of wished he had not been so eager. We hit a lot of very rough weather and he was pretty well shaken up.

Monroe developed some sort of ailment and left Tezpur for Calcutta for hospital treatment. I did not see him in Tezpur again. We had been at Kurmitola for a month or so when I heard my name being called out across the campus. It was Captain Levin again. He had learned where I was and again used this method to locate my tent.

Monroe was full of rumors. One was about a weapon so powerful it would no doubt end the war. He could not describe it but we could only believe it was some sort of gun. A little more than a month later we all knew more about the mysterious weapon which did indeed end the war.

I had been looking forward to the end of my tenure from the day I arrived in India. It came suddenly, nevertheless, for I had miscalculated my time remaining. When I left on what turned out to be my last trip, I thought I had about two or possibly three more trips to go. When the tower asked me to report to operations after landing and I was told that I had just completed my last trip with time to spare, I could not believe it. I did not argue, however; if they said I was through, I would sure go along with it. I accepted the figures they presented and left the flight line for the last time. It was a big moment. It was difficult to realize I had just completed one of the most difficult and grueling ordeals I was ever to encounter.

I couldn't help but do some summary thinking. On many trips when visibility would permit I would look down at the hostile land below. The jagged peaks, the ominous jungles, and impassable terrain were a threatening sight. I would then tell myself, "I did not learn to fly for this — this is not the goal — this is only an interim." Somehow that made me feel better and gave me hope that I would survive the missions and see my way home again. Now it was over. It was like a reprieve from death row. So many of my friends, better pilots than I, were now statistics. Why me? How did I make it when others could not? I am still meek about it all, and the most thankful person in the world.

We left the flight line for the Raiders' Roost. I threw my beer card on the bar and said, "Free beer for everyone." It was a privilege I had looked forward to for a long time.

It was almost a month from my last flight until my orders arrived to clear my transportation for the States. All efforts were now being directed to the war in the Pacific and the China-Burma-India theater. Even though I had completed my tour of duty I would not breathe a deep breath until I was well ensconced on the other side of the world. My goal was to get out and away from the CBI as soon as possible.

With not much to do except to play hearts with my tentmates when they were in, there was plenty of time to take stock of where I was, where I had been, and where I should go. It was still difficult to imagine the future. We had all been thinking war for so long the thought of its ending had not yet occurred to most of us. It was a good opportunity for me to take note of some of the things I did not want to forget.

Not all the memories were bad. We used to borrow a jeep once in a while at Tezpur and ride into the village for a meal other than the military mess. There was a Chinese restaurant in Tezpur we patronized from time to time, never sure we would be able to eat there, for it was off-limits as often as it was open, seldom meeting the standards of sanitation required by the medical inspectors.

We shopped and experienced the smells and sights of Tezpur so very foreign to us. Invariably, upon our return to the base, it was a shower and shampoo, in order to purge the lingering odors from our clothes and ourselves.

While waiting in Kurmitola I finally went to operations one

day in August to arrange for flying time so I could get my flight pay for the month. I soon got a call to fly as crew member on a C-47 trip to a rest camp located down the coast south of Dacca on the Bay of Bengal. It was called Cox's Bazaar. It was a two hour flight to our destination, but upon arrival our airstrip was under water. We had arrived at high tide and the sandy beach that was the airstrip would not be available for a couple of hours. We diverted to a British fighter strip nearby.

Here we were greeted with open arms. These poor British fighter pilots had been all but forgotten. They had nothing to do for days on end and saw no one but each other. It was enough to drive them to drink, and that is just what they had been doing. The days were spent sipping gin and tonic with a shot of lime. We were coerced into having lunch with them and, of course, we were asked to join them in a toast to peace or whatever happened to be on their minds at the time. We were not able to accept any of their hospitality except the lunch, where we exchanged stories in rapid order. It was delightful and a wonderful respite from our flight duties.

One of the most magnificent sights I have ever seen was near their officers' club. It was a huge banyan tree with mammoth roots. The most exotic orchids of every hue and size filled every fork and cranny in that tremendous tree. It was a riot of fragile beauty.

The time was gone all too quickly and we had to depart while the tide was out. We were soon back over our runway on the beach. The landing was like a dream. The moist sand slowly got the wheels turning up to speed without the sudden jolt usually felt on a paved runway. We loaded our rested GIs and returned to the land of reality, leaving the orchids and the land of enchantment behind. That trip produced over five hours of flying time, one more than enough for the August flight pay. It was my last flying until I was back in the States.

While at Tezpur with an idle Sunday to spend I got a jeep and, with Gus Keiser, probed the foothills north of our base, traveling for nearly an hour before the trail got too rough for even a jeep to traverse. We then got out and hiked a few miles more. We were in much higher ground by this time and in a fairly heavy growth of timber. On a narrow foot path right in front of us stood a group of natives. They seemed friendly and we tried to impart our friendly intentions also. We drew close enough to start, or try to start, some type of conversation. They knew no Hindi and we certainly did not know what else they used in way of language. We resorted to the age-old method of signs. A game of charades in such surroundings was quite an exciting pastime. We had heard a great deal about tribes in the hills and what they expected of us. We were told they would do almost anything for salt. We had none. We were told they loved competition. We thought we would try that. We were moving along the trail together toward what sounded like a tumbling river. When we came upon it, we found it to be too wide and too swift to swim, so we started to throw rocks out into the current. I would pick one up and throw it, then one of them would do the same thing, only farther. I would throw again, farther than he. This went on for some time to the glee of their entire group.

They led us from the river to a small living compound, where their women were engaged in various activities. One was nursing a baby; another was cooking in a pot over an open fire; and another was weaving a reddish bit of fabric on a very complicated loom. I was surprised and fascinated to see such an intricate piece of machinery in the hands of these seemingly primitive people.

The piece she was making would just about cover the main parts of one of these little people if it were to be used as a sari. Not one of the tribe was anywhere near five feet in height, and the women were noticeably smaller than the men. I suppose their size was somewhat a result of their scanty diet; they had to be living on what the forest and the streams had to offer. There were no signs of anything modern in their encampment except the loom and, curiously, a metal Coca Cola sign stashed away in one of the grass huts.

With the best sign language I could muster I tried to let the woman who was weaving know that I wanted to buy her product. Apparently I got the message across. It was two months later before I could find the opportunity to return to their village. When I arrived she saw me and recognized me, and she went directly to one of the huts, where she retrieved the finished piece of goods from a dry and protected spot up under the eaves. I was glad I returned; she had trusted me. Our advance information proved inaccurate. I tried to barter with her with salt, but she would have none of it. I tried other things, but nothing seemed to please her as much as silver rupees. Not paper—silver rupees. So for the equivalent of a few cents—the price she set—I bought the fabric and she was happy, since she took what she wanted from my open hand. I had the feeling we all would have been good friends if time had allowed.

While awaiting orders I had plenty of time to reminisce about strange happenings in India. One sad bit of irony came to mind in the case of Captain Melichor, a pilot checked out in all fighter-type aircraft while he was at Romulus. Fighter aircraft at that time were called pursuit planes and nicknamed "pea shooters."

Captain Melichor was also an avid instrument pilot and a good one. He was perhaps the only one to have made instrument approaches down to minimum limits in a pea shooter. He was reprimanded at one point for breaking minimums in his approach to Newark during a spell of especially nasty weather. Eventually he, too, was called to the Hump.

When he arrived he seemed to relish the challenges of the weather as an opportunity to add to his instrument experience. In fact, after completing his tour of duty at Jorhat he asked for a second tour. To most of us that was simply an expression of the death wish, but he successfully finished the second tour, the only man, I suspect, to have done so.

On his way home he was on the shuttle flight to Calcutta, where he would get final orders. The plane landed in Lalmarhat on a routine stop. Without the knowledge of the crew, someone put gust locks on the controls. When the plane got airborne it stalled, taking all aboard to a fiery death.

My memories of India still include the sight of wretched hordes of humanity; the exotic aromas permeating the bazaars; monkeys everywhere; moldering vine-covered temples in horrible disrepair; beggars and their plaintive *bakshees;* sacred cows wandering freely through the streets and shops; ritual bathing in putrid ponds; burning ghats of Calcutta; monsoon season followed by barren aridness; the brooding snowcapped peaks of the Himalayas; the meandering Brahmaputra and the tumbling Salween and Irrawady; and mostly the defeated and helpless expressions on the faces of thousands of people hurrying through the streets.

Homeward Bound

After a month of waiting, orders for my return to the States came through. I was to report to operations at Tezgon, the base adjacent to Kurmitola. There I was to be assigned space on a flight to Karachi, where I would receive further travel orders.

As soon as possible I started the task of signing off the base and saying good-byes. In spite of the happy thought of finally going home, it was not easy to leave friends with whom I had shared many trying experiences. I wished them well and left for Tezgon.

In Karachi we were staged to leave the theater. Nothing could be taken out that had been issued when we entered the theater, so off came my watch and all the clothes that had been issued almost a year earlier. I was never certain of this, but it is more than likely the sergeant in charge took the watches and sold them on the black market in the streets of Karachi. I happened to know enough about supplies to know they were written off and were expendable when they were given to us. My watch was a particularly good time-keeper, and I really wanted to keep it, but I soon found out that if I wanted to get a clear visa out of India I would have to part with it.

That supply function lasted almost a full day. I was one of the few pilots on the manifest, so I found a way to break the monotony by spending some time in the cockpit on each leg. Our first stop after Karachi was at the desert base in Abadan. It was eleven o'clock at night, but the heat had been so intense during the day it was still over one hundred degrees. I felt a slight burn as my hand touched the skin of the aircraft while debarking. We were glad to get airborne and back in cooler air.

We went as far as Cairo on the next leg. Here we had a delay of one day, giving me a chance to see some of the sights so famous in Egypt. We made a tour to the pyramids, saw the inscrutable face of the sphinx, climbed up into one of the empty tombs in a pyramid, and rode a nasty-smelling and badly behaved camel. We visited the Blue Mosque and had a drink on the porch of the famous Shepherds' Hotel. Like Calcutta, the Cairo streets were inundated with human beings flowing in currents in all directions. Our BOQ was very comfortable and clean, and the food took on a noticeable improvement. We were getting away from the far end of the lifeline.

Our route after Cairo took us over the southern shores of the Mediterranean. The cool air off the waters of the sea mingled with the hot dry air coming off the deserts of North Africa, producing some of the roughest air I had encountered since flying in the last thunderstorm. Here I was a passenger, having experienced the worst on the Hump, and now fighting off airsickness with a vengeance. I found the solution was staying flat on my back. I was not flying first class on a modern airliner, but rather in a gutted C-46 with bucket seats along the side walls. There was duffel piled in the center on the cabin floor, and I used it as my berth.

Stops were made along the way for fuel and food, but we covered the entire trip from Cairo to Casablanca without being able to RON. While feeling well, I was able to look out on the desert, and to my amazement, the tank tracks and other signs of the battles of 1942–43 were still visible. One could see bomb craters, burned out villages, and tracks everywhere. On the other side of the plane the view was the endless blue of the Mediterranean.

Arriving at Casablanca, we again had to face staging for the final leg to the States. I was given space in an English-type tent with several others. We were in Casablanca for several days while the records were processed and the manifests were being made up for the next leg. It was during this stopover that World War II ended.

Never have I suffered such conflicting emotions. The bomb was dropped. I was thrilled with the knowledge that it was over, but those wonderful thoughts were diluted by the fear they would find out I was a four-engine pilot, and I would be sent back to help in the endless evacuation of India. My fears were somewhat allayed when I finally got orders to report to operations for the trip assignment. I was on the passenger manifest for a C-54 from Casablanca to Belém, via Dakar.

We landed in Belém after dark, and by midnight I was on a C-47, northbound over the jungles and trackless expanse of the Amazon Valley. To pass the time I went to the cockpit, where I found two second lieutenants, obviously not too long out of advanced training in the States. They told me that they had been in Europe flying parachute troop C-47s in Europe in the Troop Carrier Command.

It was a dark night with only a small moon to shed some light on the forests below. I noticed the ADF needle quivered and then dropped to the 180-degree position. Almost at once the copilot reached up and turned off the ADF receiver. When I asked why, he replied that we had crossed the station, and he was unable to get the next station due to the great distance. He was not aware he could keep it on, and still use it as a navigational aid. Right then and there I became a little nervous. Was I going to let some poorly trained pilot finally do me in by getting lost and running out of fuel somewhere in the vast Amazon Valley?

I found they had been doing nothing but formation flying and neither of them had an instrument rating. With all the pilots in the world, why did they put two together that could not fly by instruments? I asked them what they did during bad weather and instrument conditions when they were flying in Europe. They replied, "We just get in on the leader's wing real close." I gave a lesson on that flight about how to use an ADF.

We had been making all of the approaches in China with the ADF. The approaches were designed to follow published bearings, in- and outbound on the tiny transmitter near the airport or airstrip. We followed the published procedures because they were positioned to avoid the mountain ridges on either side of our course. We tracked in and out of those stations meticulously. We believed in our ADF. We figured our bearings and headings with no mistakes, for we knew the results of carelessness in such surroundings. I passed on this information that night to two of the most amazed pilots one could imagine. We started by turning on the ADF and having a lesson in tracking out. We also had a lesson in tracking in and how to counter for crosswind. We had a lesson in how to tell how far out we were from the station by taking wingtip bearings and timing the change. They learned more than they thought was possible to learn about just one little piece of radio equipment. We made it through the night and into Puerto Rico.

We were back at Borinquen Field, the home of the wonderful daiquiris. I had been traveling with a Lieutenant Rommel, an engineer, telling him that we could expect daiquiris for fifteen cents when we got to the Officers' Club. But postwar inflation had already struck—they were now twenty cents!

Lieutenant Rommel had been in Burma for several months, walking the Lido Road from Assam to Myitkyina, surveying and laying out the way for the construction crews to build the military supply line to China. He had slept out in the open under the stars in those jungles. He said he would hear the planes going overhead, and sometimes he could see the exhaust from the four engines. He wondered what that would be like and felt he was in a better part of the war. I saw them building that same road from far above and also wondered how they could stand such duty, down there among the leeches, jungle animals, mosquitoes, poisonous snakes, hostile natives, Japanese snipers, and all the other unmentionable problems. To each his own. I would not have traded with him, nor he with me.

We both had plenty of time to enjoy a few daiquiris at the club. In fact, we were there for over twenty-four hours while a hurricane raged off the coast of Florida, blocking our way on the final leg of the long and frustrating trek to the States.

The final flight from Borinquen Field to Miami was flown by Eastern Airlines under contract with the government, in an *upholstered* C-46! We were finally arriving in style. We landed at the Thirty-sixth Street Airport, and I debarked from that last plane ride at the exact spot where I had stepped off American soil just eleven months before.

New arrivals were whisked away to the Floridian Hotel on the beach. As soon as possible I called home to let them know I was finally on the right side of the Atlantic and would be home soon. We were to stand by at the Floridian for orders to a new base assignment. I had a choice, so I chose Romulus, since it was as close as any to my home.

While awaiting transportation, I went to a milk bar where they sold malted milks and milk shakes, and I ordered a quart of plain milk, something I had promised myself while suffering the lack of milk during those months in India. I had dreamed of a cold glass of milk many times, just like a wanderer on the desert hallucinates about cold, clear water. I drank the whole quart with hardly a stop, enjoying each drop. It was also an equal thrill to go to any fountain and drink water without fear of pestilence and without the strong taste of chlorine. People cannot understand what this country is really like until they have traveled abroad and returned. It was sheer, glorious, exhilarating freedom to accept the products of sanitation and to enjoy plenty for a change.

There was only a day of waiting until travel orders came, and I left at noon on the train for Detroit, arriving at Detroit the next morning. I found transportation out to the air base, checked in at the BOQ, and looked around for familiar faces. One of the first was Flight Officer Baker. We caught up on the news and I hit him up for the twenty-five dollars he had borrowed from me before he left for the States in December. He paid. We went out that night to visit some of the spots in Detroit. He borrowed the twenty-five back, and I never saw him again.

On Monday I was at the squadron headquarters at eight sharp for further orders. I was told that I had enough points to be discharged. This was all new to me; the point system was drastically changed right after V-J Day. Having been involved in war efforts since January 1941, I was shocked to learn that it was over and I was no longer needed. I did not know what to think of all this change. I asked what the alternative would be to getting out and was told that I would be assigned to the Pacific, to be involved in evacuating personnel from that area. My past experience of long-range transportation seemed to be the right qualifications for what they would be doing next. Just thinking about those twelve- to fifteen-hour trips was enough. I faced another point of no return; I chose to get out. In short, I was given a leave to visit home, and in one week I was to report to Nashville for separation orders. I was on my final leg to home and civilian life. Somewhere a radio was playing the song "Sentimental Journey."

Unless a person has experienced a similar situation, it is impossible to know the great feeling of finally coming home. To those who have had the experience, there is no reason for me to try to explain the pure joy of it. Words cannot express that burst of emotion.

I can remember my arrival, shortly after dark in the train station at Marshalltown. The whole family was there, and I rushed off the train and grabbed my mother and then each one of the family as fast as I could. We were not a demonstrative family as a rule, but this night all rules were broken. Mom thought I had lost a lot of weight and was particularly disturbed by the jaundiced coloration of my skin caused by the Atabrine. It took several weeks for it to fade and healthy color to reappear. She was right about the weight. I was down to 157 pounds, the same weight I held while running on the track team in 1934. This time it was not just good conditioning, it was malnutrition to a great extent. But with Mom's cooking that changed in rapid order, and by the time the Atabrine traces were gone, my weight was almost back to normal.

I spent a delightful week at home renewing acquaintances and unwinding. What a contrast to anything I had experienced during the previous year! The week went too fast, and I returned to Nashville for the long wait for separation orders. This time the orders would free me from military duty.

Beechcraft D-18S and me.
From *Monsanto Magazine*, September 1946.

3
Corporate
Aviation

Early corporate aircraft *Smilin' Thru,* 1929. Owned by Automatic Washer Co., Newton, Iowa. Left to right: Harry Ogg, secretary Katherine McBride, and pilot Wilford Gerbracht. Courtesy Beech Aircraft Corp.

Interior of *Smilin' Thru.* Left to right: pilot Wilford Gerbracht, secretary Katherine McBride, and Harry Ogg. Courtesy Beech Aircraft Corp.

Prairie Wings prior
to South American
trip, 1947.

Plush interior of *Prairie Wings,* 1947.

Looking aft from the cockpit area at the interior of a Convair 240.

Monsanto pilots, 1951. Left to right: Bob Hinds, Del Clark, Dick Thurston, George Meyers, me, Paul Vance, Bob Turner. Photographed by Aaron Spotswood. Flags on *Prairie Wings* were accumulated during the South American trip.

Sabreliner N-2009 in front of the Lambert Field Terminal Building, 1966.

Civilian

The wait in Nashville was a month long. I was interrogated about the Hump and I responded with the simple truth. It was of no purpose to exaggerate my experiences or the conditions to be found in Asia. The truth was difficult enough for people to grasp, let alone any attempt to embellish it.

Days of boredom followed days of more boredom. I became reacquainted with some of the friends made prior to my overseas duty. Captain Raptis, whom I had known in Romulus, felt we should try to do something about our instrument ratings. Each of us had over one hundred hours of instrument time now, and we were eligible to get our rating changed to the green card, which allowed pilots to sign their own clearances while flying from any base. Even more important was the fact that it could be converted to an instrument rating with the CAA when we became civilians. By this route we would not have to take an instrument course all over again but could merely make a change on paper to the civilian ratings.

Raptis and I went to the training department on the line and told them of our intention. They needed something to do and were glad to cooperate as we started on a ground-school course as well as a scheduled-flight course. The trainer was a little C-45, but it was well equipped for instrument flying. With some practice we were each ready for the final flight test. We soon completed ground school and passed the final written with good grades.

In the air, under the hood, we went through all the routine maneuvers, such as steep turns, engine-out procedures, and orientation problems on the range legs and on the ADF. Finally the ADF approach was to be made using the published bearings for our final approach course to the field from the range station. The only difference from our usual approach, which we had been using in

China and India, was the fact they wanted us to do the entire problem using aural null instead of the automatic antenna setting.

During my flight test, I located myself in the area, positioned the aircraft on the published bearing of the final approach, and flew inbound by aural null to the station and from there on to the airport, all under the hood. After crossing the station I used the second hand on my watch to time my flight to the edge of the field. When my calculated time was up the instructor check pilot lifted the hood so I could see. It was a nice feeling to look down on the end of the southwest runway at Nashville. He said, "You've passed the test. Let's go in for a landing." I asked him about the accuracy of the ADF compared to the actual range legs. His reply was a little startling. He said, "You were making corrections with aural null before I could hear an off-course signal on the range leg." That was amazing, but gratifying.

My orders came through just about a month after checking in. I was to report to Jefferson Barracks, St. Louis, for final separation from the military. A train ride to St. Louis, an overnight, and the next thing I knew, I was a free civilian. I rode to Des Moines on Mid-Continent Airlines, and the family met me for the drive to Marshalltown.

During my overseas duty I had stored my Buick in Dad's double garage, on chocks so the tires would not flatten. Every Sunday Dad would start the engine and let it run long enough to warm up and lubricate the engine. I didn't know then what I know now about oil and care of an engine. The first thing I did when I returned home was remove the chocks and start the engine. It ran beautifully, but my mistake was not changing the oil, thus cleaning the engine of all the sludge that had been building up. That mistake was brought to light on a trip to Des Moines a couple of days later when a bearing burned out, and I had to be towed back to Marshalltown.

Days went by when all I did was sleep all day and stay wide awake all night. I was hit by what is today called jet lag. I was 180 degrees away from where my system slept at certain hours and was awake the other times. It took several weeks to get readjusted to the new time on our side of the earth.

It was very nice just letting the world go by without urgent and important matters to solve daily. In fact, it got to be too easy just to be there and let my mother do the cooking and provide clean clothes. It suddenly struck me that this is how a guy becomes a bum. I wondered what the rest of the world was doing. Would they all be going off and leaving me behind? I decided it was time to do something about it. I took my form five — the army flight record — and placed each daily flight in my logbook, bringing it up-to-date, starting with the last entry sometime in 1944.

I decided to go to Kansas City, where several of my friends had found flying jobs in civilian life. It was my plan to stop at the CAA in Des Moines on the way and get my license renewed. I left one morning in October, stopped in Des Moines and presented myself, the logbooks, and my discharge papers to the CAA. I asked to be reinstated as a commercial pilot with an instrument rating. I was shocked when they told me I would have to present the actual form five — which I had left in Marshalltown — for substantiation. Returning to Des Moines the next day, I presented the form five. The inspector did not even look at it. He wrote out my new ticket and I proceeded to Kansas City. This was close to the same type of thinking used in the military — bureaucracy was exercising its power.

My stay in Kansas City was not too fruitful at first. Jobs were scarce, and I found many pilots had given up and were resigned to going into other work. That was not what I wanted. I hadn't gone through everything in order to toss all that experience aside. I was determined to stick with it and do something I knew I could do well. Perseverance paid off. I got a telegram from Hubert Bloodworth, who was in surplus sales for the air corps in St. Louis. The wire said that Bill Remmert had just purchased a second UC-78 and would be needing a pilot. Hub was designated to help find that pilot. "Wire back if interested." I did and found myself back in St. Louis, just as in 1940 — job hunting.

Bill Remmert was in the process of getting his release from the navy in the fall of 1945. His wife, Betty, was secretary to Dr. Charles Allen Thomas, one of the Monsanto Chemical Company's executives. Since Dr. Thomas was a member of the committee of scientists which monitored the development of the atomic bomb, he had to make frequent trips to White Sands, New Mexico. With commercial travel very limited it seemed feasible to Bill Remmert to put a charter plane in operation, which he did with the purchase of the first UC-78 early in 1945. The little twin-engine trainer was converted to an upholstered personnel carrier and put into service, mostly flying from St. Louis to White Sands. When I arrived on the scene in November, I was given a check ride by Hub Bloodworth, accepted by Bill Remmert, and put to work.

The first trip was to Jefferson City and back with Al Ahner and Charlie Sporher, followed by a week-long trip by Monsanto's Bill Belknap and Rush Cole through the South. And so it went, Betty handling the schedules from her vantage point at the Monsanto offices and Bill taking care of maintenance in his spare time after hours with mechanics who were willing to moonlight.

Part of the reason I was put on the payroll was that I did not differentiate between flying in daylight or at night and on instruments. At this point very few pilots other than those flying for airlines had or needed an instrument rating.

Lambert Field

Records show Lambert Field in St. Louis was established on June 20, 1920. In 1923 the International Air Races took place at Lambert Field. That was one of the first major events.

Charles A. Lindbergh, a young barnstormer, arrived in 1924 and became chief pilot for the newly formed Robertson Aircraft Corporation. Other members of that organization were William, Frank, and Danny Robertson, and O. E. Scott. This group landed an airmail contract in 1926, and in 1927 the Lindbergh flight to Paris became the talk of the world.

Curtiss started building the Curtiss Robin on Lambert Field in 1928. It was powered by an OX-5 engine. In 1929 the Robin was available with a Challenger engine and was the model used by Douglas ("Wrong Way") Corrigan in 1939 to duplicate the Lindbergh feat.

During the late 1920s, Lambert was home to several pilots who became famous in their own right. They included Bud Guerney, Jimmy Doolittle, Benny Howard, and many others.

In 1929 the National Balloon Races were held at Lambert Field and the Robertson Corporation started Universal Airlines, one of five airlines which, under the guidance of C.R. Smith who was joined later by Red Mosier, became known as American Airlines.

In the early 1930s Curtiss began building the Curtiss Condor while Ralph Damon was the company president. The Monocoupe factory, which is still standing, was producing Monocoupes for the private flyers.

A new terminal building was dedicated in 1932, and Red Jackson and Forrest O'Brien set a new endurance record with a Challenger-Robin.

In 1937 the Great Depression was still taking its toll on aviation, but the International Air Races were held at Lambert anyway. In 1939 McDonnell Corporation settled in the old American Airline hangar on the southwest corner of Lambert Field.

From 1940 through 1945 Lambert Field was the setting for an intensive war effort. The first C-46 was produced there, along with many different types of training aircraft. Curtiss-Wright was a busy place.

It was during this period in 1943 that one of the most tragic accidents in St. Louis history occurred. A production glider lost a wing and Mayor William Dee Becker, William Robertson, and many other civic leaders lost their lives on the demonstration flight.

At the time of my arrival in 1945 McDonnell was taking over the Curtiss-Wright facility. Johnny Randolph was the airport manager. His office was on the second floor of the old terminal building and the door was always open. When John was offered a better position with Hertz he left St. Louis, but not before devising a testing system for his replacement. One of the tower operators took first place in the competition and served as airport manager for twenty-five years. His name was David Leigh.

During David's tenure many changes took place on Lambert Field. New and longer runways, taxi strips, and a new terminal building were all constructed during those years. Construction has been continuous since 1946. Like most major airports, growth is constant.

Dave Leigh's tenure was followed by the administration of Leonard Griggs. It was during his time that the largest and most expensive expansion took place. Extra runways, lengthened runways, and more finger ramps were added, and the East Terminal was completed.

Early in 1968 Remmert-Werner was purchased by Rockwell

127

International. Later they sold the facility to Sabreliner Incorporated. Young Aviation became Midcoast Aviation, and a former Remmert-Werner executive, John Tucker, took over from Dewey Young. Only two fixed-base operations were on the airport at the end of the sixties. The same two are there today.

The old terminal building on Lindbergh Boulevard was razed, along with all the hangars on the west side of the field, to make room for runway expansion. Even before the old terminal building was removed the rotating beacon was moved to a point over on the McDonnell operations hangar. It was not easy to see when it was on top of the tower on the old terminal building. I overheard a transient pilot call the tower one dark night to ask if the beacon was on — he could not see it. The reply was, "Yes it is on, but it is a little hard to see it at night!" Well, it is still hard to see, buried among the lights of hundreds of buildings in the vicinity of the McDonnell Douglas complex. By the time pilots have located the rotating green light they have crossed the airport and are in serious trouble with approach control.

I am certain the best is yet to come for Lambert Field. Millions of passengers pass through St. Louis each year. It took many years for the total passengers in and out of St. Louis to reach the first million mark. Growth is painful, but it is inevitable so we may as well prepare for it with sound principles and foresight.

It is very unlikely there will ever be another air race or balloon demonstration on Lambert Field. The glamour days are over and nothing is as important as moving people in and out of the airport. Air races and big celebrations were staged to develop interest in aviation. We have accomplished that, as indicated by the masses who move through the airport today. Not only is there no time for promotional activities there is no longer a need. That is progress!

Civilian Pilot

My first trip with Monsanto was taken before I had arranged for a place to live in St. Louis, and my clothes were still in my car. I had not had enough time to buy new ones, nor did I know where I was going or what kind of clothes to buy. Things did not get much better either. Except for the down time I had at Huntsville fixing a sick engine, I flew every day in November. With a few hours off one day, I did get to Ferguson, in north St. Louis County near Lambert Field. There I found a room in a nice house on Tiffin Street, just off the main drag. The room was small and had only one light bulb hanging from the ceiling for light. It was the right price—ten dollars per week. It was all I needed under the circumstances because I was in it only long enough to sleep and go back to the airport for the next trip.

December started out with a series of charter flights and there were only a couple of days when we didn't fly somewhere. On December 19, I flew to New Orleans, where we spent the night, and then went on to Havana, Cuba, on the twentieth after picking up a St. Louis doctor in Tampa. His mission was to go to Havana to diagnose a case of cancer to see if surgery in St. Louis would be feasible. On the way back the next day we ran into some pretty heavy weather between Havana and Key West. My passenger, Dr. Arbuckle, who was not too crazy about flying anyway, apologized for not going any further with me and took the train back to St. Louis. I could not blame him too much, but on the other hand, the weather was behind us and I had a nice calm trip back to St. Louis alone. He arrived a couple of days later.

While in Havana the family of the patient had asked me for a quote on moving the patient to St. Louis. I had hoped to make the trip with a demonstrator Beechcraft that was in our hanger in St. Louis. Instead, I was talked out of that and a stretcher was quickly fabricated and installed in one of the UC-78s. On December 31 we left St. Louis with both airplanes, one for the patient and one for the family. Harry Hoemeyer flew the other plane with Buzz De Salme; my copilot was Bill Short. I also had the nurse who would accompany the patient back to St. Louis. Since the family wanted to accompany the patient, they were very disappointed with the arrangement of two airplanes instead of one, but they were good sports and accepted the situation; the whole thing was sort of a last-resort type of a trip.

I don't remember where the nurse stayed that night in Havana, but we pilots all stayed in the same hotel with adjoining rooms. It was Buzz De Salme's first trip out of the country and his eyes were wide open. We had the doors open between the rooms in the hotel and Buzz was taking in everything he could see. In the bathroom he walked over to a fixture which looked a little like a footbath and inadvertently stepped on a small pedal as he looked into the bowl. The pedal did what it was designed to do and a good-sized column of water shot toward the ceiling. Unfortunately Buzz's face was in between and he took full blast from that jet of water. He soon learned about bidets, at that time much more common outside the United States than within.

Our shopping in Havana consisted of buying the usual novelties. Of course, each stocked up with a six-pack of Metusalem rum. It was six dollars.

Early the next morning we were at the airport with clearances ready, waiting to put the patient on board. By eight we were airborne and on our way to Miami for the customs inspection. This proved to be less of a problem than we had anticipated. Bringing a patient into the country sometimes creates complications. Apparently this had been planned well in advance. The weather was with us up to this point, but during our stop in Tallahassee for fuel, we found the weather around Birmingham was flyable but not too good. Since Harry Homeyer did not have an instrument rating, he had to divert to the east via Chattanooga.

During my stop in Birmingham I called St. Louis to give Bill Remmert our arrival time. I suggested the ambulance be parked in the hangar and that I taxi right into the hangar upon my arrival. Our trip from Birmingham was on instruments most of the way, and worse yet, the temperature in St. Louis was not the balmy seventy degrees we had left in Havana, but more nearly seven degrees. We landed on time; as we approached the hangar the doors came open and we shut down the engines, coasted into the hangar, and saw the doors shut before we opened the doors to the airplane. The patient never suffered a change of temperature of any kind.

February was much like January and December in that we flew almost daily. I don't know how I had the time to accomplish all that was done during that time, but it got done.

Early in 1946 we made many trips to Jefferson City to the State Department of Education to get all the requirements for an approved flight school. We already had the CAA requirements well in mind. I wrote the curriculum for the entire school. We were going for commercial licenses and would leave instrument ratings for a later date. By March we had our VA and CAA approval and were in the business of giving flight instruction to those veterans who qualified for flight training. This was a great source of revenue to a struggling aviation company.

Another accomplishment was the acquisition of a distributorship for Cessna Aircraft. This meant that all Cessnas sold in our area came through our facilities and added to the company revenue. Bill had also arranged to be the dealer in our area for Motorola radios. There were two types, a two-way aircraft radio and a simple aircraft receiver. We put the receiver in one of the UC-78s, giving us the luxury of being able to hear two messages at the same time. Although they are common today, there was no audio panel.

I had to unplug my headset from one receiver and quickly reconnect with the other. Having no marker beacon receiver, that was the system I used on instruments as I approached St. Louis from the east. The northwest leg of Scott Field crossed the east leg of St. Louis near the Spanish Lake fan marker. I would report the marker when I heard an on-course signal on each of those two stations.

It was soon obvious to me that I was lucky in having a job at all. It was also obvious that if I was to be paid regularly I would have to jump in with all time available to help make the new company go. It did pay off as they began to grow and I, in turn, received raises as fast as they could afford it.

Flying almost daily left little time for outside activities. My social life centered around various airport locations. The cafe operated by Art Schneithorst in the terminal building was one meeting place. After a busy day I would sometimes go up in the tower and visit with Paul Vinyard and Mary Alexander. Mary was one of the first female controllers. Things were a little less formal than they are today. Each airline flight number was like an old friend to the controllers.

There was a fan marker out near St. Peter's on the west leg of the St. Louis range. TWA flights arriving would report that fix as "passing the Pearly Gates" rather than "over St. Peter's marker." In time they just tapped the mike against the metal part of the pilot's seat. The result was somewhat like a bell. The controllers knew that TWA Flight 248 was over St. Peter's fan marker.

Since traffic was not dense in those days it was not difficult to associate a certain number with a certain person. Controllers soon were able to rate the pilot's ability and would expedite or slow down the clearances to satisfy the pilot. What a far cry from today's impersonal approach.

Our flight school kept growing and it became necessary to

have a ground-school instructor full time. Stacey Weeks, an experienced navigator recently separated from the air corps, took over the ground-school, much to my relief. Stacey held many different positions other than just ground-school instructor, and he stayed on the airport for the next forty years.

Remmert-Werner branched out a bit by establishing a flight school at the Starling Airport. Daily, Bob Burrell would fly a Cessna 120 to the airport in South County to work with the students. Here is where the name of Doc Sante first came up. He was operating a maintenance shop on the Starling Airport and soon became a regular in the group of our participating personnel. Doc continued off and on with Remmert-Werner for the next forty years. During that time he logged a flight from Ireland to the States in a SkyVan in the middle of the winter. That feat was comparable to some of the most noteworthy flights of earlier days because he was heading west against the wind in a slow, albeit turboprop, aircraft.

Our school was honored by Texaco's Aviation Sales Division when they chose it for the training of John C. Morgan, one of their members. He was an air force veteran but did not have commercial a license and needed the training in order to pass the flight check. At first his name did not mean a great deal to any of us; it was just another name. We learned much later who he was, but not from John, as he was much too modest to mention anything about himself.

John was the copilot on the B-17 named *Ruthie II*. They were on a bombing mission to the Focke-Wolfe factory, deep in Germany. They had just arrived in enemy territory when they were attacked by a group of enemy fighters. Another group came out of the clouds and started firing 20mm shells. One shell split the skull of Lt. Robert Campbell, the pilot, who immediately slumped forward on the wheel, causing a shallow dive. Bullets had already riddled the windshield in front of copilot Morgan, and he could barely see because of the rush of wind through the shattered windshield. John Morgan heaved back on the wheel and called for help from some of the crew members. He got none. His intercom had been shot out, as well as the oxygen system for the waist, tail gunners, and radio compartment. Sergeant Tyle Weaver, top turret gunner, came staggering to the cockpit. A shell had ripped off his arm right next to the socket. He was losing blood and rapidly losing consciousness and gestured to Morgan to take the bomber down. He stumbled through the opening into the navigator's compartment where Keith Koske tried unsuccessfully to stop the flow of blood. He helped Weaver into a chute and pushed him out through an open hatch in the floor. Morgan did not know this, but the waist, tail gunners, and radio operator had passed out from lack oxygen. Since he no longer heard their guns firing he assumed they had also bailed out.

For two hours Morgan tried to stay with the formation for fear of being easy prey as a straggler. He kept the bomber in formation with his right hand while holding the fatally injured pilot away from the control column. He flew to the target, dropped his load of bombs, and then headed back toward the North Sea. Often he had to take evasive action as the fighters attacked his unprotected tail, then back up on the throttles to regain formation position. After reaching the North Sea, Koske came up from the nose compartment and noticed the problem in the cockpit. He lifted Campbell out of the seat and into the nose compartment. With all gas gauges reading empty because of bullet holes in the tanks, little fuel remained. At the first airfield, Morgan radioed the tower, but the radio had been knocked out. He did the only thing he could. He entered the busy traffic pattern and, with the help of the tail gunner who had recovered from oxygen lack, got the gear and flaps down and landed safely.

Sergeant Weaver survived the parachute jump; he was taken to a German hospital and recovered in spite of a tremendous loss of blood. The gunners who had lain unconscious for hours also survived but suffered severe frostbite.

On a subsequent mission, Morgan was blown out of an airplane as it exploded after flak had set an engine on fire. He found himself in the air with his parachute under his arm. He managed to get it on over his head against the terrific blast of air, and by lying on his back, he got most of the straps fastened. Just as the chute opened he hit the top of a tree, which cushioned his fall. But even then, he fell thirty feet to the ground. He was captured by the Germans and remained a prisoner until the war's end.

John completed the commercial course and went to work for Texaco as sales representative for aviation products. It was several years later that I was privileged to watch the ceremony in which he received the Medal of Honor presented by General Tooey Spaatz.

In February Bob Werner announced that he had just bought a PT-19 for the company from a friend of his in Ann Arbor, Michigan. He was looking at me with a strange twinkle in his eyes, and the next thing I knew I was on the train to Detroit. His friend met me at the station, and we drove out to the airport where the plane was located.

It was a most discouraging sight. The open-cockpit airplane was in a T hangar with no front door and very little roof. The cockpits were both full of snow, so we were several hours cleaning it out and getting the engine in running order after a long inactive period in the coldest of weather. It took all day to get the plane ready to fly so I was forced to spend the night.

Early the next morning I was off the ground and heading for St. Louis. Fortunately, I still had my winter flying suit complete with heavy lined boots and leather helmet. In spite of all that paraphernalia I was not too keen on the prospects of an airy ride to St. Louis. The trip required two fuel stops and almost five hours before I rolled up on the ramp in St. Louis.

The plane served as an advanced trainer for our school and provided us with aerobatic capabilities which were not supplied elsewhere at that time. Bob Werner took some instruction from me in the plane and others showed interest also.

It was not long before Betty Remmert asked to take a ride in it, so with Bob's borrowed helmet and goggles, we got her seated in the rear seat for a ride in the airy bird. We had to boost her up with several cushions since she was not very tall in the first place. Even then she was not towering out of the cockpit, but she could at least see out.

After takeoff we proceeded north of Lambert Field to our practice area. She had asked for some aerobatics after some sightseeing. I did a loop, looked in the mirror, and saw her smiling face, so continued into a slow roll. Again I looked back for her smiling face. I almost died — there was no one in the cockpit! While staring stunned at the empty mirror, I began to see a couple of hands gripping the combing, soon followed by Betty's face! She was not smiling and her helmet and goggles were gone. When the plane had turned over, the belt was just loose enough to let her head catch the wind, which snatched her helmet and goggles away at the same time all the cushions fell out. Of course, after we were righted, she slowly pulled herself up to a position where I could see her startled face. Mine must have registered stark terror. I was almost frantic until I saw her. That ended our flight for the day.

Things were getting a little hectic from my standpoint. I would no sooner arrive from a charter trip on the UC-78 than Bill would have a student waiting for me in the Cub or one of the Cessnas. There were days when I would fly as many as four or five different airplanes. It was difficult to be in the mood to do some training and then be called out to make a charter trip. I could not complain for I wanted something to do, and I was doing it. It just became a little frustrating never to get settled down in one type of flying before another was forced upon me.

Looking back on those days with Remmert-Werner, I must treat them as a necessary transition to becoming a corporate pilot. I learned that a person cannot overdo little niceties for the passengers. I learned that I could almost always ease consternation on the part of passengers if I talked their language. When they saw me at work, they had more faith in me and confidence in my flying. I had passed another point of no return in my career. I was definitely interested in going into corporate flying rather than airline duty, which I decided would be sheer boredom. While flying charter I never seemed to make two trips to the same place in succession. Somehow, I liked the challenge of new places and new routes, new approaches and new climates.

After all the raises from Remmert-Werner, I was still not up to what I had received as a captain in the air corps. When a better position appeared, I was going to be looking for a change. I felt I had gone about as far as I could go with this job. Still, I did not want to make a change for the sake of change. I was looking for something that would be a permanent position, preferably with a large corporation.

One day a man walked into the office and asked if he could charter a plane for a round trip to Walnut Ridge. His name was Danny Fowlie. That name rang a bell with me, as I had heard about his aerobatics and his crazy pilot act at air shows before the war.

En route to Walnut Ridge he started to ask a lot of questions about my background. He was pleased to know about my association with the Livingstons as they were both good friends of his. He was most interested in the fact that I had recent experience in C-54s.

He told me the reason for the trip was to purchase a bunch of C-54s. He planned to ferry them to Texas where they would be converted to DC-4s with airline interiors. He had a market with some foreign airlines for their sale. He offered me a job as pilot to do the ferrying, for six hundred dollars per month plus expenses.

The offer was for a lot more than I had been making, but I couldn't see where the job would take me after all the planes had been moved. I told him I would have to think it over but would let him know in a couple of days.

When I got back to St. Louis, I discussed the offer with Bill. He said he could not match the offer and that sooner or later he expected me to move on. In the meantime Monsanto was thinking about hiring a full-time corporate pilot. Knowing nothing about pilot salaries, they came to Bill to see what I had been making. At that time Bill told them about the offer I had received from Danny Fowlie which later became my starting salary at Monsanto.

Monsanto

It was a very rainy day in mid-May. I had flown to Chicago Midway Airport to pick up Edgar Queeny, Monsanto's chairman, to bring him to St. Louis. Rumor had it that Monsanto was about to buy a new twin Beechcraft.

Queeny arrived and as we were rushing to the airplane through the rain, I mentioned that I had heard about their contemplating the purchase of a new airplane. If it was so I wanted to put in my bid for the chief pilot's job. His reply was somewhat of a surprise but typical of a Monsanto executive. He said, "We are leaving the selection of a pilot to American Airlines. They know how to pick good pilots, but we only know how to make good chemicals." Queeny was on the board of American Airlines and was the second-largest individual stockholder, surpassed only by C.R. Smith himself.

I felt a little rebuffed after having flown so many of the executives during the previous months, but on the other hand, I would not let anything like that stand in my way of going after a job I wanted.

The trip back to St. Louis was what could be expected on a May day — lots of rain, ragged ceilings, and more rain. We were on approach behind an American Airlines DC-3 when they missed the approach and had to pull up, so we were cleared to make our approach. I had my trusty, quick-headset-change system to find Spanish Lake and I reported that fix to the tower. I was soon at the low cone and started the turn to the west, then followed the road that would bring me in alignment with the final approach to runway sixteen. After all the hours I had instructed in the area north of Lambert Field I could recognize my location by a tree or an old barn; once in sight of the ground there was no reason for me to miss the approach. I landed in the rain and while taxiing in Queeny asked me, "How come American missed the approach and we got in?" I suggested that perhaps they had not spent enough time instructing north of Lambert Field. This event changed nothing. I still had to go through American's pilot procurement screening at La Guardia.

Early in June I arrived at the American Airlines facilities at La Guardia Airport and began the screening, which started with interviews, an IQ test, psychological testing, more interviews, and more testing. They insisted they would have to audit my logbooks, which I did not have with me. I called Betty and told her where they were. I asked her to send them to me by special delivery at the Waldorf Astoria tower suite, where I was booked for the weekend. Monsanto had kept the suite there all during the war because rooms were scarce and they needed a place for their executives to stay in New York.

On Saturday I was able to find my dentist friend Monroe Levin and have dinner with him, his wife, Vickie, and Barbara Donahue. Barbara had been the CO of the WASP contingent at Romulus, and the four of us had been together there socially on several occasions. It was a pleasant evening of reminiscing and bringing each other up to date.

My logbooks arrived on Sunday afternoon, and with nothing more to do, I went to Radio City Music Hall for a show. By Monday I was ready for the remainder of the testing.

I took the physical in the morning and the flight test in a C-45 in the afternoon. Right after my flight, I was approached by the check pilot with the offer of a job with American. They were in need of four-engine pilots, and they could have put me on the payroll right then. I had to make a decision. I could not, in all honesty, accept such an offer when Monsanto had sent me there in good faith. I had reached the point of no return once more: I was flattered but could not accept. I had reservations out of La Guardia late that afternoon for St. Louis. I was turning down a career as an airline pilot for the unknown future of a corporate pilot.

On June 12 I went to the offices on South Second Street in St. Louis and became the first pilot hired at Monsanto. They backdated my employment to June 6. Sam Allender checked me into the company with a wonderful briefing and orientation. He had been hired by John F. Queeny as an errand boy shortly after the company had been founded. He saw the growth from a company started on five thousand dollars of borrowed money to the present multimillion dollar giant. His comments imbued me with the spirit of Monsanto, which in turn helped me formulate procedures to be used in the flight department.

In the afternoon I was airborne again on the airline to Wichita. I was staying at the Broadview while waiting for the plane to be ready for delivery. The next morning the airplane was rolled off the assembly line and over to the flight test department. I was not allowed to ride on the first flight as that was restricted to test pilots. From that flight on, however, I was in the left seat and becoming acquainted with the flying characteristics while the test pilot sat in the right seat and made notes of discrepancies. This went on for five or six flights before all was in working order and airworthy.

During that period I became acquainted with the key people at Beech who had already contributed much to the Beechcraft mystique. I spent a great deal of time with Leddy Greever, of course, since he was head of marketing. I met Walter Beech and enjoyed talking about our mutual friend John Livingston. I also met Olive Beech, who was by that time well into the actual management of the company. Of course I got well acquainted with Parker, who drove the limousine, picked me up every morning, and dropped me off at the hotel every night. He stayed with the company for forty years and was either made head of personnel or given some other responsible position. They were all great people, and I was especially impressed with Vern Carsten, the chief test pilot. He was very low key, very thorough, and was a great help to me in learning what I needed to know about the airplane. They did not have a formal training department at that time as they have today. You learned pretty much on your own or you scuttled the airplane.

It was during this period of waiting that I also managed to give some thought to how I was going to run a flight department. I looked around for help and discovered there were few departments to use as a model. I began to develop some ideas of my own. Among those ideas were some of the things I had seen at Beechcraft. They ran a high-class operation. I was impressed by being picked up at the hotel in an air-conditioned limo each morning. I liked the atmosphere of professionalism found throughout the company. I had spent some time in the Monsanto offices. I saw how the executives were treated. All of this had something to do with the way I wrote the procedures manual. My dress code consisted of a well-pressed business suit or sport jacket, white shirt, tie, and shoes shined to military standards. It paid off. I was approached early by one of the Monsanto executives about uniforms. He wanted to know what I would like. I was ready with the explanation that we would prefer not to have uniforms. I remarked that a uniform in our case would mean little to anybody. The airlines had their own distinguishing insignia, but we had none in Monsanto. I suggested we would prefer to wear business suits in good taste. The idea was accepted. Consequently in almost every case we were invited to join our passengers for dinner no matter where we were. That would not have been possible if we had been in an unidentified uniform. Neither would we have been included had we been wearing what so many were wearing at that time — an old and badly worn leather flight jacket, baggy pants, a baseball cap, and dark glasses. It seemed to me the job required a little more dignity. Dignity begets respect. The topic of uniforms never came up again, and I believe the company was better pleased with the pilot staff because of it.

I had met George Meyers at Romulus while I was instructing on UC-78's and he was up for twin-engine transition. I saw him again in India, and a third time in Wichita awaiting delivery of the D-18. It was only then that I learned he had an instrument rating and the mechanic's license. I needed a well-qualified copilot who would soon be able to act as captain. He looked like my man.

On June 21, I delivered the airplane to the Monsanto people at Parks airport in Cahokia, Illinois. Messrs. Belknap, Queeny, Cole, and Thomas all came out to see the plane and then decided they had to have a ride. Mr. Cole's son rode that flight as my copilot. He had been the army acceptance officer at the Beechcraft factory for several months during the war. After the demo ride I took the plane back to Lambert Field, where we were basing it with Interstate Aeromotive. During the afternoon I took George Meyers to the office for signing in on the payroll.

On the twenty-second we flew to Montreal with Queeny and Richard Bishop, the artist, and spent the night. The next morning we flew on to Mont Joli over some of the most beautiful scenery I had ever seen. The St. Lawrence, from Montreal to its mouth, is most picturesque. From Mont Joli the passengers went by car to the Salmon Club on the Bonaventure River; George and I flew to Burlington to clear customs and then on to Washington, D.C. We had passengers back to St. Louis from Washington the next day. By July 25 we were ready for our first hundred-hour check. We were back at the factory just a little over a month after taking delivery. So it went the rest of the year, from coast to coast and with trips to Canada on several occasions. We had little time for anything but flying and taking care of the routine maintenance on the airplane.

When Monsanto had a flight department in the making they did not plan well for the future. It had not occurred to top management that the flight department would have to fit somewhere in the management structure. It did not take long for them to realize that they should give it more than just passing attention, for it was all too obvious it would take a bit of money and planning to keep the operation going.

At first the flight department fell into the pool where all other services went. For several months I reported to Sam Allender, the head of the service department. This department staffed the dining room and management of all food services, the stenographers pool, the drivers, the receptionists, telephone and switchboard facilities, and, finally, the flight department. This was a little too much for such a nice man as Allender.

I was regaled by the stories Allender related about some of his early years with Monsanto. His stories perhaps were not meant to be inspirational, but they turned out to be since I was enthralled with the way the company started and I automatically caught some of the enthusiasm Allender had for the organization.

In the early days, when the company was starting out on a

shoestring, John F. Queeny was somewhat tightfisted. According to Allender, Mr. Queeny would frequently stop at one of the stenographer's desks to see that she was using both sides of her shorthand sheets. If he found she was not, she received a long lecture about wastefulness. A second occurrence was automatic dismissal.

One day Mr. Queeny sent someone out to buy a broom. When the employee got to the store he found that brooms were forty cents apiece, but if he bought two he could have the second for twenty cents. Looking to please the boss with his sage purchase, he returned to the office and proudly announced his acquisition. Mr. Queeny was irate. He said, "Take one of them back. I told you to buy one broom, and that is all this company can afford."

Such stories and the recounting of the growth of the company gave me the feeling of responsibility. No matter what my position was, I felt it necessary to produce as well as possible to keep in step with all the great ones who had preceded me in the company. I saw to it that each pilot hired would be exposed to Allender's personality and hear firsthand some of the fascinating stories of how the company got under way and how it grew to the huge corporation it was by 1946.

Much as I liked to listen to Allender, it was not the place for the flight department. Expenses, when they came up, were out of the jurisdiction of the limits placed on the service department. Wisely, it was decided that someone with vice-presidential status should look after the flight department. The first one chosen was Oz Bezanson. Oz was one of the old-timers in the company and, of course, knew nothing about aircraft operation. We soon had a tacit agreement: he left the aircraft business to me and I let him make chemicals. He was easy to talk to when I needed an allocation of money. All I needed to do was present the request in the normal manner and it was granted. Prior to that, however, I had usually prepared him with plenty of information about the upcoming request. By adding one little phrase concerning safety, I found almost instant reception of my requests.

So the flight department found its proper niche. When Bezanson was picked to head a new company being formed with American Viscose in Philadelphia, which was to be called Chemstrand, my contact with top management had to be changed. Again I was lucky to find a receptive ear in Rush Cole.

While looking back over the way we came, I can say that we made some mistakes but did some things right. The fact that we had a connection to top management through the system of reporting to a vice president became standard procedure with many companies. It has been proven many times that the most successful flight departments are under someone in the upper echelon of management. Any of those found in a lower bracket have never been successful.

There is a strange phenomenon of "monkey see, monkey do" in corporate aviation. If a company sells an airplane, no matter the reason, other companies will take a long hard look and all too often will sell one of theirs. This phenomenon made it difficult for me to be anything but conservative. Monsanto was also known to be anything but liberal in their views about growth, expenditures, and new enterprises. The tightfisted approach initiated by John F. Queeny continued to be felt throughout the company well after I came aboard in 1946. When that philosophy changed in 1964, it was a shock to me and to many others who had been living under the conservative blanket for so many years.

Scheduling remained with Monsanto's service department long after the flight department's move to a higher level in management. Scheduling can be critical to the success of any flight department: if it is too high in the management spectrum, potential users are reluctant to request the airplane; if it is too low in the management scheme, employees tend to misuse the service. Top management can solve the problem by providing a clearly defined policy as to who may ask for an aircraft and for what purposes the aircraft may be used. When these guidelines are readily available for all to read, there is seldom any reason for doubt or questions about aircraft use. Guidelines preclude the need for a scheduling clerk to make the decision.

A distasteful item in aircraft use is titled "charges." Someone has to pay the bill and many of the lesser departments do not have budgets large enough for more than just a few aircraft trips. When a policy regarding charges is set up it should be made known company-wide so there are no surprises later on. Most companies will absorb the fixed expenses and charge only flight expenses to the user. That is sound and fair. After all, the company is getting the advantage of depreciation as well as other benefits. In order to encourage the use of the plane, "flight expenses only" must be reasonable and expected. Like many other company flight departments, Monsanto's had to go through a lot of trial and error before an equitable charge-back system was adopted.

There was a time when I felt we could get much more use from our airplanes than just a few hundred hours per year. Since the fixed expenses went on whether the airplane was used or not, it behooved me to see that we got as much as possible from our investment.

Just to be on top of things, I moved my office in with the head of the traffic department, where I could take a peek over his shoulder every morning and see who was going where. Often I found several people going to the same place at the same time, usually to a convention or seminar. By using my readout of what the costs were on each of our airplanes, I could determine the break-even point. If the cost of the tickets of the passengers equaled or exceeded what the flight expenses would be, then we put the passengers on the company aircraft. In one year we flew over three hundred hours fulfilling the needs of this particular group of travelers. That was money saved.

The ideal way to schedule aircraft is to handle all requests for transportation at the same point. When enough requests come in for the same destination then the company aircraft can fill the bill. In addition the company will have a handle on where everybody goes and for what purpose. The worst possible system allows potential passengers to write their own ticket. This can be expensive, and sooner or later the company aircraft could be idle at the airport while dozens of people are spending money for airline tickets.

Another aspect of scheduling is getting people to the right place. It was always a concern that we would have a flight going one place with the passengers wanting to go another. It finally happened to me.

During the process of getting the Chemstrand Company off the ground, we made many trips to Philadelphia and many to Washington, D.C. There was work to be done with the American Viscos in Philadelphia and a lot of government permits and red tape to handle in Washington. Most of the time Bezanson was my chief passenger, and often there were others with him. One day I was told we were going to Washington, D.C., which was not surprising, so off we went. The weather along the East Coast was lousy. Our approach to Washington National took us in a series of holding patterns from nine thousand feet down to approach altitude. After a long and tedious approach we landed and pulled up to the Butler Aviation operations line. I went back to open the door and Bezanson said, "This isn't Philadelphia, is it?"

"No," I said, "it's Washington, D.C."

He said, "I told my secretary to call you and change our destination but perhaps she forgot."

That was what had happened in St. Louis, but I had to climb back up into that mess of weather and traffic and do it all over again at Philadelphia. Just a simple matter of communications to some but to me it was a pain.

Baggage was another problem. Often when we had two flights going to different destinations, we worried about loading the wrong baggage on the wrong airplane. It happened only once but that was enough to be disastrous to the passengers with the wrong baggage or none at all.

Many different kinds of people asked for the airplane. Some were very dependable. When they asked for the plane as many as three weeks ahead of time, I could usually depend upon their going through with the schedule they ordered. Others, however, could not stay with their plans no matter when they were made.

On one occasion we were scheduled to go to Augusta, Georgia, to pick up a regular user at ten o'clock Thursday morning. The day before the trip the time was changed to eleven o'clock. We still planned ten, as if that change were never made, for fear he would want to leave at ten anyway. We had not left St. Louis on Thursday morning before another change came in: now he wanted to leave at noon with lunch aboard. We made the necessary changes and were waiting at the Augusta airport with lunch aboard well before noon, with a flight plan made out for St. Louis. Our passenger did not show up at noon, of course; he came out at eleven thirty. We were ready, and as we taxied out, we received our clearance, which began, "You are cleared to the St. Louis Airport." When our passenger heard that, he rushed up front to give us yet another change. "We are going to Memphis from here," he said. "Make that Memphis," we told the clearance delivery, "and stand by for change of routing." So with the fourth or fifth change on record, we were finally off for Memphis.

Upon arrival at Memphis we were told to be ready for a departure sometime after dinner since he had a dinner engagement. With that much time to kill the copilot and I borrowed a car from the FBO and went to a theater nearby to see a matinee. I was sitting there fully enjoying the show when suddenly I was struck by a horrible thought: What if he changes his mind again and can't find us? The hair on the back of my neck crawled with the horrible thought of it. I grabbed the copilot and said, "Let's get out of here!" I know he must have thought I was out of my mind, but a team of horses could not have held me back. We got back to the airport, turned in the car, and were just checking the weather when our fickle passenger arrived and wanted to know how soon we could take off for St. Louis. His dinner plans had fallen through! I filed a flight plan and we were airborne less than five minutes after he arrived.

Edgar Queeny was one of those people who was always on time. In fact, he was always early. Often we would have a seven o'clock takeoff for New York scheduled. He would arrive at six thirty. He was always apologetic, saying he could not sleep anyway so came on to the airport. We were ready and airborne at six thirty more times than seven. I primed copilots about his habits so they were never late either. They certainly didn't want Queeny to know they were not eager to go.

In contrast to Queeny, Dr. Thomas always had a difficult time with traffic in the mornings: no matter what time we were scheduled, he was delayed by traffic. That was as a rule, but when he was riding with Queeny, he was like everyone else in the company. He did not want to make Queeny wait on him, so he would come out early. Invariably that would be the only morning that Queeny would come sauntering in for an on-time takeoff. I think he liked to know he was causing Dr. Thomas a period of stewing.

They were not the best two people to travel together in the first place. Queeny loved to keep the temperature in the cabin on the edge of what normal people would find uncomfortably cold. Dr. Thomas was very susceptible to cold and had to have the temperature above what most people called comfortable. Between the two it was hard to adjust to a perfect medium.

I can still recall seeing Edgar Queeny wandering around the airplane in his BVDs while Dr. Thomas had not removed his hat or overcoat. Fortunately for me the heat controls were in the cabin and not a responsibility of mine in the cockpit. Problems like those have suggested the title of a book: *Care and Feeding of Executives.* I am not too sure anyone could write fast enough to cover all the cases that I encountered during my twenty-two years of trying to please the various personalities — all with their own idiosyncrasies.

We had a schedule problem only once with the Queenys. It was at the start of daylight savings time in St. Louis. In those days, country folk did not cotton to such foolishness, so Stuttgart, like other rural areas, retained standard time. I dropped both Edgar and Ethel off on a Friday night and was scheduled to pick them up on Monday morning at seven o'clock. They both specified local time. At least that is what I heard and remembered! So at six thirty on Monday morning I was on the airstrip at Wingmead ready for a seven o'clock return to St. Louis. They were there waiting when I landed. Both were very upset because I was late. I tried to explain that I was not late, that I was a half hour early. Neither would buy my explanation. For years they would suddenly ask me, "Why were you late that morning? Really?" Why they could not believe there had been a mistake in understanding the time involved I do not know. It mattered not that hundreds of times I had come almost three hundred miles for a departure and had always been ahead of time. They could only remember the time I was late.

Edgar Queeny

During my years at Monsanto, I developed a special relationship with Edgar Monsanto Queeny, a complex man who was the chairman of the board of Monsanto and the Queeny of Queeny Towers. I knew him as his personal pilot and as a friend.

I first met Mr. Queeny in the early spring of 1946 on a trip from St. Louis to his home in Arkansas, which was called Wingmead. I remember very little of the conversation for it was scarce. I do remember that his questions were quite probing and to the point. He treated words as if they were valuable expenditures never to be recaptured. If it took the normal person a paragraph to make a statement, he would work on it until he had it down to a sentence. He could also be very bored with big talkers. By asking a few questions he could learn a lot about a person, but the one interrogated would never know what he was up to.

I was called into his office one Monday morning late in the summer of 1946. We talked about airplanes. He did not seem to be satisfied with the size of the D-18 and, on the other hand, the DC-3 seemed to be much larger than he wanted. Suddenly I realized the conversation was over, but as I was leaving he asked if I could come down again at the same time the next day. During our second meeting we talked about the pros and cons of a Lockheed Lodestar versus the DC-3 and about Remmert-Werner. When it came time to leave, he again asked me to come down the next day at the same time. I did, and when the conversation ended that day, he followed me to the door and then took my arm as we walked the full length of the inner corridor of the executive suite. In those few steps he divulged the gist of our three previous conversations. He wanted to invest in Remmert-Werner and he wanted me to be the fourth partner. Before I could protest about the amount to be invested, he said he would finance my share. Within a week we were members of the new Remmert-Werner Corporation. There were four owners of equal shares: Bill Remmert, Bob Werner, Edgar Queeny, and I.

Bill Remmert, having started the original company, served as chief executive. He was a salesman of unquestionable and amazing ability. Although he often oversold, Bob Werner with his engineering department would rise to the occasion and produce whatever it was Bill Remmert said they could produce.

Bob Werner was an engineer and had many years of experience with the Curtiss-Wright organization, most of which were during the war years. He was sort of a silent partner, but developed an engineering group second to none.

Edgar Queeny was a full partner, but silent. His presence was strongly felt because of his prestige and fame as the son of the founder of Monsanto. He was instrumental in bringing much new business to the struggling little company.

Since I was a full-time Monsanto employee, I was only involved with Remmert-Werner part-time. My duties were to test-fly aircraft which were going through conversion, and when they were nearly ready for delivery I would see to the training of the crews. During the years of part ownership in Remmert-Werner, I test-flew and trained crews on the aircraft of as many as twenty major corporations.

Shortly after our new company was formed, Edgar Queeny bought a surplus C-47 which was in parts at the air base in Sedalia, Missouri. During the winter, the C-47 was converted by Remmert-Werner to a plush-interior DC-3 called *Prairie Wings* and subsequently was the showcase for selling DC-3s to corporations all over the country. During January of that year, I was sent to Ardmore,

Oklahoma, where American Airlines conducted all their training. Convairs and DC-6s were coming on the line, and I was one of the last to get an Airline Transport Rating (ATR) on the DC-3s. This was made possible by Mr. Queeny's connection as an American Airlines stockholder.

As the years went by, my association with Queeny became more and more involved. One outstanding adventure was in connection with his filmmaking. I worked as sound recorder on two different pictures. The first was *Prairie Wings,* a duck picture; the second was *Sunrise Serenade,* a picture of the grouse family's early spring mating season. Both films are now in the archives of the American Museum of Natural History. I cherish the memory of nights spent in sleeping bags under the stars on the open prairies while in search of birds and their habitats. The conversations were revealing, and Queeny was at his best — relaxed — and, compared to his usual self, he became quite talkative. It was on one of those nights he expressed his fear, due to claustrophobia, of being incarcerated for any cause. He also stated he could never tolerate being sick or having a prolonged illness.

Queeny was a perfectionist in his photographic efforts. We often visited the Disney studios and when they saw his works, they commented in amazement and said, "How does he do it?"

A safari truck was outfitted with some of Queeny's ideas, one of which was to use a gun turret as a mounting base for a camera. New and sensitive microphones were added and the truck was shipped to Nairobi. Queeny, Jack Clink, Dick Bishop, and several others were in Africa most of January and February that year and brought back outstanding footage, both sound and visual. The picture *Latuko* was made from this trip and played in many of the largest theaters all over the country. Many other minor films were made in documentary style and also rest in the archives at the American Museum of Natural History. Later, his pictures taken under the icy waters of the Bonaventure River in Quebec became known as masterpieces of photography. Never before had the salmon been pictured actually hitting the fly. This was not done in a tank. It was done live, under natural conditions, by Queeny in a wet suit!

Queeny was quiet and unassuming and actually very shy. He wrote well, but could not deliver a speech even though he might be exceptionally sincere about the subject. It was a fault he never was able to conquer. Along with his shyness was his propensity for honesty; he often said he would rather overpay taxes than ever be found short for fear of imprisonment.

He had a keen mind and could figure out design problems easily, but with a screwdriver in his hand he was lethal. If a drawer in the plane failed to open easily, it was soon shredded by the closest available tool.

A problem arose during the construction of the big Monsanto plant on South Second Street. The steam power generated at the Cahokia plant across the river in Illinois had to be transferred to the Missouri side. The engineers were trying to see whether an under-river system or overhead suspension would be best for the huge conduits. Upon hearing about their dilemma, Queeny said, "Why don't they bring it across by wire?" So now the steam is converted to electricity in Illinois, transported to Missouri on high wires, and re-converted to steam upon arrival at its destination. Simple!

Queeny was an immaculate dresser. All his clothes were tailor-made. In fact he was so much aware of cut and style that his trousers had no hip pockets. That was what the public saw.

What people saw in *Prairie Wings* after he had dressed prior to a landing was something else. Where he took off a shirt is where you found it. His socks were on the floor. He always traveled in khakis and changed to a clean shirt and business suit before arrival at the destination. His wandering from the wardrobe in aft cabin to the front not only left a trail of garments but created a constant trim problem in the cockpit.

He was a lonely man. He had very few close friends and was most uncomfortable in a crowd. I never played poker with him but understood he was a formidable opponent. In the company of a few friendly hunters or fishermen he was at home and jovial. Let one outsider come in, and he immediately withdrew to his quiet and retiring personality.

There is no doubt in my mind that he was a genius and the most interesting man I have ever met. With all of his abilities he was also very compassionate. His influence was felt for years throughout the company. Upon occasion of the Texas City disaster, and without counsel, he saw that no family suffered financially in any way from the catastrophe; his behavior became a model for other corporations to follow in cases of disaster.

The company grew under his leadership from a $150 million corporation to over a $1 billion organization. His meekness showed even to the last. One day after a board meeting on a trip between Decatur, Alabama, and Pensacola, he came to the cockpit and said, "How much is $300 million?" I quickly asked, "If you don't know, who would?" The board had just approved that much for an expansion of the Pensacola plant. He was not too blasé to admit that $300 million was a lot of money.

He was a generous man, as witnessed by the fact that there is a Queeny Tower and a Queeny Park; and many other organizations also have benefited from the Queeny wealth. On the other side, there was a touch of tightfistedness in the blood too. Jack Clink had been in Hollywood for several weeks working on film footage prior to our arrival in *Prairie Wings* with Queeny. We were scheduled to go from there to Seattle, so Queeny suggested Jack return with us to save airfare home. This threw Jack's laundry schedule out of phase and he was caught with a lot of dirty clothes in Seattle. With a day to wait before our return trip to St. Louis he did what anyone in the same spot would have done – he had his laundry done at a day laundry. When he returned to St. Louis, he turned in the bill as part of his expense account. Queeny turned it down as an unnecessary expense. The hotel bill for two nights and food for that length of time was not questioned, but the two-dollar laundry charge was too much.

We had returned to St. Louis from a trip to the east, arriving on a Sunday morning about eleven. Before landing Mr. Queeny had asked me if I could drive him home. It was a day off for all his help, including his driver, Tom. Ethel, his wife, was visiting her sister in Washington, D.C.

Having no plans for the rest of the day and being single, it was easy for me to accept the invitation to take him to Jarville. At that time Jarville, on South Mason Road, was way out in the country. On the way Mr. Queeny asked me to stay and have lunch with him. He said, "I'm not much of a cook, but I know how to make a hamburger, and with your help I think we will do just fine." He also added that he thought a good hamburger was about the best meal anyone could imagine, especially if accompanied by a large slice of onion. All of this sounded great to me.

We entered the estate from the rear gate. The drive ended in the bricked courtyard. We climbed the outside stairway to the kitchen on the main floor and found that the help had left a huge onion and a loaf of bread on the kitchen counter.

Queeny proceeded to make hamburger patties from a supply he had removed from the giant refrigerator. The finished product was approximately three-quarters of an inch thick and at least four to five inches in diameter. We fried them in an iron skillet over a gas burner to medium rare and they were still large enough to cover the first slice of bread. When we added the huge slice of white onion and the other slice of fresh bread, the Queeny production was complete. Carrying catsup, Durkees dressing, and cool beer, we moved to the spacious dining room to enjoy a meal. It was delicious.

That was the first Queenyburger for me but certainly not the last. When *Prairie Wings* was being outfitted, a vital bit of equipment was included—an electric grill installed in the galley. It was powered from a converter which brought the 24-volt system to 110 volts. It worked for many years. Standard provisions for any flight always included at least two pounds of hamburger, a loaf of bread, and a huge white onion. Hundreds of guests enjoyed Queenyburgers, fixed by the chef himself, while cruising along the airways. In time the Monsanto kitchen staff learned about the Queenyburgers and started offering them on the luncheon menu. The last time I ate in the company dining room, Queenyburgers were a very popular item.

My last flight with Mr. Queeny was in 1967, from Prince Edward Island nonstop to St. Louis. His guest on that flight was Mr. Ken Bidding. I noticed that Queeny seemed to have aged and that he stumbled while leaving the plane. His health began to deteriorate and, unfortunately, I never saw him again.

On the morning of July 8, 1968, I got a call from Dr. Perry. He said, "I have been asked to call you first, so that is what I am doing. Mr. Queeny passed away this morning." I was leaving that morning for an extended trip to the west coast with Paul Vance in the Aero Commander, so before departure I went to the funeral home, signed the book, and spent the next several days as I flew over the western states cherishing the many memories of my friend and grieving the loss of the greatest man I have ever known.

Prairie Wings around South America

In the fall of 1947 key members of the Monsanto management team made a South American tour in the newly outfitted DC-3, *Prairie Wings*. Members of the party were Edgar Queeny, chairman of the board of Monsanto; Charles Cheston, a board member from Philadelphia; John Gillis, director of international marketing; and Phil Singleton, who was based in San Juan, Puerto Rico, and who acted as our guide as far as Caracas, Venezuela. My flight crew consisted of Ralph Whitworth, copilot and Harvey Gray, relief pilot and interpreter who spoke both Portuguese and Spanish. The purpose of this trip was to survey manufacturing possibilities and to analyze the market potential in each of the countries visited.

The itinerary was to travel southward along the east coast of South America and return northbound along the west. Our first stop was in Havana, Cuba. Then we spent two full days in San Juan, Puerto Rico, followed by overnight stops in Caracas, Venezuela; Port of Spain, Trinidad; and Belem, Natal, and Bahia, Brazil.

Most of the trip en route to Natal was routine, but there a magneto went bad on the left engine. Since there were no maintenance facilities at the airport, I had to change the points myself. Upon our return I reported this to our mechanic, George Toelke, who said it was necessary to remove the magneto from the engine to change points. I replied that I was glad I did not know that or we would still be in Natal. I was afraid to take the mag off for fear of getting the engine out of time. I worked with the aid of a mirror in the hot burning sun. My hands still tingle at the thought of that ordeal.

We were slightly behind schedule when we arrived in Bahia, a unique city in that it is situated on two levels separated by several hundred feet. Shortly after checking in at our hotel we were met by Jay Wiggins, who seemed extra glad to see someone from the States. Jay had been on a sales trip to Brazil in a Norseman aircraft with Canadian registration. He was caught in some weather and had to land on the beach, which resulted in some damage to the aircraft. He had been there over six weeks, trying unsuccessfully to clear the paperwork. We spent a wonderful evening at the Taberice nightclub, adjacent to the hotel, trying to get him to forget his woes at least temporarily. Several years later, Jay became one of the original pilots for the newly formed airline in St. Louis called Ozark. He remained with them for thirty years in management and operations and as a pilot. During our frequent fishing trips together we often recount our memorable night in Bahia.

Our arrival over Rio de Janeiro, Brazil, was above an undercast, and with no published instrument approach, we had to go out to sea to let down. We broke out at a point just above four thousand feet and proceeded back toward the city on a beautiful approach passing the spectacular Sugar Loaf Mountain. Even in the rain we had a clear view of the famous Copacabana beach and, finally, the airport, located on a peninsula almost in the heart of downtown Rio. It rained all during our stay, as the intertropical belt of weather was hanging over that area.

Most of our stops included meetings with business representatives followed by a social hour and sumptuous dinner. Our new plane was often discussed and many side trips were cooked up in order to impress the local people, or in some cases the local people cooked up the side trip to be guests on the opulent flying palace. I was somewhat averse to taking side trips. We were following the routes laid out by Pan American Airways before World War II, and even though they had retired their DC-3s, the routes were still feasible and partial maintenance facilities were available at most of the stations. To divert from this well-planned system seemed to me to be jeopardizing safety.

While in Rio one such trip was planned whereby we were to fly some guests to São Paulo, Brazil. This was not a great distance, but weather with low clouds was lying right along our course. São Paulo did not have an instrument procedure, so I chose to fly along the coast and try to stay below the clouds. My chart showed São Paulo to lie at almost three thousand feet above sea level. We started out and the clouds forced us lower and lower. Finally we had only enough altitude to make turns, so I began to circle, hoping for a break in the weather. Suddenly I spotted an airstrip and we landed in heavy rain. To our surprise we were accosted by a jeep bristling with rifles, bayonets, hard hats, and harder glares. We parked and Harvey went back to face the belligerent soldiers. It seems the airport was new and had not been opened, and we were in trouble. I told Harvey to try to tell them nicely that we would

153

leave as soon as possible, which meant when the weather improved. They reluctantly agreed to let us remain overnight. We sent the passengers on to São Paulo by bus while we stayed at a resort hotel on the beach. It rained and stormed all night and the banging of the shutters in the practically deserted hotel reminded us of the worst horror movies. Morning dawned clear, so we made the short hop to São Paulo, checking the terrain all the way. If we had taken the advice of the passengers and flown in the clouds at fifteen hundred feet we would have never reached São Paulo. Our charts were correct and the passengers were wrong.

After one day in São Paulo we made a fuel stop at Porto Alegre, Brazil en route to Buenos Aires, Argentina. We saw little of the city since we were on alert for a trip to Montevideo, Uruguay. We spent almost all day every day at the airport waiting for the call to go. It never came. On the last day of our stay the trip was finally canceled and we were invited to a large ranch for a barbecue. The host had more than one hundred guests to help entertain the travelers from the north. When we arrived we saw huge pits filled with glowing embers over which were spits loaded with halves of beef, goats, sheep, and pigs. They were being basted with mixtures of juices and exotic condiments. There were four long tables laden with crystal and silverware on pure white linen tablecloths. Down the center of each table, as closely as they could be arranged, were bottles of wine. There were whites, reds, roses and champagne — and beer in cooling containers. Groups of strolling musicians and native dancers entertained us. The demonstrations of horsemanship were exciting as the gauchos roped livestock with bolas.

Another highlight of the Buenos Aires stop was an audience with the Perons. Apparently it went well without too much debate about how to run a country, for the Perons opened the fishing season at Bariloche two weeks early so our group could take advantage of the great trout and landlocked salmon fishing. This was one side trip I did enjoy, as it was in clear weather and eight hundred miles to this Garden of Eden. We fished the afternoon of our arrival and all the next day amid the breathtaking surroundings. The season was closed as we left.

Leaving Bariloche, we could have crossed the Andes at four thousand feet then followed the coast to Santiago, Chile. However, Mr. Queeny had read a great deal about the pass between Mendoza, Argentina, and Santiago made famous by Pan American Airways and also by the brilliant descriptions written by Antoine de Saint-Exupery. Thus our route was back to Mendoza for the night and then into Chile the next day. It is not a long flight, just high. We flew east after takeoff and then turned westward for the remainder of the climb to sixteen thousand feet. At this elevation the DC-3 struggles. The trip also calls for a very careful bit of navigation: a wrong turn could lead to a dead-end canyon without room to turn around. We had hoped to locate the beautiful Christ of the Andes statue but it was not to be. Between our preoccupation with critical navigation problems and the fact Mr. Queeny passed out from lack of oxygen the statue went by unnoticed. With application of pure oxygen Queeny recovered and immediately started to take pictures as if nothing had happened. Anyone having pressure chamber experience knows that his reactions were normal, but to the day he died he would never admit he passed out. Our altitude of sixteen thousand feet was well below several of the peaks, such as Aconcagua, which rises to nearly twenty-three thousand feet.

In Santiago, Harvey Gray located a friend who had accompanied Jimmy Doolittle on his tour of South America many years before the war. We were invited to his home for dinner one night and heard an account of one of Jimmy Doolittle's escapades. They were having a cocktail party on the second floor of an apartment. Some of the people were making bets on how long they could walk on the railing of the balcony. Jimmy slipped during his turn but grabbed the railing and called for help. By this time everyone thought he was fooling and finally he had to fall to the patio below, which broke both ankles. He was scheduled to fly a demonstration flight the next day in competition with a German manufacturer. He forced our host, who was his mechanic, to bolt the casts to the rudders so his feet would not slip off during the violent maneuvers necessary during his demonstration flight. He won the competition. This was an indication of the type of man who thought up the idea of taking B-25s off an aircraft carrier in order to bomb Japan.

The day before we were to leave Santiago another side trip was arranged. The host of the party was the publisher of the main newspaper, owner of many oil wells, and otherwise an influential local citizen. Worst of all he was an amateur pilot. We were to fly his guests to Valparaíso, a resort town on the coast for a luncheon. While checking with Pan American's operations, I found they had long ago abandoned flights to such a small field. Furthermore, they informed me that the field would be closed by fog until almost noon and again after four in the afternoon. It was eleven before there was improvement in the fog condition. I finally called the passengers to the airport hoping we could arrive over the airport at Valparaiso as soon as the clouds had drifted off.

Our host, being a pilot, was invited to sit on the jump seat in the cockpit. It was only ninety miles to Valparaíso and we were soon over the airport and found the clouds were clearing on schedule. Our pass over the field in this large airplane only took a few seconds and it was difficult for our host to believe that we could land in such a small field. He began to renege and apologize for getting us into this situation. I thought to myself, "You got us into this mess, I hope you squirm." One can perform amazing things with a DC-3 on a short runway. I was able to land with room to spare, but I was quite disgusted having been placed in such a spot. Queeny knew my feelings and was trying to apologize when a commotion outside the plane called our attention to the fact that the President of Chile's plane was about to land. Queeny said, "Why don't you come with me and meet the President of Chile?" I facetiously replied, "You will have to bring him over here as I am too busy cleaning up to greet him." I was placing the aileron locks on the plane when I felt a nudge. It was Mr. Queeny with a twinkle in his eye saying, "I want you to meet the President of Chile."

The next day we flew just off the coast between Santiago and Arica, Chile. The country was bleak and arid, a dreary sight. The only interesting event on the trip was seeing schools of whales and a huge manta ray. On the next leg to Lima, Peru, we reencountered the intertropical belt of bad weather and we were out of sight of the ground for most of three hours. When we arrived, Lima was suffering from a water shortage. Heavy rains in the mountains had caused landslides, cutting off the water supply to the city. We were glad to leave as washing teeth in soda water was becoming quite a bore. We arrived for an overnight in Guayaquil, Ecuador, shortly after noon, and my memory of Guayaquil will always be that of endless sheet iron roofs, palm trees, steamy heat, and squalor.

Our arrival in Panama City was like a step back into the United States. We could drink the tapwater and enjoy many other freedoms not available elsewhere in the area. We spent a pleasant night. Early the next morning we were en route to Guatemala City over dense jungles dotted with thousands of volcanoes, some of which were active and spewing their smoke in spirals into the blue skies above. Guatemala, at much higher altitude, was cool and refreshing compared to our more recent stops. Music of the marimba bands could be heard hour after hour on the streets. My favorite was their version of "Managua, Nicaragua," a song I have never heard played as well since.

Our next stop was for two exciting and rewarding days in Acapulco, Mexico. We fished both days with beginner's luck. None of us had any real experience. I had read Zane Gray's accounts and had seen newsreel pictures of leaping sailfish and marlin. The crew each caught a seven-foot sail the first day and ran into a school of tuna the second. Ralph Whitworth hooked a blue marlin, which he fought for over an hour before it finally broke away. Another highlight of Acapulco was watching the divers at the Mirador Hotel, diving at night with torches in their hands to show their trajectory into the water far below. All this to the haunting tunes of Le Mer made a memorable evening.

It was very hot the morning of our departure for Mexico City, so I was down to my shorts while we loaded the baggage, as were most of the others in the group. In the rush I forgot to get dressed and flew to Mexico City in my shorts. After parking at the ramp I looked out into the lens of a newsreel camera which was filming our arrival. Queeny was also in shorts, so we hurriedly dressed. In a short time we were seen debarking down the steps in full business suits. I often wondered if people in the theater had any idea what we had looked like just minutes before the final scene.

We spent one full day in Mexico City and on November 8 we departed for San Antonio, Texas, to clear United States customs. We dropped Queeny off in Stuttgart, Arkansas, where he spent the weekend with Mrs. Queeny. We had been gone six weeks, traveled over thirteen thousand miles, and visited twenty-three different cities and countries in South and Central America. It was the first such trip to be conducted by any corporation and the results were felt for many years. Manufacturing plants established in Buenos Aires, the Mexico City plant was enlarged, and sales offices were opened in most of the cities we visited. The trip helped open doors in those areas for several years thereafter.

Corporate Aviation

Part of my introduction to the world of corporate aviation came during the airshow I attended in Grinnell, Iowa, in October 1929 when I was a high school senior at nearby Le Grand. One aircraft in particular caught my fancy: a new six-place Travel Air owned by Automatic Washer Company of Newton. It was the largest airplane on the field, powered by the seemingly monstrous three hundred horsepower J-6 Wright. Its interior was absolutely palatial; the spacious cabin was equipped with a movie projector and screen, a dictaphone, individual lights at each plush chair, and many other deluxe items of the time. It was a true corporate aircraft and forerunner of things to come.

Automatic Washer's Travel Air was not the only corporate aircraft operating in the late 1920s. Standard Oil and Monarch Foods were already using Ford Trimotors for customer-relation trips. Phillips, Gulf, and Shell each had established flight departments. In my home state of Iowa, the Des Moines Register and Tribune operated one of the first Pitcairn Autogyros, and their Fairchild monoplane was a common sight overhead at many sports events. The famous George Yates was a flying photographer extraordinaire. They rushed back to Des Moines to process the pictures, which were seen the next day in the Sunday sports section. Flight departments like these continued to expand during the 1930s but were curtailed by the onset of World War II and the war years that followed.

The end of hostilities in 1945 signaled the reemergence of corporate aviation. Highly paid executives who never dreamed of having flight departments soon found that poor railroad service, overcrowded commercial airlines, and travel priorities made owning a corporate airplane a downright necessity. The large number of surplus aircraft and former military personnel made setting up a flight department easy and cost-effective.

Dominating the business aircraft scene at the time were the ubiquitous UC-78s, C-47s, C-45s, and a variety of Lockheeds. Also a variety of two- and four-engine bombers were converted to

"Corporate Aviation" is reprinted with permission from *Professional Pilot* magazine.

domestic use. A corporation of almost any size could find an aircraft suitable for conversion that would meet its needs. Continental Can, for example, flew a converted B-26 Martin Marauder. They also had a C-87 which needed little conversion since it was already a conversion from the Liberator to a cargo and troop carrier. It carried tonnage over the Hump far in excess of any other type aircraft.

Tennessee Gas also flew Martin B-26s. Troestel Leather and Gaylord Container flew converted B-25s for their business travel needs. A B-17 owned by the Chicago newspaper magnate, Colonel Robert McCormick, was a familiar sight at airports around the country. The Colonel's plush chair, ever conspicuous, was located in the bombardier's plexiglass nose station.

The business of converting warplanes to luxurious executive planes was a new and thriving business. Air Research, Southwest Airmotive, L. B. Smith, and dozens more joined Remmert-Werner in competing for this new facet of aviation. Conversions were the foundation of many new companies.

In time the converted war birds gave way to an interim breed of aircraft. Despite a growing demand for equipment designed specifically to meet the needs of the corporate fleet, confidence in corporate aviation at this time was far from widespread. Nevertheless, Beech came up with an improved C-45 and called it the D-18. They also built a four-engine, twin-prop plane but scuttled plans to produce it when it was lost on a test flight.

Cessna also designed a four-engine, pressurized aircraft while developing their full line of smaller aircraft. It, too, was scrapped. The decision was made at ten o'clock in the morning, and the prototype was in small bits and pieces before lunchtime. Market research indicated that it was well ahead of its time.

Monsanto took possession of their D-18 in June 1946 at a cost of sixty-eight thousand dollars. Equipment aboard was a two-channel transmitter, tuneable receiver, and deluxe ADF, plus marker beacon receiver. What more could a pilot want? There was nothing else to be had at that point; that was the state of the art. Before the year was up, we had to purchase a new spare engine in preparation for engine overhauls. We bought it from Pratt and Whitney for nine thousand dollars. While installing it in the spring of 1947 we also added a new gadget called a tuneable omni receiver. It was one of the first on the market. This new bit of equipment made it possible to navigate without having to compute mentally the bearings to produce fixes. What progress!

The DC-3 called *Prairie Wings* and owned by Edgar Queeny was used as the showcase for Remmert-Werner to demonstrate the luxury and convenience of owning a corporate aircraft. It was roomy, dependable, comfortable, and had a safety record second to none. It had been the workhorse for the airlines and then the military all through the war years.

A few of the companies and their pilots who benefited from the Remmert-Werner conversions were Olin with Bill Heaton and Bill Hobin, Matheson Chemical with Neal Fulton, Pittsburgh Plate Glass with Buck Newton, Dow Chemical with Ted Merchant, Hercules Powder with Owen Mayfield and Bill Hobson, Celanese Corporation with Howard Zbornek, Armco Steel with Walt Pague, Texas Illinois with Harvey Glass, International Harvester with Bill Dotter and Raoul Castro, John Deere with Tom Roche, and many others. Almost all of the crews were in need of transition from smaller aircraft to the larger DC-3.

Owen Mayfield later became the chairman of the National Business Aircraft Association and was instrumental in elevating that organization to the prestigious position it holds today.

Dee Howard's engineering firm made great improvements on the Lodestars and the Venturas. He finally was able to streamline them to speeds in the three-hundred-mile-per-hour class. He pressurized the cabin, and the resulting aircraft was called the Howard 500. It was a high flying, pressurized scooter, which set goals for newly designed aircraft. Few were able to match its cost, speed, or comfort in the years to come.

There were many attempts to pressurize and modify the sleek and fast Douglas A-26, not to be confused with the Martin B-26 Marauder. The A-26 became known as a B-26 after the war. Company pressure was constantly on me to come up with an airplane that would go faster and higher with pressurization, so I studied all the new conversions with great care. When making inquiries at Douglas about the A-26, I was told quite bluntly that the aircraft had been designed as a weapon and not as a personnel carrier. I felt that was a good way to explain that they wanted no part of trying to redesign the airplane. This and other cases made it more encouraging for people like the Grumman firm to start from scratch to design a corporate aircraft. Early in the fifties they did just that with their famous Gulfstream I.

Frequently in the design for a new aircraft, the power plant is chosen and the airplane built around it. Grumman did it in reverse. They designed the cabin first and for some time ran out of ideas about power. Finally, in desperation, they went to England and revived an engine Rolls Royce had scrapped as being too inefficient. They used it for the new power plant. It was the first of many DC-3 replacements to come on the market. Monsanto decided to go with the Convair 240 rather than take the big leap to the G-1 with Rolls Royce turboprops. The Convairs introduced in 1947 were converted from a thirty-seat airline configuration to fifteen-seat luxury liners. Equipped with television, beverage bar, full galley capable of providing hot meals for twenty or more, acres of luggage space, soundproofing, pressurization, beautifully colored fabrics, and other items of airborne opulence, they helped hold off the day of the jet a little longer.

When Lockheed put their first two-engine Jetstar on the market in 1957, corporate acceptance of the jet accelerated. Because the twin-engine Jetstar was underpowered, they added two more engines. This necessitated the large tanks on the outside of the wings to give it the range needed. After all the leapfrog improvements, it was not until 1974 that a new engine installation gave the aircraft a better-balanced performance. There will be those who try to improve the Jetstar as long as it lasts.

In 1962 the Jetstar had to meet some competition with the advent of the Sabreliner. North American had contemplated entering the corporate market for some time. They had one of the finest little jet aircraft for the military; it took very little change to make it a corporate aircraft, backed with hundreds of hours of military experience. Other companies followed, such as Rockwell with their Jet Commander, and Learjet. The DH-125, the Falcon, and the Hansa represented the foreign bid for the corporate market.

Those were exciting times. When everyone thought they had a piece of the action, the prices started to soar, so another one entered the fray. Cessna, after a long and thorough market study, came up with the Citation 500, aimed at the altitudes above the turboprops and below most of the other jets. It was also priced to hit the market between jets and turboprops; the first were delivered for around seven hundred thousand dollars. Lear started out by saying, "Bring your light twin in to us in the morning and go out in the afternoon in a jet." The Citation, under Jim Taylor's genius,

161

thrived to the tune of hundreds per year. Strangely enough, most of the manufacturers could not live up to the advance sales pitch in performance, in ease of transition, or in price. But companies bought aircraft. They were ready and waiting for the jet age at any cost.

Looking back a bit, we find progress made a strange twist somewhere along the line. Logically, one would have expected corporate flight departments to begin with turboprops and gradually inch up to pure jets. Not so. Turboprop aircraft developed alongside their pure jet brethren and today are not considered a stepping-stone, but a permanent arm of the fleet, providing economical short-range service. Now King Airs, Merlins, Turbo Commanders, MU-2, and Cheyennes are a major part of many business fleets.

With deregulation of the airlines came a sudden spurt in feeder line growth. Trunk lines dropped the whistle stops, but feeder lines closed the gap. Now the skyways are inundated with turboprop aircraft bringing hundreds of passengers from off the beaten track to the hubs of major airlines.

Hollywood

On September 24, 1950, we arrived at the Burbank airport with several of the Monsanto board members and some of the public relations staff. Our man on the coast had been doing a great job of contacting the right people.

It was a Sunday night, and we were all staying at the Beverly Hills Hotel on Rodeo Drive. In this posh hotel is a room called the Crystal Ballroom. On the night of September 24, the Hollywood crowd had planned a costume party which was to be a benefit for the school for hearing-impaired children. In the middle of all the plans was one Hedda Hopper, the famous gossip columnist. Our West Coast representative, Ed Schuller, knew Hedda Hopper very well and through mutual planning, the Monsanto delegation was invited en masse. That included the pilots of the two aircraft that were on the trip. Betty Hutton and Esther Williams personally presented the invitation—perhaps in hopes of receiving a sizable donation from the company or each person.

Pilots were Paul Vance, George Meyers, Carl Christensen, and I. We stood in the lobby of the hotel not knowing what the occasion was for so many celebrities to be passing through. It was an enjoyable pastime which brought a new star to our view every few seconds. While there, gawking like tourists, we were told that we were to be included in the festivities in the Crystal Ballroom. It took little time for us to accept and attend. Our table reservations were at the very table of the Queen of Gossip! No greater prestige did we need than that. We didn't have to go to the stars, they came to our table to pay homage to their Queen. We were introduced upon each occasion and of course, being from the Midwest, we sank deeper and deeper into this land of make-believe.

Our table backed up to a table described by Hopper as that of the new crop of stars-to-be. Most had never been heard of before this period. Members of that party included Janet Leigh, Tony Curtis, Lex Barker, Arlene Dahl, Shelly Winters, Joan Freeman, Debbie Reynolds, Elizabeth Taylor, and Nicky Hilton. We visited with all of them. Others within our line of vision were Lucille Ball and Desi Arnez. Lucille was heavy with child and, being their first, it had to be Lucy. The Ladds were with the MacMurrays or the other way around. Edgar Bergen paraded each of his dummies to the delight of even the old-timers, and Red Skelton gave his Guzzler's Gin salesman act, which paralyzed us all. Dorothy Lamour sang a few sultry songs in a sarong, and Les Brown's orchestra played throughout the party.

It was easy to tell who was working at the time and who was not. Those who were working were gone by nine thirty and the others stayed until they closed the place. It was a western costume party, and that added more to the lack of inhibitions. Finding Gary Cooper alone for a little while, I had the nerve to go over and start a conversation about airplanes. He had been one of my idols after I saw him in *Wings* and *Lilac Time*. He was as interested as I was in aviation and regretted that he had never soloed. He remembered the occasion at Grinnell during the festivities and the air races we attended in 1929. Wherever we glanced, we were looking at brilliant stars of the 1940s from MGM, Twentieth Century, Warner Brothers, and Paramount. What a night! I am not too sure I would have had the opportunity for such a gala affair had I been an airline pilot. Being a corporate pilot, I was one of those included in the social life of most of the Monsanto occasions.

National Business Aircraft Association

NBAA (National Business Aircraft Association), nee CAOA (Corporate Aircraft Owners Association), was founded in 1949 by a handful of ambitious flight department managers and pilots interested in having a voice in a rapidly growing segment of aviation. I had proposed we join at its inception, but was rejected by my conservative management group on the grounds we should wait and see what direction the organization would take. Perhaps they were right, but on the other hand, we could have joined and had an influence on the direction.

The first meeting I attended was in Chicago in 1952 when only about fifty were present. Members of the board at that time were Walter Pague of Armco Steel and Bill Belden of Republic Steel, both founding members. Others were Del Rentzel, former CAA administrator, Henry Boggess of Sinclair Oil Company, and Cole Morrow of J.I. Case, who was the president of the organization and instrumental in keeping it on the right track for many years. By this time Monsanto could see where the organization was going and had given me permission to participate. Tony Zuma of Tennessee Gas and I were elected to the board at that meeting. Tony became preoccupied with aircraft conversions and to my knowledge did not attend another meeting of the board.

Key people who kept the organization going in its early years were Bill Silsby, who acted as executive until his death, and the Henry Publishing Company, whose publication *Skyways* became the official voice of CAOA. Herb Fisher followed Mr. Silsby but was snatched away from the organization just before the 1953 meeting in St. Louis. Herb was replaced by Jean DuBuque, who served until 1956, when Bill Lawton was made the executive secretary. Finally, in 1966 John Winant left his job as a corporate lawyer with Sprague Electric Company and took the newly created post as executive director of the NBAA

The 1953 meeting was held in the Chase Park Plaza Hotel in St. Louis, and Lea Dorrance and I were cohosts. Two new events were introduced by their sponsor Henry Boggess. The safety award program as it operates today made its debut at that meeting and the award for outstanding contribution to aviation was introduced. Charles Lindbergh was the first recipient of that award and until the first day we thought he would attend. When it was learned he would not we did the next best thing by calling on E. Lansing Ray to accept for him. E. Lansing Ray was one of the last living backers of the Lindbergh flight. Other recipients have been most worthy people, including Jimmy Doolittle, Eddie Rickenbacher, Igor Sikorsky, Grover Loening, and J.S. McDonnell.

A common topic in the early years was getting top management people involved so that the organization would not be just another pilots' club. A look at the presidents over the years will attest to the fact that top people were selected to perpetuate the organization. It has prestige and clout at the highest levels and has accomplished a great deal in preventing negative legislation and restrictions. The benefits are unlimited to all operators regardless of their being members or not. It is hard to understand why anyone would refuse to join, as the membership fee is infinitesimal compared to the benefits. Almost every member of the Fortune Five Hundred belongs to the NBAA.

John Winant has made outstanding contributions to the organization. His analyses of problems were hallmarks and his solutions were acceptable to all concerned. Problems such as noise abatement, slots in the air traffic control system, fuel shortages and allocations, adverse legislative proposals, and proposed Federal Air Regulations were handled in a prompt and efficient manner. Without him many of the problems would still exist today.

Quiet Birdmen and Other Aviation Organizations

The first time I saw the insignia of the Quiet Birdmen (QB), it was being worn by John Livingston. Later I saw Ralph Hall with the QB wings on his lapel. When I finally asked, John explained what they stood for.

Right after World War I, when barnstorming pilots were trying to make a living with a Jenny or some other surplus aircraft they could afford, they were constantly being harassed by noisy motorcyclists. The motorcyclist would tear into town wearing helmet, goggles, riding breeches, and boots almost identical to what the well-dressed airman was wearing at the time. The pilots, having a living to make, realized the value of a good image. They could not be identified with boisterous and irresponsible acts. To develop and maintain a good image, they took the quiet approach and the feeling grew that it was necessary to be identified as a group. At a meeting in a restaurant in New York City, the name Quiet Birdmen was eventually adopted and the wings were designed. World war ritual was adopted whereby at each meeting or gathering of the members a toast was made to all pilots who had "gone west."

The idea and membership grew until now there are over twenty thousand members. Each town or area able to provide enough potential members may apply for a charter from the national committee; if they meet the requirements, they are granted a charter and the "Hangar" is registered with the nearest post office. Members are welcome at any hangar and develop many long-lasting friendships during their travels.

The QB is not a club which admits anyone who wants to join. The entry requirements are quite restrictive, admitting only experienced pilots. It often takes years after being invited as a guest before the process of becoming a member can be completed. I have been a member since 1946.

It was also my privilege to become a charter member of the National Pilots Association, which was sponsored by such aviation leaders as George Haddaway, Leighton Collins, Paul Vance, and others of their caliber. Paul Vance was also instrumental in starting the Missouri Pilots Association, of which I am a charter member.

When qualified I joined the Silver Wings Club, which is available to anyone having been a licensed pilot for over twenty-five years. The OX-5 Aviation Pioneers was formed in the early fifties and my sponsor was John Livingston, one of its founders. He could certainly vouch for the fact that I worked on OX-5 engines, cranked them, and took my first airplane ride behind one in a Travel Air. It is also a matter of pride that I hold life membership #18 in the Hump Pilots Association.

Monsanto Copilots

Pilots who flew for Monsanto often matured and went on to start flight departments of their own. Early pilots included Bob Burrel, who started the Tretolite flight department. Ralph Whitworth and Hank Haddock started the Falstaff flight department; Ralph later started the Coca-Cola flight department at Atlanta, taking with him Joe Strubb, a pilot-mechanic, who became chief pilot before retiring. Carl Christensen left to fly the Mellon bank plane as chief pilot; later he left Mellon for Eastern, where he retired. Bob Turner flew copilot for Dick Thurston in Springfield, Massachusetts, and left early in the fifties for the Sears flight department in Chicago, where he retired. Dick Young took the chief pilot's job with a construction company in Georgia. Lee Snow, after several years in the Springfield operation, left and headed the flight department for the Cutler-Hammer corporation in Milwaukee. Out of so many it is not too alarming that one was a little less than we had expected.

My first encounter with Tim (not his real name) was in 1945 while I was flying charter. At that time he was heading the instrument school for the Brayton Flying Service of St. Louis. He was fresh out of the army as an air corps sergeant in his mid-forties. According to him, he would have been a commissioned officer and pilot had it not been for eye problems. Still, thanks to his demonstrated airmanship, the air corps had given him unlimited authority to instruct in any aircraft it operated, so he said.

The CAA—FAA's predecessor—also issued Tim an unlimited

rating, he said, a distinction reserved for a very few pilots with the highest qualifications. When flight activities waned Tim signed on briefly as a consultant to an insurance company. His duties consisted of giving check rides to corporate pilots. Monsanto's flight department was one of those examined by Tim.

That year when vacation time came and I needed a replacement pilot, I thought, "Why not avail myself of the very best?" I called Tim and he accepted. I used him as my copilot so he could become familiar with our procedures, and then I planned to put him in rotation with other pilots. Lo and behold, I was shocked to find this unlimited-rated pilot was unable to land an airplane. On several occasions, I had to take over the landings to save my favorite DC-3. I was completely amazed but tried to analyze the problem. I felt it was a combination of poor eyesight, poor judgment due to a lack of experience, and a dreadful fear of the airplane. Each attempt at landing was a complete debacle. The discovery disturbed me a great deal, but I kept him under my wing as co-pilot to make sure that he would never be in a position to fly as pilot-in-command.

Tim's tenure came to a quick end a few weeks later after a particularly nasty trip involving icing. We began to pick up ice in clouds at four thousand feet. Soon the props were throwing the stuff, and because of uneven release, excessive vibration resulted. The instrument panel was dancing crazily and the sound of ice hitting the fuselage just aft of the cockpit was disconcerting to someone not inured to such goings on. I had asked Tim earlier to contact the center for a change in altitude, but he seemed to be in a strange coma. He could not channel the radio and when I got the proper frequency for him, he was unable to talk. He sat there stiff, staring straight ahead, beaded with sweat. I realized suddenly that this man was in a state of shock.

I could not for the life of me understand this strange development. Not only could this great pilot not land an airplane, now I found he was of no earthly good to me when I needed help.

I had listened to his long lurid tales of bad-weather flying in B-17s and B-25s, over mountainous terrain with thunderstorms and icing thrown in. I had listened to long and detailed accounts of his prewar experiences flying the Lockheed Vega for MGM studios. In those days the Vega was the epitome of aircraft sophistication and required highly skilled pilots to fly the intricate high-performance aircraft. Furthermore, he boasted of his intimate relations with such superstars as Jean Harlow, Marlene Dietrich, Carol Lombard, and others. According to Tim, his skills as an airman were held in great esteem by such male stars as Wallace Beery, Spencer Tracey, and Charles Boyer—all regular passengers. It was difficult not to be impressed by that background. But now I was in an airplane with him under wretched conditions and in need of help, and he was useless!

Loaded with ice, we finally got to Lambert Field. The storm window was covered also, but I was able to move it just enough to see through the slight gap for the night landing on runway 34. This runway was blacktop and hard to see in good conditions, let alone at night with two inches of ice to look through. With Tim's "experienced help," we could have kept the windshield clean with glycol and could have had alcohol on the props to keep them clean of ice and in balance. Without his help, we got a little behind in our duties, and I was glad to get the trip over and get on the ground safely. This was certainly not my first encounter with icing, and I knew what should have been done and when. Obviously, Tim had never been in actual icing conditions, and when he faced them head on, he panicked.

By the time I parked the airplane, I had made up my mind. I would not make a big noise about this, I would just not use Tim anymore as my copilot. Who was I to pass judgment on a pilot with an "unlimited" rating? He just was not right for me—let somebody else blow the whistle.

A few weeks later, I learned that Tim was in big trouble. It seems he had buzzed a farmer right off his tractor out on the St. Charles flats. The farmer finally had to take cover in a grove of trees. Tim misjudged his pull up and hit the tops of the trees, damaging the airplane. The finale was the farmer suing for damages and the CAA looking into the damaged airplane. The investigation revealed the truth about Tim. He never held a legal pilot rating of any kind except a student permit. He could not pass the physical. The license number he used turned out to belong to a commercial pilot in the vicinity of Erie, Pennsylvania. In those precomputer days, the inconsistencies of name and number had gone unnoticed by the CAA's record keepers, and Tim's fraud had continued year after year.

I was certainly not proud of having kept him as copilot as long as I did, but at least I had checked out his flying ability before sending him out as pilot-in-command. Others were not so discriminating, and their faith could easily have been rewarded with tragedy.

The entire bizarre episode was clearly a case of imagination run amok. When Tim was a kid he would stand at the Burbank airport fence and watch airplanes come and go. No doubt he would see the MGM plane with its star passengers arrive and depart. His fantasies began and were magnified by the hysteria of the times. War came and Tim signed up, eventually rising to sergeant-instructor in an air corp instrument school.

Here his imagination really went to work as he gave students hypothetical weather and situations to be solved in the Link Trainer. He made these situations as realistic as possible with the application of "rough air" and by giving a thorough briefing of weather situations before the lessons. There were thunderstorms, heavy icing, and capricious winds to be dealt with in the closed confines of the Link Trainer Room.

Finally his fantasies became real. Tim came to believe his dreams were actual experiences. Those prewar and wartime fantasies were carried into civilian life, and from those fantasies his "unlimited" rating evolved.

The fantasies and harsh realities both came to an end just three weeks after his trial and conviction. Tim, the airman extraordinaire, died in his sleep. There was only one Tim—I hope.

Transition to Convairs

By 1960 we had studied the possibilities of moving up to more sophisticated aircraft. The Gulfstream I was built by Grumman and had been on the market for some time when we received a demonstration flight. It was a little smaller than the roomy DC-3 but had more than enough space for our purpose. It had speed somewhat less than they advertised but much higher than the piston-powered aircraft of the time. The big advantage was its pressurization.

After a great deal of thought and a comparison of the initial and operating costs, we decided to forgo the turbine-powered Gulfstream for an interim aircraft and when the time came to go straight jet. The interim aircraft selected was the tried-and-true Convair 240. Remmert-Werner had converted several 404 Martins and several 240 Convairs, so we could make a good comparison. We chose the 240 not only for the appearance, but also for its better performance.

We purchased a retired airline airplane from Australian Airlines. The hull had over fifty thousand hours but was still airworthy. They gutted the interior and installed plush furnishings for fifteen passengers. The galley was left intact, with service for the original thirty or more passengers. A radome was added, which made the airplane look like a 440 Convair. Radar and autopilot were new to us, as was the pressurization system. The speed was much faster than the DC-3, and with pressurization and two-stage blowers on the engines, we were able to get above a lot of the weather that had been impossible before. This provided passenger comfort and weather avoidance, which was worth a lot to all of us.

It was decided George Meyers and I would get our rating early enough to be ready when the conversion was completed, and in July we completed a two-week course provided by Flight Safety Incorporated at La Guardia. It was our first trip in a jet of any kind. We were booked on TWA, and our plane was a 707. We were impressed with the sound level. In fact, we were not really aware of the instant when the engines were started. The motors and dynamotors, already humming and audible to the passengers, drowned out anything from the outside. The tremendous thrust of acceleration we felt on the takeoff roll was far beyond anything we had experienced in even the most powerful aircraft. We were a little more prepared for that deck angle than the other items of performance, for we had watched the airplane take off for several months and had marveled at the angle of climb.

We found the speed of the aircraft kept up with our imagination. When we thought we might be over Indianapolis, we were. In a short time we saw Dayton and Columbus go by. All of this happened in the first hour, and soon we were on our way downhill into La Guardia. We were not ready for the next surprise. After being airborne for almost two hours, we got to La Guardia and found there were no gates available. That was a harbinger of things to come. The state of the art had reached a wonderful level in speed, but the traffic control and ground facilities had not adjusted to the new era. That was in 1960, and they still are not able to keep up.

In our course we faced a lot of subjects we had not encountered before: pressurization, water injection, weight and balance and performance charts, a new and complicated electrical system, the two-stage blower on those huge Pratt and Whitney R-2800 engines, propeller functions and operational procedures, auto feathering, propeller reversal, nose steering, rotation speeds, windshield heating, use of cowl flaps in temperature control, and speed. We had to absorb these subjects and more in two short weeks of ground school. We never got off the ground during the two weeks, but when the airplane did arrive on the scene, it only took about four more hours for us to have our rating in our new bird.

In just a week, Joe Panetta was in St. Louis to give us our final time in the aircraft itself. In nine hours, which George and I split between left and right seats, we had our refresher and flight check from the FAA.

My first reaction to this airplane was, "Why didn't somebody tell me this wonderful airplane had been available all this time?" Its stability was demonstrated with flaps. With power on one engine only, it could be stalled and recovered by application of 25 percent flaps. It could be stalled again and recovered by the addition of more flaps and so on until the airplane had full flaps and was still hanging there waiting for somebody to do something right and give it a chance to fly. This was a real confidence builder and something I had never experienced in any other airplane. It had some characteristics that were not strange to me in that it had the same wing as the B-24, and the feeling on final approach was a comfortable reminder of what the Davis wing was like.

I flew the airplane every day for the rest of the week after my rating ride. By the eighteenth I reluctantly had to give up the joy of flying for the NBAA convention in Los Angeles. In addition I had agreed to join a tour to Hawaii with several of the NBAA members right after the convention. The group included Betty and Walt Pague; Cole Morrow; Lois Henry; Lila and Scotty Miller; Scotty's secretary, Grace Burke; Marilyn Bell; and my wife, Kay, and me. Although it was a terrific week, I felt cheated out of flying such a great machine at a critical time.

One of the highlights of the Hawaiian trip was being the guest of Admiral Ramsey and his wife for a Saturday night party in their home. Admiral Ramsey was the commanding officer of the entire Pacific Fleet. We were picked up at the hotel by a navy car and driver and whisked off to the admiral's home along with Dr. Crane and his wife and a long-standing pilot-friend of the admiral's. He was a Pan American pilot who had come from Paris without stop, except to change planes, and was around to the other side of the world. He brought along some very special cigars for the admiral, but after delivering the box he slowly melted away into a deep sleep for the rest of the evening.

Before we left that night, the admiral asked if we would like a tour of Pearl Harbor the next morning. We did, so on Sunday morning at ten we were at the navy pier in Pearl Harbor, where his special yacht awaited with full crew. We had an unlimited tour of the harbor with an excellent description of the entire one-sided battle of Pearl Harbor. Even in 1960, the thought of the attack was quite repulsive. The hulk of the *Arizona* was still visible just below the surface, and many other scars remained for the viewer. A few days later we saw the harbor again with the tour group. We took the ride but were deprived of our cameras and were allowed to see only certain things. I never did understand; I had used my camera freely on the first tour, but it was taken from me before entering the harbor on the next. Strange.

On another tour of the island by bus, we saw Mount Pali. The thermals were evident — in fact there was a glider soaring over the windward side of the pass. He rode back and forth across the gap and seemingly could have done so indefinitely. Here the northeast winds prevail and furnish a natural air-conditioning for the entire Honolulu area. One day the wind quit and the results were unbelievable. It became unbearable. I have never felt such humidity. Everybody was praying for the breeze again before the day was over.

Our bus tour took us around the island to various landmarks. One was the blowhole, where the waves are forced up into a narrow chute and the water spews up like a blowing whale. We also stopped in the national cemetery, in the Punch Bowl Crater. This is a volcanic depression high above downtown Honolulu. It is perhaps the most serene place on earth, or so it seemed. By nature of the terrain the sounds of the city below are cut off. The only sounds were of birds singing. The grounds were manicured to the

173

last blade of grass. Markers are at ground level and spread over the entire natural amphitheater. When I stepped off the bus I was immediately struck by the silence. Everyone must have felt the same for no one spoke for many minutes. I looked down at the markers. The first one I saw was that of Ernie Pyle.

I was glad I had come to Hawaii. The trip was something I had needed and didn't know it. When I returned I went back on schedule and flew all but three days in the month of October. I soon caught up, and with every flight felt more and more at home with the new aircraft. I had often wondered, after flying *Prairie Wings* for so long, how I would feel leaving it. Strangely enough, the thrill of a new airplane and its challenges dimmed the regret of leaving an old friend.

Transition from Convairs to Jets

There is no such thing as a perfect airplane for every company. First the needs of the company have to be considered. Are there to be five or fifteen passengers? How far are they going on one trip? Nonstop? What type of performance is required? Are the airports off airways and unimproved? Those are just some of the questions that have to be answered in a study made by the chief pilot. By 1964, I finally determined the kind of jet Monsanto would accept.

In May 1963, Remmert-Werner finished the interior and avionics installation of the first Sabreliner to be offered to the civilian market. It was the first nonmilitary Sabreliner built, and in one month it was completely outfitted with soundproofing, interior, and the latest in avionics.

I was chosen to be the privileged pilot to fly with the technical crew to Pompano Beach, Florida, where the plane would be on display and used for demonstrations during a symposium for business pilots. Since it was my first trip in any jet other that the 707, and then only as a passenger, it was especially exciting to be placed in the left seat. Later I would know how easy it was to fly the plane from either side. It was May 5 when we left St. Louis for Pompano Beach. In the right seat was Art DeBolt, and George Eremia was in the jump seat. Seated amid parts and materials in the back were Al McMahon, technical representative for North American, a mechanic by the name of Smith, also from North American, and Roy Lynck, who had been able to crowd all the new avionics package in the little space available.

The lack of sound and the ease of taxiing were impressive, as was the takeoff. For the first time I was not fighting torque. Rotation was effortless, and the plane assumed a climb angle almost by itself.

The short time needed to reach thirty-nine thousand feet was phenomenal, and then the ground speed was impressive as it increased and kept increasing until we were easily gliding along, almost soundlessly, at over four hundred miles per hour.

Checking out in the Sabreliner inspired me to write an article about my experiences that was published in the May 1965 issue of *Flight* magazine. The article is included here because it expresses not only my genuine enthusiasm for the new business jets but also a few of the technical details an experienced pilot would need to master in order to make the transition to jets.

Traveling by horse and buggy as a child, riding in my family's first automobile in 1919 and taking my first flight in an OX-5 Travel Air at seventy miles per hour are experiences as clear as if they had happened yesterday. All of this has made just a little more meaningful the tremendous thrills I am experiencing at the controls of my first modern business jet doing five hundred miles per hour, plus. I feel grateful for being a part of the great transition from horse-and-buggy days to private jets, and I also believe anyone who has flown for fifteen years or more deserves this pleasure, for I can say from experience that the transition is not too large an order for any old-timer. My company took delivery of its first jet in September 1964. It has been such a phenomenal success as a practical and efficient aircraft that I would like for people without jets to realize what they're missing.

Most of the troubled ones who spread so many tales about the difficulties for pilots in making the transition to jets are possibly the same people who found difficulty advancing from one to another piston-type aircraft. Early jet-age stories came from eager tellers trying to leave the impression they had to be superior in physical and mental attributes to cut the mustard. Not that there wasn't basis for some of the apprehension. Among jet-age birth pangs, tragedies occurred simply because they had not perfected fuel controllers as now, so when power was applied incorrectly it could bring on disaster. Today's controllers meter fuel automatically to keep power output within the realm of the engines' capabilities, allowing for sudden throttle acceleration or deceleration without a calamity. Flameouts are rare and, in the case of the Pratt & Whitney JT-12-6A, with which I am familiar, only one is on record in the entire test history of the engine as installed on the Sabreliner. It was induced by the most drastic methods possible.

Let us remember one important thing: a jet is still an airplane. The difference between it and its predecessors is that the jet is much better.

This fact may be clouded by some of the strange lingo which surrounds the jet set; get to understand it and things suddenly become clear and less remote. For instance, E.P.R. (Engine Pressure Ratio) is sort of like manifold pressure—it is the differential between the air pressure at intake and the air pressure at the tail pipe.

Mach: This is the term for speed measurement when altitude errors get too big. Mach readings are percentages of the speed of sound—Mach 0.75 is 75 percent of the speed of sound, Mach 1 being the speed of sound.

V Speed: Velocities may make this better understood. Vs is stall speed; V1 is stall speed times 1.1; V2 is stall speed times 1.2; Vne is never exceed speed; Vfo is flap operation speed.

E.G.T.: Exhaust Gas Temperature (Tail Pipe).

Compressibility: This condition is reached as the aircraft nears the speed of sound.

Flat Rated Limits: EPR limits regardless of altitude or temperature. This provides the manufacturer's safety margin.

The point is that the application of these and many other jet terms a few times will make them old and fast friends and in short order you'll be tossing them off as if you had been flying in this realm all your life. It is good to know, at this point, that some of the mystery is gone and understanding takes over.

The best way to get past this stage is to enroll in a preliminary course called "Jet Indoctrination," which will take about a week of ground school. In it you will learn the theory of jet engine power and of flight of swept wings, compressibility and its dangers, and other new facts. You will be introduced to the foibles of high altitude weather and winds. The jet stream will become a reality to you, rather than a myth. You will understand why turbulence can be expected when you encounter the jet stream. "CAT" means clear air turbulence and you will be educated on how to cope with it. You'll learn compliance with regulations pertaining to flight at upper levels and you will learn of your chances for cabin decompression and its dangers. You should have some supervised experience in the pressure chamber to understand the mechanics of sudden decompression. You will understand why both pilots of a jet aircraft are required to wear oxygen masks while operating above twenty-four thousand feet. But as we said, remember: the jet is basically just another airplane.

On to ground school, a course which will take another week, perhaps longer. Now you will learn of all the limitations imposed upon the aircraft by the regulations—how it was certificated, requirements it met in the process, the airplane's various systems (fuel, hydraulics, electrical, cabin pressurization), and the back-up for each. Now you will learn that this is just about the best engineered, the best equipped, and the best constructed airplane ever flown.

You can't wait to fly it, but first why not look into its reliability compared to the older aircraft you know about. For instance, did you know that the average piston engine has a history of failure once every 2,000 hours? That is pretty good, but not nearly as great as the jet engine, which has a history of over 175,000 hours between failures.

Most accidents involving engine failure were on training missions where the engine was cut to simulate failure. Actually, seldom is an engine failure experienced in several years of operation. But let's fly!

Your flight curriculum is complete and identical to the ATR course of any modern airplane, with jet conditions included. You will learn about hung starts, which come about when battery voltage is too low to supply enough RPM and ignition at the same time. The results will find burning fuel in the hot section but not enough RPM to give it thrust. It just stays there and cooks. If the condition lasts too long, you have an engine change staring you in the face. Correction is to shut off the fuel but keep the engine rotating to expel all the fuel and fire. Trying to start an engine with insufficient voltage may end up in a hot start and the ensuing engine change—a very costly mistake.

In the flight curriculum you will have normal takeoffs but not many. There will be single-engine takeoffs and frequently. Here your procedures will differ from those in piston aircraft operations. In the latter you first reach Vmc and then V1 and V2, and at any time up to V2 you abort in case of an engine failure. In a jet, you don't! In a jet you reach V1 first, then rotation speed (Vr) for pulling the nosewheel off the ground assuming a climb angle, then you reach V2. In case of engine failure, you abort any time up to V1. If there is an engine failure after that you go, but you hold the aircraft on the runway and accelerate to Vr and then to airborne, reaching V2 as soon as possible. When all terrain can be cleared easily, you then accelerate to en route climb speed. The jet has real performance with one engine out.

You will have single-engine climbs, normal climbs, VOR tracking, and holding, both at intersections and with DME fixes, and here again you will run into strange territory. Regulations state you must have reduced from cruising speed to 200 knots at altitudes below six thousand feet, 210 knots from six thousand feet to fourteen thousand and 230 knots from fourteen thousand above.

You will practice the entire list of stalls and you will be impressed by the help given you by the design engineers. If you are fortunate enough to be flying a wing with automatic slats on the leading edge, your work will be even easier. The stall is smooth, recovery quick and efficient. There is no tendency to roll or tuck under. This is so well-designed into the aircraft we used for training that a full traffic pattern was demonstrated with the "stick shaker" functioning, full slats extended. You will do steep turns at twenty-nine thousand feet. Emergency procedures will be stressed throughout the course. You will handle all types of simulated failures—electrical, hydraulic, radio, pressurization—and practice them until you are no longer startled by the idea.

Emergency descent as a result of simulated fire, smoke, or decompression is as fine an aerobatic maneuver as you have had since riding a Mustang or a P-40 during World War II. Briefly, the procedure is to pull power off while actuating the speed brake and roll over on the back, letting the nose fall through the horizon. Thus you can end up in an almost vertical nose-down attitude without exerting negative "G's." Your descent is made holding the airspeed right up against the red line all the way down. At fifteen thousand feet you switch to "ram air dump" position on the pressurization system. At eight thousand feet you level off and open the side window to expel smoke, if that was the reason for the descent. You have been wearing the smoke glasses and straight oxygen during the entire descent. Time for this maneuver from twenty-nine thousand feet is less than two minutes.

Also in your flight curriculum you will experience full nose-up-trim "runaway" go-arounds and a flight pattern to a landing. You will do the same with a landing in full nose-down trim. This brings us to a trait of our particular airplane which should be incorporated in all. If all the lights are off on the warning panel, you are O.K. for takeoff. The worst situation possible could be a full nose-up or full nose-down trim. This will not be shown on the warning panel. But it can be handled. If it is not a malfunction, you can trim it out during your takeoff roll. If that fails, you can still handle the airplane throughout takeoff and landing. For instance, if it is a full nose-down trim situation, you use a low airspeed — say 120 knots full flaps and gear down — and you will find it of no consequence to complete the pattern to a normal landing.

Yes, you will do canyon approaches with the single-engine pull out. Furthermore, if you don't goof it up too much, you will get back over the fix at original altitude and heading. Remember when you were satisfied just to hold altitude? You will do every type of approach — VOR, ILS, ADF — and do landings with crosswind, low visibility, and with and without hydraulic braking.

All of this flight curriculum will take approximately fifteen to twenty hours, depending upon your instrument flying ability. It is a foregone conclusion that you are an instrument pilot and a fairly good one before your transition to the new jets.

To safely flight plan your business jet, you will be back to ground school learning about performance charts in your manual prior to the flight check. In compiling our check list to follow in flight planning, we saved hours of time by lifting the charts needed from our manual and placing them in proper check list sequence.

Here is an interesting point: flight planning a business jet is intriguing — you are eager to see how near to your flight plan the actual trip turns out and it is always closer than you have ever come before! The reason is that your speed is such that a large percentage of error would be necessary before it would show up on the overall time of the trip.

The oral exam on the aircraft will take the best part of a day and the FAA inspector's thoroughness and helpful attitude will impress you. Since the first business jet came out, it was obvious how seriously the FAA was observing the new program, doubtless to make certain that nothing happened to cause negative public reaction to the use of jets in business aviation. It was our experience that Les Cooling's oral exam covered almost every phase of the quiz. After such thoroughness our first flight check was almost anticlimactic.

During my flight check, I was pretty busy for an hour and forty minutes. I suddenly realized I had made the last landing. Believe it or not, it was the first one I had made since starting the course when both engines were running and no lights were on the warning panel—it was a real shock.

Several things stand out in my mind as a result of this training. One is the unusually high angle-of-attack attitude on final approach. After looking at the flaps and slats in the out-and-down positions, I understood. Soon it was as natural as a normal glide in a J-3 Cub. At first the angle of attack for breaking ground was a little uncomfortable and seemed extreme. After a couple of single-engine climb-outs, I could accept this also as being normal.

To push those power levers forward and feel the terrific thrust is a thrill, but it's a real surprise when you discover you don't have one rudder against the stop and all of one aileron turned into torque correction. You just sit there, and she goes straight down the runway. In emergency go-arounds, the response to power application is surprisingly quick and effective. This was in contrast with all I had heard from many sources. Single-engine go-around in this aircraft is not an ordeal at all, and engine-out performance is comparable to that of most two-engine go-arounds in a piston-powered aircraft.

There are many rewarding experiences in flying the new business jet. You will be aware of one of them when you are at thirty-seven thousand feet, look down to see the towering cumulus reaching up for you, and visualize all the piston-powered planes dodging around down in the nasty stuff and getting the wits scared out of the uncomfortable occupants. Then, too, you will appreciate the almost soaring-like silence backed up by the tremendous feeling of thrust from vibrationless power plants.

You will thrill to the vistas on those few clear days when perhaps you can see from your jet all of Lake Michigan or the entire state of Florida. At night with nothing but you and the black sky and a million bright stars atop the undercast, you realize you are probably as close to the sensation of being in orbit as most of us will ever be. Crossing the great Rockies, you will find they resemble the Ozarks or the Appalachians, appearing as mere ripples on the plains.

Another compensation that will soon be over is the eagerness on the part of the visitors to the airport who gather around your jet. During barnstorming days the curious were impressed by an airplane no matter what color, horsepower, or speed, and it was fun to answer their questions. Then the public became blasé, remaining so until just recently. At Mt. Pocono airport on some of our first trips in the jet, Sunday afternoon drivers stopped just to see the strange new aircraft with no propellers. They thronged the ramp, and suddenly it was like barnstorming all over again to experience their eagerness and renewed interest in flying—to learn they have not changed. One friendly sort was soon relaying my answer to the natives as if he were an old timer in jets himself. He was most helpful when we needed advice or a lift into town. Just as in the happy days of yore, he turned out to be the local undertaker and I am sure he was not being friendly just because the airport was at two thousand feet elevation and only four thousand feet long and it always had a turbulent crosswind—or was he?

Business jet flying impresses everybody at every level. Think what it means to go nonstop from St. Louis to Mexico City in less than three hours; to fly from St. Louis to New York City in an hour and thirty-six minutes instead of ruining a full half day getting there in a lumbering DC-3.

It isn't only the long hauls that impress people using business jets. One day we made eight flights—not one or two—eight. All but three were under one hour each. This day we flew 2,169 miles in six hours and four minutes averaging 357 miles per hour and burning 270 gallons of fuel per hour. In the first place no other airplane could have done it in one day. We did it in our little jet at costs no other airplane could come close to. Long or short haul, the business jet is opening the eyes and minds of those who once were skeptics. Pilots, public, and patrons are impressed and so are those who pay the bills.

Since history began man has wanted to fly like a bird. Who has not seen the wild geese, after a long migratory flight, set their whistling wings and with feet out, come gliding into some haven from the cold altitudes? You, too, will come in over town some clear day with altitude to spare, power off, silent except for whistling wings — wheels out and reaching for the runways at the end of a fast trip. This is about as close as humans can come to emulating the beautiful bird flights we all admire.

I well remember when the sound of the horse's clip-clop was still common as we traveled along dirt roads and I was here when the sound of the jet was first heard by the world. Our age has truly been blessed and everyone who flies deserves the great pleasure of experiencing the jet before retiring.

This is how Sabreliner N-2009 spent the week of December 14–18, 1966.

On Monday, with no flights scheduled, I was trying to catch up on some paperwork in the flight office when the phone rang. Someone wanted to know if the Sabreliner was busy; if not, how long would it take to get it ready for a flight? I told them it would be ready to go in thirty minutes. Where to?

It seems a furnace in the plant in Soda Springs, Idaho, had gone awry and needed some special attention. Two Monsanto engineers needed to get out there as soon as possible. They left the office and packed, and it was three forty-five before we were airborne. With a stop at Salt Lake City to put on more fuel, we flew to Pocatello, Idaho, the closest airport to Soda Springs, dropped our passengers, and made it back to St. Louis by eleven fifteen that night.

So Monday, which was to have been a light day, ended in 2,563 miles and six hours and sixteen minutes of flying time.

Tuesday morning we took off at nine for EWR, dropped four passengers, ferried to Kennedy, met an overseas passenger, and left for St. Louis at three thirty. We arrived in St. Louis at five fifteen. Thirty minutes later the plane left for Galveston with a new crew and a load of passengers, and came back empty. The totals for Tuesday: 3,354 miles, seven hours and fifty-nine minutes of flight time.

Wednesday morning we were off for La Guardia at eight and back in St. Louis at twelve thirty. At three we were off for Albany, Georgia. We dropped the load and ferried back to St. Louis for more passengers, arriving back in Albany at nine o'clock that night. Totals for Wednesday were 3,742 miles and eight hours and twenty-six minutes of flight time.

On Thursday afternoon the plane left Albany at five thirty with a full load and was met in St. Louis by a new crew and new passengers for a flight to New York City, with a stop in Pittsburgh. This trip ended in St. Louis around four in the morning. Totals for that day were six hours and twenty-nine minutes flight time with 1,920 miles traveled.

On Friday afternoon another round-trip to Albany, Georgia, completed the week. During the morning and early afternoon, the Remmert-Werner maintenance crew ran a complete hundred-hour inspection on the airframe and engines and left only a couple of minor things to finish up on Monday. Total time on Friday was only three hours and mileage a mere 1,300.

The week ended with 13,434 miles flown in thirty-one hours and twenty minutes. The average ground speed was comfortably over four hundred. Those statistics clearly show the superior capabilities of a jet.

That was a week. That really was.

Memorable Flights

Anyone having flown for several years will remember some of the outstanding flights, while others will fade and be forgotten. Some of the flights that are still fresh in my mind are a mixture of unique, frightful, and gratifying, and all are somewhat nostalgic.

To be a happy and successful corporate pilot it is necessary to roll with the punches, take the good with the bad, and to accept what comes with grace and style.

One evening Paul Vance and I landed at the Virginia Beach airport. We were whisked into town in an elegant limousine and ushered into the posh hotel by a gentleman attired in regalia reminiscent of a banana republic dictator. Our bags were taken by his underlings. We signed in and were escorted to our rooms by uniformed bellboys.

We had dinner that evening in the quiet and serene splendor of chandeliers, white linen, crystal, and glistening silverware. Waiters, busboys, and even the maître d' hovered over us as if we were indeed royalty. The service and food were impeccable.

It was the same display of opulence upon our departure the next morning. We felt honored and very important.

That night found us on the Mont Joli airport after dark. Mount Joli is far out alongside the St. Lawrence River on the Gaspé Peninsula. It was late, and there were no services available at the airport; no telephone, no transportation, no lights, nothing. We found a conveyance obviously designed to move aircraft from point to point. We were pleased to find it would run, since we were more than a mile from the hotel in town. Balancing our bags and ourselves on the contraption, we drove to town. We pulled up in front of the main hotel to see about rooms. Much to our chagrin the hotel was booked full with mining personnel waiting to go to the Ungava mine country in northern Quebec. They suggested we try the other little hotel just a block away. We grabbed our bags and walked, leaving our vehicle in front of the hotel. We were lucky — I think — as they had one room left.

One light bulb hung dejectedly from the center of the ceiling in our room and the bed, which we were to share, was of the old style iron variety — ornate, but not necessarily comfortable. Upon testing it we found all points led to the center; it sagged. The wall separating our room from the hall was made of mismatched boards, and gaping holes gave us full view of any hallway activity.

The toilet facilities were communal and found at the end of the hall near the stairs to the lower level, with only a chest-high barricade, which provided little privacy.

The dining room at the main hotel was closed because they had run out of food, so we purchased the only thing available from a street-side stand. It was potatoes, in a form they called chips but which we call french fries. That night we called them our dinner. Neither of us slept too well that night. We both fought to stay on our own side of the bed. The traffic in the halls sounded like it was right in our room and it looked that way too.

What could we do? We adapted. We laughed and remembered the wasted elegance lavished upon us the night before.

We were on a trip to the West Coast when we ran into icing problems in the vicinity of Butte, Montana. We elected to stop and wait for improvement in the weather before continuing the remainder of the flight to Seattle. Our passengers were Dr. Thomas, Felix Williams, Lupe Wolfe, and Jim McKee.

After spending the night in a hotel, the passengers took the train to Seattle the next morning while we waited for improvement in the icing conditions. We finally noted an improvement in the ceiling, so if it became necessary we felt we could get down into clear conditions beneath the clouds. We left Butte and played a little game we both had learned in India and China called "Dodge the Rocks." By staying under the overcast we had good visibility and by following the canyons we were soon well on our way to Seattle.

We spent some time in Seattle with personnel from our newly acquired Laux Company then planned our returned trip through Salt Lake City and Cheyenne for convenience in refueling. Having a full load of passengers and baggage, we could not take on a full fuel load. This was in the early winter, which usually means icing in the clouds, as was the case in Butte.

The minimum altitude out of Salt Lake City eastbound is eleven thousand feet. In order to climb as fast as possible we had deliberately left the carburetor heat off. Unfortunately the icing began well before we expected it, and at nine thousand we were accumulating ice at a fast rate. One engine began to lose power, a sure sign of icing in the carburetor. George was in the left seat. I tried to put the heat on and was successful on the left engine but the controls were frozen on the right. The engine lost more power and we were not even at our required altitude for the area we were in. Here we dangled under-powered, overloaded for the conditions, and at an altitude way below what is considered safe in clear weather. We struggled and worked on the good engine and tried to get heat on the other. Finally, in desperation, I whacked the heater control with my fist as hard as I could. I thought, "So what if I break it off, it is doing no good the way it is." The blow broke the frozen control cables loose in their housing and the heat came on. The engine surged back to life, and we climbed up through the overcast into clear air and the safety of altitude. It was cold in the cockpit but both of us were sweating profusely. The passengers, being so close to the cockpit, were aware of our plight. Fortunately they realized there was nothing better they could do for us than keep out of our way and be silent. We appreciated that.

The remainder of the trip went as planned. We stopped in

Cheyenne for more fuel and then continued nonstop into St. Louis in fairly good weather. That little incident proved something to me: no matter how many hours a pilot has and no matter how skilled he is, there is always something more to learn about flying.

While learning to fly I was repeatedly told to keep away from thunderstorms. Due to conditions beyond my control, I have found myself in thunderstorms more often than I would like.

Between the fall of 1944 and late summer of 1945, I flew over sixty round-trips over the Hump. During that time I probably acquired more thunderstorm experience than the average pilot encounters in a lifetime. I have been in several storms in the States, in Canada, and in South America since then. There is only one thing storms have in common: they are never alike. Some are more violent than others, but all are dangerous and can tear an airplane to pieces.

An experience of the most violent type occurred one fall when my arrival over Centralia, Illinois, in our DC-3 coincided with the arrival of a tornado. We had no weather radar to warn us of the impending danger, and ground-based radar was inadequate to cover this particular area.

We were en route from Nashville to St. Louis with a load of customers and guests. We had just been cleared from six thousand feet to four when things began to happen. The airspeed and rate-of-climb indicators made trips from limit to limit. Instead of getting down to four thousand feet, I saw seventy-five hundred, and then, in a matter of seconds, forty-five hundred feet. After five or ten minutes we finally broke out north of Scott Field approximately on course. I was surprised that we were still in the air and in one piece. Monday morning's newspapers carried the headline "Tornado Hits Centralia." It could have read "Corporate Aircraft Scattered Over Wide Area."

Surely everyone at one time or another has looked out to see a thunderstorm approaching, and those with courage have looked up into one as it passes over. The clouds are black and boiling. Lightning is flashing within the clouds and from the clouds to ground. It looks nasty, and it is! The energy generated in one of those storms is immeasurable.

This section is reprinted from *Air Facts* magazine.

In 1949 Remmert-Werner completed a conversion of a Lockheed Lodestar from a cargo configuration to a plush, corporate interior with seating for ten passengers. James S. McDonnell, with several of his engineers, wanted to go to the Naval Air Station at Norfolk, Virginia. Here on May 9 they were to board the aircraft carrier *The Franklin D. Roosevelt.* On May 10 they would watch firsthand the competition between their Banshee and the plane supplied by Grumman. This would be the first carrier-based jet in history, so it was a momentous occasion for J.S. McDonnell and his staff. Bill Remmert was to serve as my copilot and Betty was cabin attendant. This trip was scheduled about a week in advance.

I had watched the weather carefully for several hours before the scheduled flight, and at every check I felt that I should cancel the trip. Thunderstorms dominated the area and there was no sign of improvement anytime in the next twenty-four hours. I kept informing J.S. about the weather situation, starting with my first check at 6 A.M. on the ninth. My comment was always, "There is no way to get there without penetrating thunderstorms."

We were due off at one o'clock on May 9. At eleven I called for the last time and told him we would have to cancel due to the extreme weather situation. J.S. asked if with my experience over the Hump, I didn't think I could get through if I were to go alone. I made the mistake of saying, "Yes, I could get through, but I wouldn't like it." He said, "O.K., I am going with you. Bring the airplane over to our ramp for loading about twelve thirty." Regretfully, I was there and we loaded.

I remember distinctly that we had penetrated our first storm before we got abeam of Scott Field. We hit two more before Nashville, and after that I lost count. I had filed instrument flight rules (IFR) but had to divert many times. I would cancel and then have to refile as I was unable to maintain VFR conditions. In time all the radios were wet out. They were located in the nose section and took a beating. The only radio I had left by the time we passed over Richmond, Virginia, was the ADF. It was dark by the time we got over Richmond, but I was reading a fairly strong signal on the Navy Base at Norfolk. We finally saw the split green beacon denoting a military airport, and after crossing over the field we were given a green light from the tower. We lined up on the lighted runway and hoped it was not a downwind landing. We happened to guess right and landed without further problems. I taxied into the hangar line and quickly got out so that I could run into operations to clear the flight plan and paperwork. It seems they had been able to follow us pretty well most of the way. They had held the admiral's gig, which was scheduled to take J.S. McDonnell and his staff out to rendezvous with *The Franklin D. Roosevelt,* already at sea. I was relieved and was beginning to relax when J.S. scurried in from the airplane with his little duffel bag and quickly thanked me for such a wonderful trip. I looked at him in wonderment and said without thinking, "If you think that was a great trip, you have to be completely nuts!" He was the type of person who was oblivious to the weather en route and had his mind on the next day's competition. Everyone else in the cabin was sick, and Betty Remmert, who had been a passenger on many occasions, did not feel too well either. She assured me she had never been in anything like that much bad weather, and Bill agreed.

The little McDonnell jet won the competition and became the first carrier-based jet. From there McDonnell kept going up and up.

During one of the training and test-flight sessions with the Hercules Powder DC-3, Owen Mayfield, Sam Massey and I ran into a little excitement — we lost an engine at twenty-five hundred feet over St. Charles, Missouri. As we turned back toward Lambert Field I told Owen to call the tower and tell them we would be returning on one engine. Over the Missouri River the other engine quit, and I told Owen to tell the tower we would not be landing at Lambert after all.

Fortunately it was just before dark and a grass strip called Kratz Field was just about below us. It was only two thousand feet long but it looked a lot better than the surrounding tilled farm land, so we deadsticked in amidst several trainers practicing touch and go landings.

The next morning we discovered the cause of the trouble. If we had had twenty thousand feet of altitude I doubt that we could have found the three hundred gallons still aboard. The fuel tanks had been removed for testing and reinstalled without much attention to the proper seating of the selector forks. I had asked for a hundred gallons in each of the four tanks before we started our series of tests. The left front fuel gauge was faulty and never did leave the one-hundred-gallon mark. It turned out that when we were on the left tank and left engine, we were indeed on the left tank as intended. However when the right selector was on the right front tank, it was also drawing out of the left front tank. Two engines were pulling fuel from the same tank and we were unable to see the depletion of the supply. There was no warning. We did know that when we tested each position on the first flight, the engines would quit, except when on left main and right main. So we had squawked about the problem on our checklist. According to the record the mechanics had fixed the mistake. Perhaps they had found the mistake but it had not been corrected. Had we gone to an off position on either engine we would have received fuel from the rear tanks, but again, even if we had had plenty of altitude, I doubt that I would have thought of going to "Off." We later heard that several instructors and students were somewhat surprised to find a DC-3 in their pattern; seeing both engines dead gave them an extra start.

In December 1948 a group of people decided to spend New Year's Eve in St. Petersburg, Florida. I don't know why that particular spot was chosen, but it turned out to be a nice warm weekend.

Sunday dawned clear and mild again for the weekenders. I had checked the weather en route and in St. Louis and found nothing to be alarmed about, except St. Louis was improving slowly from a foggy weekend. The improvement was a good sign, so I fueled for the trip in order to stay well within the maximum gross weight.

After arriving at the airport, I made one last check on the St. Louis weather. It had improved very little in the past hour but was above VFR minimums. Realizing we would be arriving in St. Louis after dark made me give the fuel load more consideration. We were about a hundred gallons short of being full, so just to be on the safe side, we added the extra fuel even though it put us a few pounds over gross. I figured that we would be well back into the approved limits shortly after starting the climb. I felt more comfortable with the additional fuel.

The trip was more or less routine until we were in the vicinity of Nashville. I listened to the weather and found St. Louis was not as good as it had been an hour earlier. This was very alarming; improvements usually can be expected to continue. We were in the soup by this time, and it was dark.

We were somewhere in the vicinity of Evansville when I got in touch with St. Louis radio and asked if Bill Waldhauser was on duty in the weather bureau next door; I wanted first hand information as to what was going on. Bill came on and explained that the front we were in had become stationary and then had started to back up. This was causing St. Louis and environs to deteriorate to conditions found twelve hours before or even worse. This was new to me and to him. We had to do something right and in a hurry. I asked about Springfield, Illinois, but Bill said it was like St. Louis. "How about Columbia? I have a limited amount of fuel aboard!" He said they were giving twelve thousand overcast and five miles. I told him to give me the controller again so I could request Columbia as my alternate. By the time we got over St. Louis it was zero-zero, so on we went to our alternate at eight thousand feet.

We listened to the weather and got all the specials as the weather at Columbia began to come down. First it was ten thousand feet, then eight, and then we were in it. By the time we reached Columbia it was down to two thousand feet and two miles visibility with light rain.

The range station was located five miles west of the airport and there was an approach from the west straight into the east-west runway. In the clouds at the high cone, we broke out momentarily in the procedure turn, hit the low cone at the minimum altitude, and were in and out of the clouds; we could just barely make out the runway lights ahead. It was raining pretty hard by this time. The cockpit was full of pilots who knew better than to ask a lot of questions. Our wheels finally touched down on the dark, wet runway. We rolled out near the hangar which had a light on the windsock high above the door. Before I got the engines shut down, the light and the sock went out of sight in the fog. Close! We would have never made it to Columbia without the extra fuel.

We arrived over the strip at Wingmead, which was completely covered by fog. From our vantage point it was thin enough to see through while looking straight down. From the ground, I was told, it looked impenetrable. Having seen the trail made through cloud tops by aircraft starting their descent, we decided to give it a try and see if we could hurry the fog movement. We lined up with a tree sticking up through the fog which we knew to be about a mile off the south end of the runway. We flew right down on top of the fog, the full length of the field. We made a turnaround, and sure enough, the flight across the top of the fog had cleared it from the strip, but by the time we were on final, a light breeze from the west moved the opening across the entire span of the strip. Not to be foiled so easily, we made another pass, this time on the upwind side about the width of the wingspan.

Our plans worked exactly, for as we turned final, the opening was just arriving over the runway and we made a VFR landing. After coming to a stop to board the passengers we learned that they had never seen the airplane, due to the density of the fog. They asked, "How in the world did you find the strip?" All we could say was, "Do not cut the tree down that stands at the south end of the runway if you want an all-weather flight service here at Wingmead International."

We made many trips to various places for pictures and hunting, but one in particular stands out because so many different things happened. We had arranged a trip to Mexico with the help of a representative of Remington Arms who lived in Mexico City and loved to hunt. The main passengers were Queeny and Richard Bishop.

We left Stuttgart, Arkansas, on January 8, 1949. The first night was spent in Monterrey and the next in Mexico City. Our host from Mexico had arranged for the services of a professional hunter, who supposedly knew all the right places to hunt ducks and geese in all of Mexico. We met our White Hunter in Irapuato and it was decided we would fly to Aguascalientes, northwest of Irapuato. From there we proceeded by rented cars north about a hundred miles to a region called Salinas. The road at times was almost indistinguishable from the countryside.

It was the dry season. Dust rolled down the windshield and windows like water in a heavy rain. There was no traffic, but of all things we found ourselves following a bus loaded with people and livestock. Our Great White Hunter never did understand that we would have preferred to let the bus gain ground on us so that we would have less dust. He tailgated the bus doggedly, mile after mile.

Luckily, he saw some geese flying, so he stopped and observed for awhile. He soon developed a plan of action. There were some shocks of maize in a row and the geese appeared to be trying to land to feed in the field with the shocks. We spread out along the shocks with the Great White Hunter in the lead. We each crouched down behind a shock, intending to let the geese come in close before we started to shoot. The huge flock circled and came in toward us right over our fearless leader. Guess what happened next! He shot at the very first goose that came within his range. The geese, of course, all flared and were gone. Things were a little strained after that, but I am not too sure the Great White Hunter ever did catch on that he had done something wrong.

We continued our drive and finally, well after dark, arrived at a little village which had no electric lights. Our hotel was like a medieval inn. It was completely walled. We entered a courtyard through a huge wooden gate, which was closed as soon as we were inside.

Each of us had a room, more correctly called a cell. It was equipped with a wooden bed on which was a very thin pad instead of a deep mattress. A single lamp was the only source of light. We had to go to a nearby cantina for dinner, which consisted of the only thing they had that we felt we could safely eat — eggs and bacon. It was a far cry from the opulence we enjoyed in the luxurious hotel in Mexico City two nights before.

The next morning was fairly interesting. Stationed at a waterhole, we waited for ducks and quail to arrive. Our shooting was extra good, and I shot until the gun got too hot to hold. I kept thinking about the horrible trip up and that it had to be repeated to go back out. I started to look around and found a dry lake bed which gave me ideas. I took one of the cars and drove all over it, measuring the length in all directions. It would do.

I was about as dirty as I had ever been on the farm, and getting dirty was something I never did like. That was one of the reasons I left the farm. At lunch I told Mr. Queeny my plan. My copilot and I would go back with one of the cars to Aguascalientes, spend the night, bring the airplane up the next morning, and have it ready when they quit hunting for the return to Mexico City.

It sounded like a good idea to him so we were off for civilization. That night I luxuriated in a full tub of clean water in the hotel in Aguascalientes.

Early the next morning we checked out of the hotel and cranked up *Prairie Wings* for the trip up to the dry lake bed near Salinas. It was not too hard to find, and I could see the tracks I had made the day before, when I had driven over the sands. We landed, and in minutes people started to arrive in every kind of conveyance possible. They came on burros, horses, bicycles, and in rickety cars. It was like barnstorming in the thirties, but these people had no money and we were not giving rides. One particularly beautiful black stallion took my eye. The owner had it adorned with a fancy saddle and bridle. In the best Spanish I could muster, I asked if I could ride it. He quickly got off, and I got on and rode out across the salty flats feeling like I had returned to the days of Pancho Villa.

We had to land in San Luis Potosi for fuel but found it would take some time to get permission by wire from Mexico City before they could sell it to us. Having time to kill, the party got a cab and toured the city. I did not go with them as I had to stay and refuel when the clearance came back from Mexico City. I only know what was told to me when the passengers returned.

During their sojourn the name of our passenger, Bishop, came up and the cabdriver, being a good Catholic, could not let that go unnoticed. Facetiously they said he was the Bishop of St. Louis. Wow! What an effect that had on the driver. Suddenly he was the most important cabdriver in all of Mexico, and worse, he could do no wrong! So the speed increased, the horn never stopped blowing, and traffic was scattered in all directions at every intersection. Passengers were nearly having heart attacks. To this poor soul, having the bishop aboard would certainly insure his entrance to the promised land, and apparently the quicker he could get there the less chance he would have of missing the opportunity.

My passengers arrived back at the airport with this story, still badly shaken from the wild ride through the streets of San Luis Potosi. The rest of the trip was all quite tame.

Early in 1964 John Tucker obtained the use of a DC-3 in airline configuration from Remmert-Werner and suggested that we put a group together for an island-hopping tour of the Caribbean. In the middle of a St. Louis winter, it sounded like a good idea. I called a few people and so did he until we had ten couples. There were three couples from Marshalltown, Iowa. They were Ethel and Mike Lynch, Betty and Larry Collison, and Mable and Doc Watson. From Alton, Illinois, came Betty and Mal Walston along with Thelma and Harry Nimmons. The St. Louis couples were Lucy and

John Tucker, Kay and Jim Connaughton, Jamie and Dick Vorhoff, Wanda and George Harriel, and Kay and Ralph Piper. Most of this group had met for the first time on this occasion.

The only request made of passengers was to be on time for all departures; otherwise there were no set tours or schedules to follow. During our first overnight stop in Fort Lauderdale we all went our separate ways. The next day and night were spent at West End in the Bahamas. Suddenly for some unknown reason the crowd jelled and became one solid group of friends. From that time on we all played and traveled together. Upon our return many tears were shed and promises made to get together again. Often that type of promise is never kept. However, in this case it was, and we have had several reunions since. On one occasion, all except the Walston's traveled to Marshalltown in another old DC-3 for the wedding of Jane Lynch and Robert Baur. At each reunion events and stories are recalled and the strains of the island song "Yellow Bird" are heard again and again.

We were on a trip to Seattle in *Prairie Wings* in the late fall. I had checked the weather and knew we would be traversing a cold front somewhere out in central Nebraska and before our fuel stop in Cheyenne. All was going as scheduled, and sure enough, we began to pick up dark clouds ahead, which indicated we were closing in on the front. At that point, Queeny came to the cockpit with an empty martini shaker. He said, "Where is the ice?" I looked at Bob Hinds, my copilot for the trip, and from the redness creeping up his cheeks, I knew there was no ice aboard. He apologized, but I said, "Wait a few minutes, Mr. Queeny; I will get some ice for you!" He looked at me incredulously, but nevertheless turned around and left the cockpit. We were soon bouncing through the cold front.

There is an anti-icing system installed around the windshield — a system of tubes which decant glycol across the windshield, preventing the formation of ice. I chose not to turn it on, as I needed all the ice accumulation I could get for a serious problem aboard. As we wallowed through the turbulence which accompanies a cold front, we began to collect ice. The windshield became opaque and a nice bit of rime began to build up on the tubes that normally carry the glycol to the windshield surfaces. In due time we emerged from the other side of the front into cold, clear, crisp air. I opened the sliding window on my side, reached out into the frigid slipstream, and gingerly loosened an accumulation of ice which had formed on the glycol tube. It came off, and I carefully lifted it away and into the safety of the cockpit. I closed the window and called Queeny forward to the cockpit. Believe it or not that piece of ice fit the opening in the martini shaker exactly. It was precisely the right thickness and length to fill the shaker. He added the gin and a dash of vermouth and really began to smile. Seeing his mirth, I was relieved and so was Bob, but a little at a loss as to the cause of that much glee. Then Queeny said, "Boy, this is something! Now I have had a martini made with the newest ice possible, to match the time I made martinis from the ice found in one of the oldest known glaciers on this continent." He had been on an extended trip to Alaska and frequently used ice from a famous glacier at cocktail time.

We were off the hook for having forgotten the ice, and a new record had been set by one who was always pleased to have blazed the first trail no matter if it was at eight thousand feet over central Nebraska. Those who fly the modern corporate jets at forty thousand feet will have a more difficult time if the boss runs out of ice!

In October 1960 the prince of Belgium and his entourage were paying a visit to the United States. Their tour included St. Louis and particularly Monsanto, which had a sizable investment located in Brussels. The well-known citizen and Belgian consular official, Casey Lambert, acted as guide and host to the royal party while they were in St. Louis.

Monsanto executives were hosts at luncheon on October 13. It occurred to one of the executives that they should enhance the hospitality by offering transportation for the group back to the New York area. I was alerted to the proposal and in short order my friend Casey and I were busy trying to work out the details. Such things as special preparations for hors d'oeuvres for the cocktail hour and other niceties were arranged, as well as limousine reservations at the other end of the line. Our plans were to fly into Newark in order to avoid almost certain delays at La Guardia.

Our trip started at five in the afternoon and ended at Newark Air Service ramp three hours later. During the trip the prince came to the cockpit and seemed to be fascinated with procedures, while listening to the conversations between us and the controllers en route. His wife, Fiona, also spent time in the cockpit.

When we arrived at the Newark Air Service ramp the limos were waiting and, unfortunately, so were dozens of reporters and photographers. It took some time to get the royal party off and on their way to New York City.

After departure of the entourage I was interviewed. The reporters were interested in anything I could tell them firsthand about royalty. I could not help but remark about the fact that the chief passenger was certainly a prince of a fellow.

Our farm near Le Grand was just east of three different Hoover families, all of whom were cousins of Herbert Hoover. There was another living in Le Grand everyone called Uncle Davis. On many occasions we would see a black limousine parked in front of Uncle Davis' house and we would know his illustrious nephew was making a call. On one occasion while I was going by with my mother in a horse and buggy we noticed they were shooting movies of the family on the front yard. Herbert Hoover had two sons, Herbert, Jr., and Allen, both of whom were present that day. In 1962 Dick Thurston and I flew Herbert Hoover, Jr., and his family from Craig, Colorado, in the Monsanto Convair. Mr. Hoover was a member of the Monsanto board and the purpose of this trip was for them to attend the dedication of the Hoover library, which was being donated to the community of West Branch, Iowa, near Cedar Rapids.

En route to Colorado the next day our climb took us over the little town of Le Grand. We were at about twelve thousand feet when I called Mr. Hoover to the cockpit and pointed out the little town below. He remembered the day of the movie-making and was intrigued by the fact that I had seen him in his youth. He went back to the cabin, perhaps to dwell with his memories and I took the opportunity to do the same.

I saw the village square and the road leading north to the cemetery, where there is a place reserved for my worn and weary body when the time comes. I remembered the Ira Gaunts, the Merrit Gaunt family, the Manships with a family of teachers and coaches, Dr. Mills' wonderful family, the Duncans, the Rhodes, Radloffs, Smahas, Adairs, and then we were looking down on the east end of Quaker Lane. The Hibbs' farm on the left, Tom Keens' farm, Perishos, Swensons, Knudsons, the Hoovers, and then the Rubenbauers and finally the Wolkens.

We crossed just south of Marshalltown and saw Albion to the northwest and our former farm just east of it. I recalled my departure from that point on a bleak day in January 1941. Ahead was State Center, Ames and the huge campus, but by then we were leveling off at sixteen thousand feet, our assigned altitude, and I had to bring my mind back into the cockpit and to the present. There were RPMs to reduce, manifold pressure to lower and mixture controls to adjust, cowl flaps had to be trailed for proper cooling on the huge R-2800 Pratt and Whitney engines. It was probably the day I graduated that I passed the point of no return at Le Grand, and I could only go back temporarily as I had just done—in my memories.

One day we flew over Nashville and crossed Chattanooga, ninety miles east, nine minutes later. I was reminded of a trip to Minneapolis in the fall of 1938.

Doctor Seth Walton and I drove from Hampton, Iowa, to Mason City early in the morning of October 15. We rented a Cub from Sylvan Hueglin and Bud Kramer. My logbook shows we took off at ten thirty and landed, 120 miles north, at Wold-Chamberlin Field at noon. We took a cab to the Minnesota Stadium, where Minnesota was hosting the Michigan Wolverines.

We watched Michigan topple Bernie Biermans' great Gophers that day, mostly due to the scampering of a newcomer by the name of Tom Harmon. He was a sophomore and this was one of his first games. It was also just a token of many more afternoons like it for the next two years, for Michigan.

On Sunday the sixteenth we left Wold-Chamberlin at eleven thirty in perfectly clear weather. But the wind blowing from the south was so strong that when we leveled off at two thousand feet we had not left the boundaries of the airport. We could see that it was going to be a long afternoon, and our spirits became lower and lower as we watched trucks pass us while going up the long, high hills south of the Minneapolis airport.

By two o'clock we had to look for a place to stop for gas. I picked a likely looking pasture near Geneva, Minnesota. After some cajoling we managed to get a replenishment of our fuel sup-

197

ply from a farm lad. He drew the gas from his father's tractor tank. We paid him, of course, and we were soon on our way against the unbelievable south wind. At four fifteen we taxied up to the little hangar at the Mason City Airport.

Computations show our speed was eighty miles per hour on the way to Minneapolis, and thirty miles per hour on the way back. I was reminded of the trip while in the Sabreliner when I clocked my speed between Nashville and Chattanooga. With a tail wind our time between Nashville and Chattanooga was nine minutes and the distance was ninety nautical miles. Corrected to statute miles the ground speed was six hundred and ninety miles per hour. In 1938 such speeds were never even dreamed about by the most optimistic engineers. In those twenty-nine years a lot had happened in aviation and I was right in the middle of it all.

Twice I have had the eerie experience of watching the moon rise twice in the same night.

The first time was on a flight from India into north China. We had been above an overcast, and just before starting our letdown we watched the eastern sky lighten and then saw the moon pop up. Our descent blanked the moon from our vision, and we continued to the dark valley and onto the airstrip stretching between two mountain ranges. The overcast drifted west and cleared the top of the eastern range, the horizon began to lighten, and the moon rose over the mountain range.

The second occasion was upon our return from a West Coast trip. We were over western Missouri when the moon came up and flooded the dimly lighted cabin of our little jet. It was a beautiful sight. As we made our descent, the moon went out of sight; we landed and parked on the ramp on the west side of the field. As each passenger was on the ramp, we all noticed the moon rising in the eastern sky—again.

On March 16, 1966, another emergency occurred at the Soda Springs, Idaho, plant. Engineers and specialists in St. Louis were needed to get the furnace back on the line. For every hour the plant was shut down it cost the company a sizable amount of money.

It was late in the afternoon before they could gather all the equipment needed and arrive at the airport for departure. I remember little about the trip out since everything went according to plan. Merle Current flew that leg and we landed at Pocatello, Idaho.

The passengers disembarked as we unloaded the parts and tools. We refueled for the return trip to St. Louis. It was my turn in the left seat. We were climbing out by eleven o'clock that night and had contacted Salt Lake center. The center asked us for our first checkpoint and our heading. We answered with "Fort Bridger, and 120 degrees." The next question was, "Would you like radar vectors to St. Louis?" We had noted very little wind effect on the way out and the night was clear with moonlight flooding the mountains. "Why not?" They then told us to turn to 109 degrees, which we did. In a couple minutes they came back with a correction, which was to turn further left to 104 degrees. We turned left to 104 as we were leveling off at our assigned altitude.

There were no more transmissions. It was calm and smooth, and the stars in the black sky above looked like they were in our cockpit. We were a part of the night. Silent. Only the wind whistling over the windshield and the dynamotors whirring in the radio compartment. Silence. We saw the glow of lights where Denver should be, then Boulder and Fort Collins. There was Cheyenne right under our nose.

During this period the only radio communication was when Salt Lake cleared us to the Denver center. Way out over eastern Colorado I suspected we had been abandoned. I called Denver for assurance that we were still being monitored. "Loud and clear!" was their reply. "There's nobody else out there tonight." They soon gave us the frequency for Kansas City center. More silence.

We began to see the lights of Kansas City and Omaha, and to the right, Springfield, Missouri. More radio silence and a big sky with no one in it but us. Kansas City finally called and gave us our descent clearance as we passed through their area. Power levers back, almost to idle, and even deeper silence pervaded. The lights of Jefferson City on our right and the lights of St. Louis over the nose identified our position. Kansas City center cleared us to contact St. Louis approach control, whose clearance was, "Turn right to 120 degrees for vectors to the final approach to runway 12 right." This was the first heading change since Salt Lake had asked us to turn to 104 degrees.

We had covered more than a thousand miles and glided across most of the state of Missouri in silence to touchdown. I don't believe the two of us spoke two words during the entire flight. Both of us were caught up in the spell of the silent night. There were only the two of us to appreciate the magnitude of it all—no disturbances in the air or on the radio. Only silence and the night prevailed. Then the trip and the spell were over.

Final Approach

The decisions I have made through the years were not based on criteria used by exceptionally ambitious or greedy persons. To be a millionaire was never my goal. One can only eat so much, or drink so much, and what does it matter after sleep comes whether the room costs one hundred or twenty-five dollars.

Once my career was launched there was never a time when I went hungry or lacked necessities or comfort. I always gave the job 100 percent of my attention, but never did I allow it to enslave me.

What I call success is attaining goals. My goals were never solely based on money, although I wanted enough to be comfortable. For many years in early life I had no money; yet a lot of those years provided happiness far beyond what money could have bought.

Success is comfort, security, and respect. Once I felt security was established I began to freely enjoy life. Stature, based on money, had nothing to do with it. Stature, based on the respect of others, did.

For many years I have been able to observe the life-styles of those living in opulence. None were ecstatic. They were happy in their own way, perhaps, but I didn't sense they were truly happy people. Most let me know at one time or another that they envied my freedom.

I faced a point of no return many times. Each time the decision was made I never looked back. I am happy and comfortable; I enjoy the company of many friends; I enjoy life to the hilt! Respect, comfort, and security are my goals and always have been. I am not smug; I am not frustrated; I am, in my own mind, successful and happy.

When I started to fly I thought I was in heaven. When I began to make it a career, I kept saying, "How can anyone have this much fun and still get paid for it?" The money was not the reason I was flying. I was happy before the money. Money was merely a bonus. It was my responsibility to make my job one of the best in the country. When that was established, respect came along as people recognized the job I was doing. Had I been doing poorly at my job, I would not have received respect. With respect, I was comfortable and secure.

Successful corporate pilots must assume the attitude of professionals.

A professional pilot is what the name implies, just as surely as the doctor, lawyer, architect, or minister is a professional.

Professional pilots are as meticulous and precise in their work as a surgeon in the operating room. They treat their airplane and its instruments as delicate tools and strive to obtain maximum return from their use.

Professional pilots plan every approach with utmost care. They prepare their instruments and themselves as the surgeon lays out tools and plans for an operation. Emergency equipment is readied as well. In both cases lives are at stake.

Professional pilots are able to assume a bedside manner with new and apprehensive passengers as easily as the successful general practitioner.

Professional pilots are as sure of their position as the trial lawyer standing before the judge and jury. Just as the lawyer must foresee every possible block from opposition, so the professional pilot must be prepared with an alternate at all times.

Professional pilots are as loyal to their boss and company as ministers are to their Maker. They represent their company and its best interests above personal wishes.

Professional pilots' respect for safety is as sincere as the architect's regard for proper material to insure strength of construction. Neither will compromise at any cost.

This section, "What Is a Corporate Pilot?" is reprinted with permission from *Professional Pilot* magazine.

Pilots are professionals if they can go from A to B quicker and safer than other pilots. Pilots are professionals if they can start their descent at the correct time so as to enter the traffic pattern at the correct altitude and speed.

Pilots are professionals if they study for improvements and upgrade their ratings; if they evaluate and apply the capabilities of new equipment to the needs of the company; if they recommend improved instrumentation rather than gadgetry.

Pilots are professionals if they take pride in their profession without giving the impression of arrogance. Their love for their work should serve as an inspiration to younger pilots.

They are professionals if they recognize the delicate margin between respect and subservience; if they can be warm yet not familiar.

Professionals are honorable people in love with their profession and having the respect of all who come in contact with them. They are a credit to those who call themselves professionals.

These are the components of a professional pilot.

All flight preparations have one common goal — to land safely at the destination. Sometimes, due to circumstances beyond the control of the pilot, landings have to be made at points other than the one planned. Changes in routing are also not uncommon.

I can remember the time we were leaving St. Louis for Philadelphia with Edgar Queeny and Dick Bishop aboard. As usual, we had filed our flight plan and while taxiing out we received our clearance. Queeny overheard the part of our clearance regarding Philadelphia and hurried forward to tell us we would be going to Washington, D.C., first. We asked the controller to alter our destination and to stand by for the new routing. Before we received confirmation for our requested changes Queeny came up again and asked that we take them out over the Quiver Club to look for early fall ducks. "Sure, no problem," I said. We called the controller again to tell him we would pick up our clearance on the way eastward, after circling the St. Charles area. It is always well to know where you are going. Often the pilot is the last to know such privileged information.

This was somewhat parallel to the career I had established for myself in Monsanto. Most of the plans had been working out fairly well. I was one of the few employees to have stayed at the same base for so many years. My flight plan was being followed fairly closely until the Chemstrand arrival.

During my six years on the board of directors of the National Business Aircraft Association the subject of pilot retirement had been discussed at some length. Most people are aware of the fact that pilot longevity is somewhat less than that of the ordinary employee. A pilot is good for another year each time he can pass the FAA physical, but during the time General Manuel Quesada was administrator of the FAA, he set sixty as the mandatory retirement age for all airline pilots. This was something that has been contested every day since it was introduced. Nevertheless it became a guide for corporate pilots, although not a regulation.

The thinking on the part of most of the NBAA board members was that the pilots with less longevity than others should be given the opportunity to pay in toward retirement at an accelerated rate and retire at the arbitrary age of sixty with full benefits. In that manner a pilot would have the same retirement benefits as an employee who stayed until the regular age of sixty-five.

After much debate, trial, and error, the people in personnel began to see my point. The plan also included an age fifty-five optional early retirement with fewer total benefits. I had been planning for over ten years to take early retirement from Monsanto and start another career as an aviation consultant, specializing in something I knew, corporate aviation.

I felt particularly well qualified for such a career since I had made my share of mistakes and found the reasons for them and the corrections. I had also been the victim of forced moves much against my better judgment. So both negatively and positively I had learned a lot about corporation aviation. I had watched it grow from infancy to a giant industry. I had played a part in shaping its destiny with my close connections over many years with the NBAA.

Here I was, loaded with experience, and it looked as if I had something to offer corporate aviation in the role as a consultant. The age of fifty-five appeared to be more and more golden as time rushed along.

With the Chemstrand merger, takeover, or whatever history decides to call it, came many changes in the philosophies throughout the company, including the flight department. I thought my retirement at fifty-five was settled. Not so. Chemstrand took over as soon as possible, and all retirement plans were put aside and new ones were developed. When they discovered an excess of engineers, they offered bonus settlements as incentives for them to leave the company early. It was not a part of my long-range planning that I found myself included in the incentive program to retire. Having spent more than ten years planning my retirement, I did not find it difficult to see it through, whatever the plans.

Most of my last three years with Monsanto were spent flying the Sabreliner. This was the most enjoyable flying I have ever done, and the most rewarding. I needed jet experience to round out my qualifications as a consultant. After I had the three years of jet experience I was almost satisfied.

Another strong contributing factor to my retirement was the long waits that came with the jet. The out-and-back-in-one-day trips were the rule rather than the exception. We were making one-hour flights to the destination, waiting all day, and flying an hour to get home. Two hours of flight for eight hours of waiting. I felt useless, and for the first time corporate flying was losing its allure.

The Chemstrand retirement plan took more than another year of fine-tuning and adjustments. Even after the initial announcement, many amendments were added to the original plan. Little of the Monsanto plan remained.

The final plan, in essence, was to give the retiree an option of a fixed monthly income or a minimum guarantee plus an additional amount keyed to the cost-of-living index. This fund was invested in stocks and bonds and the income from such investment was believed to be more flexible with the times. I chose the latter which produced the desired results. The income from that section has increased many times since the plan got under way. When my age reached fifty-five, my flight plan was activated.

On October 26, 1967, I had a trip with Gerry Gamble to Raleigh-Durham and back. It was my turn to empty the honey bucket at the Raleigh airport. I did it and we flew back to St. Louis with passengers. I took care of the paperwork, closed the desk, and walked out the door. After almost twenty-two years I was the only one to know that that was my last flight for Monsanto. I had passed the point of no return again. I did not look back in regret. I looked forward to the wonderful life of an independent consultant. I had a new career staring me in the face and I had to get started on it as soon as possible.

When I started at Monsanto I felt as if I had suddenly found my home. I could not imagine being with any other company. I liked what I saw; I liked the potential; I liked those who ran the company and the way they treated the people in the company. My close association with Edgar Queeny was a particularly rewarding experience. It included a weekend with Edgar as the guest of Glen L. Martin at his farm home in southern Maryland. It included a special occasion as a dinner guest hosted by the famous general of World Wars I and II, General William ("Wild Bill") Donovon. Queeny, Ned Putzell, and I were the guests. Ned had been the general's aide during the war.

Other notables I was privileged to meet through my association with the NBAA were Eddie Rickenbacker, Igor Sikorsky, Jimmy Doolittle, Barry Goldwater, and many other important people in aviation.

The Hollywood party as the companion of Hedda Hopper was a memorable event, probably impossible for most pilots.

It was also fascinating knowing Sam Allender, and hearing tales firsthand about the way it was with John F. Queeny, the founder of Monsanto.

The flight with Herbert Hoover, Jr., and his family was thrilling, enabling me to touch base just a little with our roots.

Six years on the board of the NBAA and fifteen more on the technical committee helped make friendships that have survived these many years. Watching the growth of the organization from a few members to the thousands of great corporations today gives me pride in having been a part of a tremendously important part of aviation's growth. I shared the thrill of checking out the crews of at least twenty corporations in newly converted DC-3s. That alone brought my acquaintances and friends in aviation to a huge total.

It is an accomplishment to have landed in every state in the contiguous United States, as well as all provinces of Canada. To have flown all around South America, all over Central America and the Caribbean, was, to me, a unique opportunity.

The trip with J.S. McDonnell to the Norfolk Naval Air Station is one of the flights I shall never forget. Nor will I forget the long, sad flight from New York to Texas City to see the devastation created when the freighter *Grand Camp,* anchored in the harbor adjacent to Monsanto plant, exploded, leveling the Monsanto plant and leaving no trace of the ship.

The trip in a C-46 from Memphis to Calcutta and my Hump

experiences defy comparisons, but millions of dollars would not entice me to do it again under the same circumstances or with the same equipment.

Starting with the first sight of an airplane back in the second decade of this century, the path has taken many interesting turns. If the time I have spent in the air were to be lumped into one continuous block it would total almost two full years at the rate of twenty-four hours per day. Two months and eleven days have been spent on instruments, out of sight of the ground, and most of that out of sight of the wingtips. Another three months and nine days have been spent flying at night.

I count my blessings. What a privilege to have lived from the horse-and-buggy days to this point. I have met and had long conversations with Neil Armstrong, the first man to have walked on the moon. More has been accomplished in science during my lifetime than all the years of recorded history preceding these years. My life has been rewarding and exciting. And now, as I approach the last decade of this incredible century, I just had to tell about it.